Women's Theology in Nineteenth-Century Britain

LITERATURE AND SOCIETY IN VICTORIAN BRITAIN
VOLUME 3
GARLAND REFERENCE LIBRARY OF THE HUMANITIES
VOLUME 2055

LITERATURE AND SOCIETY IN VICTORIAN BRITAIN

SALLY MITCHELL, *Series Editor*

Women's Theology in Nineteenth-Century Britain

Transfiguring the Faith of Their Fathers

Edited by
Julie Melnyk

Garland Publishing, Inc.
A member of the Taylor & Francis Group
New York and London
1998

Library of Congress Cataloging-in-Publication Data

Women's theology in nineteenth-century Britain : transfiguring the faith of their
    fathers / edited by Julie Melnyk.
            p.   cm. — (Garland reference library of the humanities ; v. 2055.
    Literature and society in Victorian Britain ; v. 3)
        Includes bibliographical references and index.
        ISBN 0-8153-2793-5 (alk. paper)
        1. Theology—England—History—19th century.   2. Women and
    religion—England—History.   3. Women authors, English—19th century.
    I. Melnyk, Julie.   II. Series: Garland reference library of the humanities ;
    vol. 2055.   III. Series: Garland reference library of the humanities.
    Literature and society in Victorian Britain ; v. 3.
    BR759.T73   1998
    230'.082'0942—dc21   97-34074
                                                                     CIP

Printed on acid-free, 250-year-life paper
Manufactured in the United States of America

To my father and his faith,
to my mother and hers.

Contents

Acknowledgments

I would like to acknowledge some of the many people who contributed to my work in editing this volume. First, I thank the contributors themselves for their fascinating, groundbreaking research into nineteenth-century women's theology. I thank Sally Mitchell for suggesting this collection on women's theology and supporting me generously with her advice and encouragement. At the next stage, Joy Dodson cheerfully and intelligently helped me force my computer to produce camera-ready copy; without her, I could not have completed my task. And finally, I thank my husband Andrew for his patience and his support and his faith in my work.

Introduction

Julie Melnyk
Central Methodist College

RELIGION AND THEOLOGY

"It is beginning now to be understood that theology is not religion;
but not so very long ago, the two were miserably confounded."
Christian World Magazine (1871).

Recently, literary critics and historians have turned their attention to
nineteenth-century women's religious writing. Few, however, have
discussed Victorian women's theological writing, perhaps because there isn't
supposed to be any. Women's writing on religious topics -- those related to
devotion, conduct, worship -- was tolerated and even encouraged. Most
Victorians held the essentialist view that, in some sense, women were
spiritually superior, "temperamentally better suited to learning [religious]
truths than are men" (Krueger 26): either innately, perhaps connected with
the biological function of motherhood, or as a result of social circumstances,
their exclusion from the corrupting marketplace or the increased
opportunities for edifying suffering offered by their social position. William
Wilberforce, the most prominent Anglican Evangelical of his day, provides
an early expression of what was to become a dominant view: "...that
[female] sex seems, by the very constitution of nature, to be more favorably
disposed than ours to the feelings and offices of Religion" (434). Thus,
religion was regarded as one of the few socially acceptable areas of interest,
experience, and even a degree of predominance for women.[1] Women
responded by pouring their energies into religious life and religious
literature.

But this encouragement of women's religious work and literature did not
extend to theological writing. While Victorian religious discourse was
gendered neutral or even slightly feminized, theology, "the study of or
science which treats of God, His nature and attributes, and His relations
with man and the universe" (*OED*), remained a clearly masculine discourse.
Nevertheless, Victorian women had original ideas about God's nature and

attributes and his relations with man (and woman), and some found socially acceptable ways in which to express these theological ideas.

The overlap between religious and theological writing, the confusion noted in the epigraph, provided opportunities for women writers to engage in theology. Barred from university and pulpit, they were also forbidden to write in the traditional genres of theology, the treatise and the sermon. Their theological ideas appear instead in nontraditional genres, in letters, novels, pamphlets, devotional manuals, and in the increasingly influential periodical press, disguised as uncontroversial religious writings. These women authors almost never claimed to be writing theology, and, naturally, they did not propose overarching, self-consistent theological systems, but they did reinterpret the nature of God and of Christ, the relationships between God and humans, and the Scriptures. The essays in this collection identify and analyze Victorian women's theological thought in all its diversity, demonstrating the ways that women revised, subverted, or rejected elements of masculine theology, in creating theologies of their own.

RUSKIN REACTS

The exploration of nineteenth-century British women's theology is intrinsically interesting and provides valuable insights into women's religious experience and their gender ideologies. But women writers did not contribute directly to masculine theological discourse: with few exceptions (see Mark M. Freed's essay on Mary Arnold Ward), their work was neither cited nor discussed by academic theologians, and they were not often quoted from the pulpit. Most Victorians would have been unaware that women were writing theology. So did women's theology have any impact on Victorian culture? I claim that it did: through its accumulated influence on its readers, women's theological writing quietly began to transfigure Victorian Christianity.

But I am not alone in seeing the transformative action of nineteenth-century women's theology. John Ruskin's dictum that theology was the "one dangerous science for women" is often quoted, but the passage from "Of Queens' Gardens" which it introduces indicates not only that Ruskin was aware of women's participation in theological writing but also that he perceived it as influential enough to pose a threat.

> There is one dangerous science for women -- one which they must indeed beware how they profanely touch -- that of theology. Strange, and miserably strange, that while they are modest enough to doubt their powers, and pause at the threshold of sciences where every step is demonstrable and sure, they will plunge headlong, and without one thought of incompetency, into that science in which the greatest men have trembled, and the wisest erred. Strange, that they

will complacently and pridefully bind up whatever vice or folly there is in them, whatever arrogance, petulance, or blind incomprehensiveness, into one bitter bundle of consecrated myrrh. Strange in creatures born to be Love visible, that where they can know least, they will condemn first, and think to recommend themselves to their Master, by crawling up the steps of His judgment-throne, to divide it with him. Strangest of all, that they should think they were led by the Spirit of the Comforter into habits of mind which have become in them the unmixed elements of home discomfort...(73)

Ruskin begins by reaffirming that theology is an essentially masculine discourse. He asserts not only that the science of theology is dangerous for women who practice it, but that it is uniquely dangerous among the disciplines. In fact, he portrays it as a kind of sacred ark of the covenant or, perhaps more appositely, a forbidden fruit that will cause death, or loss of innocence, to the woman who dares approach it. He does not specify the nature of this danger to women, but only refers vaguely to such profanation.

Ruskin regards theology as uniquely dangerous because it is the one subject that women discuss with confidence -- they doubt themselves, remain at the "threshold" of other sciences, but in the realm of theology they are willing to speak. Here Ruskin becomes more violent in his accusations, losing whatever detachment he might have claimed; in his next sentence he accuses these theological women of complacency, pride, vice, folly, arrogance, petulance and "blind incomprehensiveness." Notice how strange, how unnecessary this violence seems: surely ridicule, particularly when wielded by such a well-respected member of the literary establishment, would have been a weapon strong enough to defeat a collection of devotional books, novels, and magazine articles. But, however gratuitous Ruskin's attack might appear to the modern reader, he clearly felt that the threat warranted such a strong reaction.

Each accusation is carefully chosen, and each deserves equally careful consideration. "Complacency," a charge which often attaches itself (sometimes justifiably) to the stereotypical Victorian, merely restates Ruskin's earlier complaint that women seem insufficiently afflicted with self-doubt when they write about God: their presumed spiritual equality or superiority has made them over-confident. They are "prideful" because they believe they have something worthwhile to say about God, and perhaps also because what they say tends to glorify their own position as women. With "vice or folly" he accuses these pious women of either the moral sin of "vice" or the intellectual sin of "folly," and implies that these two possibilities do not merely taint, but fully exhaust the contents of their writings; he then elaborates this description with "arrogance, petulance, or blind incomprehensiveness."

"Arrogance," of course, is related to pride, but it has more precise connotations: "arrogance" derives etymologically from "arrogate," meaning to claim or seize without right, to appropriate to oneself, most often used to describe the appropriation of power or superiority; it is a political word. In choosing this word, Ruskin implies that these women regard themselves not only as competent but as superior and powerful in this realm; they appropriate theological utterance and power for themselves. "Petulance," though, seems a strange word to choose in describing theological documents; it denotes forwardness and immodesty, charges often brought against women engaged in public discourse, but it further connotes impatience and irritability, the reaction of a small child to being balked of its desires. To characterize these writings as petulant is to recognize that many of them manifest, not complacency, but discontent, even annoyance; despite the belittling connotations of his diction, Ruskin proves himself a good reader, one who can discover the subtext of protest beneath the surface of conventionality. And, finally, he accuses these women of "blind incomprehensiveness." On one level, this reiterates his charge of "folly," but again the connotations refine and complicate his meaning. First, incomprehensiveness can mean a failure to understand or even a disposition not to understand; but it also implies narrowness, a failure to be comprehensive. Here Ruskin may perceive women theologian's concentration on women's experience of God as a failure to encompass men's experience. Failing to take into account women's experience was standard practice; failing to take into account men's was intellectual crime, "incomprehensiveness." This bundle of vices and follies is "bitter"; again, Ruskin realizes that what these women have to say is not all pious sweetness. Sometimes the subtext is acid.

The political ramifications of these texts, and the nature of the danger that Ruskin fears, become clearer in the next sentence. First, he portrays women as by nature incarnations of Love, analogous to Christ, but only in respect of his selflessness, and, by implication, his suffering. But these unnatural theological women claim more of the attributes of Christ. They attempt to climb onto his throne, his seat of power; Ruskin accuses them not merely of claiming the power exercised by male theologians, but of claiming the very power of Christ. But the power that women claim is specific: it is power to judge. The throne of Christ is identified as the judgment throne, and Ruskin complains that these women "condemn first" "where they know least." He may again be objecting to women's presumption in making intellectual judgments about the merits of specific theological positions, but the judgments usually associated with Christ are moral rather than intellectual. He objects to women who used their theological or religious writing to condemn certain practices of society, of the government, and of the church, women who claimed the power to judge the behavior and institutions of men. (For such uses of theological discourse, see especially Flammang's "'And Your Sons and Daughters Will Prophesy': The Voice and Vision of Josephine Butler"; Mumm's "Ellice Hopkins and the Defaced Image of Christ"; and Goslee's "Religion as Contextualized Critique in the Letters of Harriett and Jemima Newman.")[2]

The final sentence of Ruskin's dense critique manifests his anxiety about one of the most powerful, empowering ideas of Protestant Christianity: the will of God. Nineteenth-century women used the will of God to justify actions (and words) that might be considered unacceptable according to social conventions; they were "led" or "called" to behave against prevailing standards -- to take up a profession, to speak in public, to write theology. Such claims of "leading" could not be verified or refuted, but only accepted or denied. Ruskin here denies the validity of the "leadings" of the grounds that they come from the "Spirit of the Comforter," and yet in their results they tend to make him, and other men, uncomfortable. What theologically active women do, justified by their claims about the will of God, disturbs Ruskin, but he feels largely powerless against it.

Ruskin's excessive, almost obsessive attack on women's theology indicates the cultural power that these theologies were laying claim to, the masculine power that Ruskin was defending. So in addition to its intrinsic interest for feminism and for religious history, a study of women's theological thought can provide important insights into a significant, often-neglected influence on Victorian Christianity and into the power-struggles within Victorian culture.

VICTORIAN WOMEN'S THEOLOGY

The essays that follow are remarkably diverse. They examine the theological thought of women writing in different genres and for different ostensible purposes, claiming allegiance to different religious sects or parties, and revising different aspects of the masculine theologies they challenge.

While they were not permitted to write academic treatises, many women writers found less strongly gendered forms of nonfiction prose in which to express their theological ideas. In "Envisioning Equality, Asserting Authority," Robert M. Kachur discusses devotional prose by (mostly Anglican) women which reinterprets the Apocalypse, presenting a new vision of the New Heaven and New Earth. Frederick S. Roden compares the devotional prose of High Anglican Christina Rossetti to the writings of medieval mystics in "The Kiss of the Soul," finding in them similar experiences of the Divine, similar doctrinal emphases, and similar strategies for authorizing the woman's voice. Kimberly VanEsveld Adams's "The Madonna and Anna Jameson" discusses art-historian Jameson's interpretation of Mary as a powerful Christian goddess, an image of feminine power and virtue within patriarchal Christianity. L. Robert Stevens finds Julia Wedgwood's intertextual theology in her articles for the periodical press, while David Goslee analyzes the letters of Harriett and Jemima Newman as they argue with their newly converted brother J.H. Newman.

Fiction as well as nonfiction could serve as vehicle for women's theological ideas. In "Evangelical Theology and Feminist Polemic," I discuss Emma Jane Worboise's *Overdale* as a "woman's sermon," demonstrating how her version of Evangelical theology drives her simultaneous anti-Tractarian and feminist polemics. Virginia Bemis's "Reverent and Reserved" analyzes the sacramental theology in the novels and periodical articles of High Church writer Charlotte M. Yonge. Finally, in "The Moral Irrelevance of Dogma: Mary Ward and Critical Theology in England," Mark M. Freed argues that Ward introduced the British public to the ideas of German Higher Criticism, but moved beyond it to formulate a "theology of action."

The unorthodox theological ideas that underwrote the campaigns of important late-Victorian women reformers can be found in their polemical books and pamphlets. In "'And Your Sons and Daughters Will Prophesy'," Lucretia A. Flammang analyzes the heterodox theology of Josephine Butler, its Evangelical roots and it apocalyptic visions. Susan Mumm analyzes the "theology of altruism" taught and lived by purity reformer Ellice Hopkins in "Ellice Hopkins and the Defaced Image of Christ."

The final section of this volume moves "Beyond Victorian Christianity." Sarah Willburn reveals the theology of spiritualist practices, while Susan Thach Dean looks at the controversial revisionist work of Buddhist scholar Caroline Rhys Davids.

In all this diversity, however, common themes and interests emerge. Unsurprisingly, many of the women writers are centrally concerned with the authority of the woman's voice in religious life, with their own right to pronounce on theological topics. They present arguments, some based on Scripture, others on personal experience of "call" or "leading," to justify their participation in religious and theological discourse, particularly their right to read and interpret Scripture independent of masculine authority. Most also stress the fundamental equality of men and women before God.

A second, less obvious theme in women's theology is the centrality of the second Person of the Trinity. God the Father represents too clearly the power of the patriarchy to figure largely in these feminizing theologies. God the Holy Spirit, while important in twentieth-century feminist theology, plays a clearly subordinate role in the nineteenth century. But Christ appears repeatedly and centrally in women's theologies, in a variety of roles. Perhaps the most significant for mainstream Christianity was the feminized Suffering Saviour, with whom women and other socially disadvantaged groups could readily identify. His suffering encouraged identification, and his resurrection and reign promised power. This figure is particularly prominent in the theology of reformers Josephine Butler and Ellice Hopkins.

Christ also appears in the work of the reformers as the model for Christians, the model of a (feminized) man. In this context, what matters is the Incarnation, the embodiment of God, rather than His suffering. Many of the women writers see Christ as possessing all virtues -- "feminine" virtues as well as "masculine" ones -- and thus as a model of androgynous life. For the apocalyptically minded, Christ provides a preview of the new humanity who will inhabit the New Earth.

Finally, for women mystics, medieval and Victorian, Christ is the Bridegroom of the feminized Soul, the perfect Lover. (See especially Frederick Roden's "The Kiss of the Soul: The Mystical Theology of Christina Rossetti's Devotional Prose.") Mystical or not, however, women's theology focusses on Christ as Love itself, as Love embodied. The women writers agree with Ruskin in identifying their own natures and duties with those of Love, but they regard Love itself as powerful and transformative.

Even more striking than their intense identification with Christ is the tendency of these women writers to advocate the centrality of action to theology. The most explicit and well-developed examples are Mary Arnold Ward's "theology of action," expounded in Mark M. Freed's essay, and Ellice Hopkins's "theology of altruism," discussed by Susan Mumm. However, many of the other women writers examined in this volume also emphasize the importance of lived theology: Jemima Newman's challenges to her brother's claims of transcendence rely on an extra-textual, contextualized component of theology, as do Emma Jane Worboise's claims for experience as the criterion for religious authority and Josephine Butler's calls to active participation in the creation of the New Earth. Even Caroline Rhys Davids's reinterpretation of Nirvana and of Buddhism itself as active and progressive rather than as contemplative and static argues for theology as the experience of revelation through action, through becoming. To some extent, of course, this emphasis results from women's exclusion from traditional theological discourse, the demand that women focus on religion and moral action rather than theology and intellectual contemplation. But it is also a reaction against what these women perceive as the sterility, even the self-centeredness of academic theology. (See especially the conflict between Oxford theology and theology of action in "Evangelical Theology and Feminist Polemic.") Far from concentrating on the compensations of the afterlife, these women's theologies focus intently on this world, its problems and joys.

In fact, when these women writers do posit an afterlife, or a millennial Paradise, or a mystical sphere beyond common sight, it is often a way of setting up a transcendent standard by which to judge present social conditions -- and most often find them wanting. Their New Jerusalems are not escapist fantasies, opiates to dull the pain of social oppression, but models of equality and harmony and love which rebuke the patriarchal order and inspire the Christian woman to bring them into being.

TRANSFIGURATION

With the possible exceptions of the spiritualists and the reformers Butler and Hopkins, none of these women set out to "transfigure" masculine theology: they were complementing, revising, reinterpreting orthodox doctrines. If challenged, they might well have denied contributing to theology, let alone transfiguring it. Nevertheless, the cumulative effect of all their writings, all their revisions, may well be called a transfiguration. They countered repressive elements of "masculine" theology with a vision of gender equality and with images of the Feminine in the Divine and the Divine in the Feminine; in doing so, they empowered their women readers with a transcendental justification for public speech and public work. In their claims for women's religious and social equality, their feminized Christs, and their theologies of action and commitment, women writers changed the emphases of Victorian religious and, eventually, theological thought and laid the foundations for feminist and liberation theologies of the twentieth century.

NOTES

1. Obviously, this spiritual predominance did not translate into much institutional power, particularly within the patriarchal Church of England. It did, however, justify many forms of public work for women and increase the potential authority of their religious writing.

2. It may seem strange for such a devout anti-capitalist, himself intent on changing many Victorian institutions, to protest against this kind of protest, but Ruskin perceived these women as an even larger threat: yes, women should use their influence to soften capitalism and to prevent wars -- that is the thesis of "Of Queens' Gardens" -- but they should do it privately, not publicly, from a position of acknowledged submission, not from one of assumed power.

WORKS CITED

Christian World Magazine. Ed. Emma Jane Worboise (Guyton). London: James Clarke, 1866-1887.

Krueger, Christine L. *The Reader's Repentance: Women Preachers, Women Writers, and Nineteenth-Century Social Discourse.* Chicago: U of Chicago Press, 1992.

Ruskin, John. "Of Queens' Gardens." *Sesame and Lilies.* 1865. Philadelphia: Henry Altemus, 1899.

Women's Theology
and Nonfiction Prose

Envisioning Equality, Asserting Authority:
Women's Devotional Writings on the Apocalypse, 1845-1900

Robert M. Kachur
University of Massachusetts, Lowell

> *I am lost in the profound wisdom of God in [the book of Revelation's]*
> *constitution, that to some it should be an open page, and to others a*
> *sealed book.* -- The Orb of Light; or, The Apocalyptic Vision, by a
> Lady (1860)

To some an open page, to others a sealed book. With that characterization
of the biblical Apocalypse, the anonymous "Lady" author of *The Orb of
Light* reveals the key to the last book of the Bible's enduring appeal: the
paradox of its being both open and sealed at once. Although "Apocalypse"
means "unveiling," the book re-veils even as it reveals. It promises a glimpse
into the transcendentally true; but because it seeks to represent spiritual
realities for which there is no adequate language, it uses arcane symbols that
need to be decoded.   No wonder, then, that the Apocalypse[1] has been
capturing the religious and literary imaginations for centuries: because it
wrestles with the unutterable, it abounds in allegory and symbolism whose
hermeneutical instability has allowed writers to use the authoritative Word
for their own purposes.   Reviewing the history of Apocalyptic
interpretation during a series of lectures in 1913, University of London
professor R.H. Charles lamented the book's subversive potential: the
moment people began rejecting the literal sense of the Apocalypse, "the
meaning assigned to the text became wholly arbitrary, and each man found
in it what each man wished to find" (12).

This is not to say, of course, that the Apocalypse has always been used
in similar ways, or even that levels of public interest in it have remained
constant.   Britons seemed to have been particularly engrossed by the
Apocalypse during certain periods; the mid-to-late Victorian era is one of
these. As Mary Wilson Carpenter and George P. Landow have documented,
"interest in prophetic exposition reached an unprecedented peak of
popularity" around 1860 (303).   Between 1845 and 1900, British writers
published hundreds of commentaries, devotional guides, tracts, sermons and

lecture on the Apocalypse -- a flurry of writing about Last Things not seen in Britain since the apocalyptic rise and fall of the Commonwealth two centuries before.[2]

Even more interesting, a significant number of the Victorians writing about the Apocalypse were women. Although women were officially prohibited from offering original biblical exegesis within the Anglican church and most Dissenting congregations during the nineteenth century,[3] they published at least two kinds of prose intended to illuminate the Apocalypse: adaptations of Apocalyptic exegesis done by men, simplified for laypeople and children, and the ecclesiastically sanctioned form of "devotional meditations" on the Apocalypse.[4] In defining "devotional meditations" I follow theological historian Margaret R. Miles in referring to "manuals of instruction in the practice of Christianity" which "do not often argue theological issues; the advice they give is usually concerned with changing their readers' behavior" (2). Thus, women's texts of the Apocalypse were by definition supposed to be unremarkable echoes of men's texts -- translations of what the last book of the Bible means, or suggestions of how those already established meanings should affect one's domestic affairs and private worship.

No less than thirty such pieces of women's non-fiction prose on the Apocalypse written during the second half of the nineteenth century have been preserved in the British Library alone. These texts reinforce what a variety of contemporary sources (from articles in the *London Times* to the private correspondence of the young George Eliot) suggest: that women writing biblically-centered texts during the mid- to late-Victorian era were indeed drawn to the Apocalypse in significant numbers.[5] In some cases, this fascination with the Apocalypse among female Christian writers is mentioned in these texts themselves. In her opening "Advertisement" to *The Sevenfold Book* (1853), Catherine Gauntlett refers to the surprising number of women engaged with the Apocalypse:

> Since the commencement of this little work, some others on the same subjects have been published; but the author nevertheless ventures to send it out, with the hope that, by the blessing of God, it may not wholly miss its design. The successive, and almost simultaneous, issue of volumes on the Apocalypse, may be regarded as a providential direction to a more general, systematic, and diligent study of the book itself. (iii)

In addition to testifying to the increased number of women writing "little works" on the Apocalypse such as her own, Gauntlett -- whose text is a simplified adaptation of clergymen's exegesis -- provides a record of the perceived characteristics of women's religious writing as a whole: "These hints on the Revelation were begun with the design of aiding young enquirers in the study of this divine book; and of making it plain to a class of readers, who have not time for lengthy volumes, or works of research and controversy" (iii). According to Gauntlett, women's religious writing does not put forth an argument: it "hints" at possibilities. It is written for "a class of readers" which include the young and those inexperienced at Bible reading. It includes neither "research" nor "controversy."

In this essay, I challenge these widely held assumptions about Victorian women's religious texts in order to make a more specific argument about the function of women's *devotional* texts on the Apocalypse. I seek to demonstrate that female devotional authors -- unlike Gauntlett and other women who attempted to write faithful adaptations of men's exegesis -- were attracted to the Apocalypse precisely because it allowed them to begin to articulate arguments with controversial implications. Within their devotional prose, in other words, these women do, indeed, try their hand at original biblical exegesis. Furthermore, their interpretations of the Apocalypse make explicit what is implicit in their very choice to become exegetes: that Christian women should be repositioned as authoritative readers, writers, and speakers within the church and within society at large.

Before examining how exactly these writers use the Apocalypse to critique gender ideology, the larger question of why these women were drawn to the Apocalypse at all must be addressed. As feminist biblical scholars such as Tina Pippin and Adela Yarbro Collins have pointed out, the Apocalypse is in some ways an especially misogynist biblical text. In its narrative, the two vilified female figures, Jezebel of Revelation 2 and the Whore of Babylon of Revelation 17-18, are killed; the Whore is, additionally, stripped, burned and eaten. Even the book's two "good" female figures, the Woman Clothed with the Sun of Revelation 12 and the Bride of Revelation 21, are marginalized by ultimately being excluded from the narrative in important ways.[6] While some feminist biblical scholars, such as Elisabeth Schussler Fiorenza, take issue with Pippin's contention that the Apocalypse is too inherently misogynist to be recuperated for women, all agree that it at least seems to reinforce unacceptable gender assumptions -- not the least of which is the representation of women as either saints or whores, a dichotomy which met with widespread acceptance during the mid- to late-Victorian era. Why then women's attraction to the Apocalypse as a resource for making critiques of gender ideology during the latter half of the nineteenth century?

In this essay I will attempt to show that it is the Apocalypse's fantastic, controversial allegory and its utopic vision of the New Earth that enabled women to make critiques of gender ideology -- and to cloak those critiques within a veil of orthodox respectability which would allow them to be published and read.

Although all books of the Bible have been subject to multiple interpretations, the Apocalypse's bizarre, dreamlike quality has generated an especially large number of conflicting interpretations and the greatest amount of controversy since its inclusion in the canon.[7] Even the voluminous *Catholic Encyclopedia* laments that "[it] would be alike wearisome and useless to enumerate even the more prominent applications made of the Apocalypse" (598). Thus for women writers who were prohibited from doing straight biblical exegesis, the Apocalypse's open-ended quality made it easier, rather than more difficult, to interpret than other books of the Bible. Because there had not typically been "one" overarching interpretation of the Apocalypse accepted as orthodox within the Christian community, women who would otherwise not be allowed to publish biblical exegesis would be allowed -- indeed, required -- to make explicit exegetical choices when writing about the last book of the Bible. Unlike New Testament books not dominated by controversial allegory, in other words, the Apocalypse is so radically open-ended that to write about it *is* to interpret it.

Women writing devotional texts on the Apocalypse between 1845 and 1900 were, in fact, exegetes who developed their own hermeneutic -- one interpreting religious allegory in terms of the female reader-exegete's immediate circumstances and response. Using this exegetical approach, women used Apocalyptic allegory to envision new possibilities for themselves. Despite devotional texts' marginalization as "feminine" and "practical" within the larger body of "serious" exegesis on the Apocalypse, their generic conventions more easily allowed women to position female experience as a source of authority, as well as to articulate desires for equality within the Christian community. In addition to the freeplay of meaning afforded by its allegory, the Apocalypse provided women writers with a provocative glimpse of the utopic afterlife that loomed so large in Victorian imaginations, but is rarely and usually only fleetingly described in the Bible. The New Jerusalem's close identification with the Bride of Revelation has led to its construction in various eras as a distinctly "feminine" place (Pippin 35). Furthermore, its emphasis on the redeemed's unification as one body under God provided a way for women (much as it had done for Socialists of both sexes)[8] to justify their vision of an egalitarian community. Ultimately, this essay seeks to show that this group of devotional writers, producing texts over a span of fifty years, represents a significant movement anticipating twentieth-century attempts to construct a biblical feminism. The pages that follow examine the writings of women speaking through the Apocalypse to articulate an authoritative, yet "orthodox," Christian female voice.

It is important to emphasize here that the progressive devotional writers discussed in this essay were not revolutionaries. Although their entry into original biblical exegesis is in itself a critique of contemporary gender ideology, they do not typically announce it as such. Nor do they often call special attention to the feminist implications of their exegesis. Instead, these writers clearly seek to remain "orthodox" Christians; rather than breaking with Christian orthodoxy, they try to inscribe their feminist impulses into it.

This complicity with established church systems distinguishes these writers in an important way from the more radical "Apocalyptic" feminists of the early nineteenth century, whose Socialist activities Barbara Taylor details in *Eve and the New Jerusalem*. Those who did interpret Socialism within the framework of Christian eschatology -- "Mother Ann" Lee, Mary Evans, Luckie Buchan, Sarah Flaxmer and Joanna Southcott, to name the most prominent -- were anything but orthodox. Their radical, heretical belief that Christ was ushering in a new egalitarian world order through female messiahs fashioned after the Apocalypse's Bride and Woman Clothed with the Sun obviously placed an insurmountable gulf between them and established Christian churches. Like bright burning flames, these highly visible feminist messiahs made an intense impression on small groups of people outside established churches for a short period of time.[9]

By contrast, the Apocalyptic writers being examined in this study were like smouldering coals emitting more heat than light: they sought to change the way their Christian readers *felt* about women, slowly, without making their feminist impulses too overtly visible. Although these writers do not directly condemn the heresies of the earlier Apocalyptic feminists, the fact that the only women in recent history who had attempted to use the Apocalypse to make feminist claims were infidels and heretics surely discouraged them from explicitly calling attention to the controversial implications of their claims. The devotional writers examined here, in fact, uniformly avoided all labels that were considered incompatible with Christianity within the established churches, even when the label might have been somewhat accurate. A number of these writers for example, envision not merely egalitarian, but socialist-sounding utopic societies, yet roundly condemn Socialism as an infidelity-breeding evil. This inconsistency makes sense if we consider that their project was to construct a biblical feminist theology that would not be associated with fringe radical movement (Socialism, female messianism and the like) but mainline Christianity itself -- a theology that could not be dismissed by the majority of Christians as heterodox and peripheral. To do this, they had to do away with labels that, in Mikhail Bakhtin's words, had become "already enveloped in an obscuring mist...of alien value judgments and accents" (276). Indeed, although attempts to envision a Christian feminism date back at least to Hildegard of Bingen and other medieval writers,[10] these Victorian writers are distinctive precisely because they articulate such sentiments while remaining "ordinary" Christian women writing from respectable positions within mainline churches. The attention roused by visionary abbesses like Julian of Norwich or messiahs like Joanna Southcott would defeat their larger purpose. In order to make universal claims for Christian women, their personas, their callings, and their abilities must appear unremarkable.

READING REVELATION AS MEN AND WOMEN

To build an argument about Victorian women's devotional writing on the Apocalypse, it is first necessary to understand a few fundamentals about the exegetical context in which it appeared. In developing a devotional hermeneutic, how were these women responding to male-dominated interpretive approaches? Although Victorian exegetes often combined interpretive methods and moved between different methods within a single reading of the Apocalypse, my research suggests that Victorian exegetical methods can be grouped in ways that further our understanding of the relationship between Apocalyptic exegesis and gender.

Given Victorian proscriptions against Christian women doing scholarly biblical exegesis, generic distinctions between men's "scholarly" texts which interpret the Apocalypse and women's "devotional" texts which apply the accepted meaning of it to everyday practice are hardly surprising. These generic distinctions, however, obscure more than they reveal on several levels. First, the notion that all "orthodox" Christian women during the Victorian era limited themselves to the genre of the devotional is false: some men wrote primarily devotional works on the Apocalypse, and, as mentioned above, a small but significant number of women wrote adaptations of clergymen's exegesis for uneducated laypeople and children.[11] Second, the generic distinctions of scholarly texts and devotional texts, like all totalizing distinctions, breed a degree of inaccuracy. Scholarly exegesis and devotional writing do not exist as pure and discrete categories of religious prose. Just as men's sermons and commentaries on the Apocalypse sometimes discuss implications for practical application, the affective and experiential content of women's devotional guides and daily meditations were predicated on implicit, and sometimes explicit, exegetical choices.

Even more importantly, the oversimplified notion of devotional writing as non-interpretive can lead to an inaccurate assumption about religious women writers who did choose to stay within the acceptable genre of the devotional: that they were ideologically conservative about women's roles. This does not survive scrutiny of their texts. As we shall see, it was women writing devotional texts on the Apocalypse who more commonly used its allegory to make unorthodox bids for equality and authority; by contrast, the women who did publish recognized (albeit simplified) exegetical works were, with a few important exceptions, mouthpieces for male clergy who reinforced prevailing ideas about Christian women's roles.

Thus the familiar gendered binary of "scholarly" male texts and "devotional" female texts is inadequate as a basis for understanding the relationship between Apocalyptic exegesis and gender. Rather, devotional writing must be understood in terms of its position in relation to different binaries: scholarly versus popular interpretations of the Apocalypse, and literalistic versus spiritualized interpretations of it. Because these binaries are used to distinguish between different types of Apocalyptic exegesis written primarily by men, I will lay a foundation for understanding Apocalyptic devotional writing by briefly identifying the dominant, "male" exegetical approaches to the Apocalypse being published at the same time as these devotional texts.

Reworking hermeneutical categories suggested by biblical scholars Bernhard W. Anderson and E.F. Siegman, I organize male-dominated exegesis of the Apocalypse during the mid- to late-Victorian era in terms of four broad approaches organized around the period John's vision is thought to describe. *Historical-allegorical* exegetes work from the premise that the Apocalypse's allegory largely describes past events; the last book of the Bible is approached as a map of church or world history. *Spiritual-allegorical* exegetes also work from the premise that the Apocalypse must be approached as allegory, but assume that the book describes timeless spiritual realities rather than specific historical events. *Literal-eschatological* exegetes, rather than approaching the Apocalypse as an allegorical document at all, contend that it describes events which will be literally fulfilled in the future. Although these three popular approaches were most widely used by laypeople and clergy throughout the nineteenth century, *historiocritical* exegesis (which still undergirds modern scholarship on the Apocalypse), had become entrenched in the academy by the very beginning of the century. Influenced by the German Higher Criticism, historiocritical exegetes work from the premise that the Apocalypse offers a cloudy window into the biblical writer's contemporary circumstances -- nothing more.

Christians outside the academy, though anxious to preserve the Apocalypse's integrity as a divinely inspired document offering more than a cloudy window into the biblical writer's world, were often fierce in their declamations of popular approaches to interpreting the Apocalypse which conflicted with their own. Critics of the literalistic and historical-allegorical schools of interpretation often complained that such a "narrow" method of interpretation, which allowed for no allegorical open-endedness, "forced its adherents to do violence repeatedly to the obvious [moral] sense of the text" (Charles 45). Critics of the spiritualizing camp, on the other hand, complained that an ahistorical exegetical approach resulted in "unbounded licence in the interpretation of the Apocalypse...[which] destroys its significance for its own immediate age or any other" (Charles 23-24).

At first glance, devotional writers may seem to have written outside this fray. This is not to say that their writings were not clearly "popular" rather than scholarly, of course: as writers of what were packaged as personal meditations on Revelation, they emphasized the book's potential as a guide for everyday piety and as an affective aid for worship and spiritual reflection. But because they wrote personal reflections of Revelation rather than "public" documents arguing about the book's ultimate meaning within the larger Christian arena, they were hardly considered exegetes at all. As such, they escaped the notice of scholarly exegetes, who did not reference them. Even more importantly, they largely escaped the censure of exegetes in the literalizing and spiritualizing camps, who would have believed that devotional meditations on Revelation complemented, rather than competed with, their own exegesis. Conservative Christians who disagreed about the Apocalypse's ultimate meaning agreed that it, like all Scripture, has tropological value: it is, in other words, "profitable for doctrine, for reproof, for correction, [and] for instruction in righteousness" (2 Timothy 3:16). Thus, though women's devotional meditations on the Apocalypse were marginalized as "feminine" and "practical," they occupied a unique position: they were read by, and could influence, a wide cross-section of Christians. [12]

The "safe," generically conventional appearance of women's devotional prose on the Apocalypse during this period, however, belies the fact that women were stretching and redefining the genre of the devotional by using it to engage in biblical hermeneutics and thus to re-envision what their roles as female readers and writers should be. Ironically, it was the female Apocalyptic writers who were bold enough to try their hand at male-dominated exegetical approaches who overwhelmingly reinforce prevailing ideas about the Christian woman writer's role. Reading women's non-devotional Apocalyptic texts written between 1845 and the end of the century helps us understand why this is so. Clearly, these women felt that in order to be published, they had to ally themselves with male exegetes and their readings: they had, in fact, to become "male" exegetes. The gender anxiety manifest in Mrs. J.C. Martin's historical-allegorical work *The Revelation of St. John Briefly Explained* (1851) is typical. An almost ridiculous series of assurances that she has been taught by and seeks to emulate male exegetes comprises the bulk of her preface:

> Having had my attention...directed to these prophecies, in the library of my father, the late Bishop Mant,...The valuable work of Bishop Newton upon the Prophecies...is [alas!] too elaborate and expensive for ordinary students....Mr. Elliott's recently published work seems

indeed, to be the classic book on the Apocalypse: and, besides constantly referring to it in the following pages, I wish generally to acknowledge the pleasure and profit with which I have read it....But [Elliott's] "Horae Apocalypticae" is, from its size alone...inaccessible to a multitude of students: and therefore, I have been induced to submit this little hand-book drawn up, at first, exclusively for my own satisfactionn, and amidst a variety of domestic and parochial occupations -- to the indulgence of the public... (iv-vi)

Rather than making a case for her position as a female exegete, Martin resists that identity: she is, rather, an editor and conveyer of men's exegesis for less educated -- and, we can assume, predominately female -- readers. A careful reader will be assured that she has not willingly published this book at all: she has been "induced" to make public an unusually astute specimen of private meditations of Scripture, which were acceptable for women otherwise properly engaged in "domestic and parochial occupations."

Of all the Victorian Apocalyptic texts by women which do critique gender ideology, the anonymously authored *The Orb of Light; or, The Apocalyptic Vision, by a Lady* (1860) stands apart as one of the very few pieces in which a woman attempts to use a "male" hermeneutic to do so.[13] Although *Orb* is an anomaly, it is valuable to study for that very reason: it testifies to the tremendous degree of pressure female Apocalyptic writers who used a "male" hermeneutic felt to deliver a familiar, "male" reading, and it helps provide a context for understanding the very different rhetorical strategies used by devotional writers. By "male" hermeneutic, I refer to the four broad types of Apocalyptic exegesis mentioned above, which, during the second half of the nineteenth century, were predominantly written by men. Women generally only pursued these exegetical approaches for one purpose: to make accessible, and thus perpetuate, exegesis done by men.

Interestingly, the *Orb* author remains anonymous about her identity except for one important detail: her sex. Because female religious writers who do not give their names more commonly try to downplay gender by using initials, this author's foregrounding of her position as a woman reading the Apocalypse seems significant. Indeed, her text reveals a preoccupation not only with what it means to read Revelation as a woman, but with what's at stake for women in contemporary readings of Revelation. Indeed, unlike the devotional texts we are about to examine, *The Orb of Light* is itself a very threatening feminist manifesto. The Lady author not only offers exegesis of the Apocalypse to a general audience, but claims to have a boldly original "vision" of what John's vision means -- an entirely new type of historical-allegorical exegesis. Standing alone against the majority of historical exegetes, who believe that most of the Apocalypse has already been fulfilled, she posits that the Victorian era, though marking the end of a 2,000-year epoch, only marks the end of the third biblical epoch within a larger succession of seven. Her initial identification of herself as a Lady prophet with a new interpretation of the Apocalypse is quickly followed by these comments:

> In presenting this little work to the public the writer is deeply moved at the position she occupies....Is such a commission [to reveal the meaning of Revelation] a trifling one? No; the writer must be a presumptuous, bold fanatic, an evil angel, or God's messenger; and thus it is that she submits it to the patient reading of the public, to be impartially judged....And she would ask for the work that, *if it be* scriptural...it may rather receive the verdict of time than of impulse or preconceived opinion...When we are told by the generality of Publishers, "Bring us a story and we will publish it for you, but for theological works there is no sale unless they are written by -----, and -----, and -----, and ----- we are discouraged, and truth and humble service are almost afraid to lift their heads: but that does not prove that they should retire ashamed, or that they are any the less needed. (v-vii)

Given the plethora of commentators who make no apologies for attempting to reveal Revelation's meaning, the Lady's concern that she will be considered "presumptuous" or even "evil" for doing so seems odd -- unless we consider that she has decided to offer the kind of exegesis that only men such as "----- and ----- and -----" are generally allowed to publish. (Compare Thomas William Greenwell's brief reference to the unconventional nature of some of his exegesis in *The Illustrated Apocalypse* [1884]: "Many of the ideas are original, and are put forward entirely on [my] own responsibility.") "Preconceived opinion" would not only expect the Lady's "little book" to be littler than it is at 348 pages, but devotional in its tenor, helping the reader to an affective experience of the Apocalypse described by L.B. in *Short Notes on the Revelation* (1886) as "ecstasy which overwhelms thought" (35). This Lady's attempt to discuss Revelation in a very unladylike way causes her to address the reader's anxiety with admonitions to remain open-minded throughout her text. "Should I be accused of dogmatism and presumption," she writes toward the end of her book, "I answer, that this work is one of more than ten years of prayerful, humble research" (340).

What makes the *Orb* Lady's highly defensive rhetoric necessary is not that she, as a woman, does original allegorical exegesis per se; as we shall see, female devotional writers regularly do this without verbally arming themselves for battle. What causes the Lady to anticipate such a high degree of opposition is, rather, that she does original allegorical exegesis by way of a "male" hermeneutic, which forces her to make her stance explicit. Because the *Orb* author transgresses the exegetical norms of the historical-allegorical approach by reinterpreting the Apocalypse's historical timeline, she calls attention to herself as a woman doing "female" exegesis.

But why, we might ask, does the *Orb* author identify herself as a "Lady" author at all? If her purpose is to put forward a new historical interpretation of the Apocalypse, why does she foreground rather than obscure her gender, a major obstacle to its acceptance?

The *Orb* author's declaration of gender only makes sense if we consider that part of her purpose in rereading the Apocalypse is to redefine gender roles within a Christian context. The degree of unresolved tension resulting from the Lady's attempt to employ "female" exegetical strategies within a "male" exegetical framework makes *Orb* a singular text -- one particularly helpful for elucidating points of conflict between "male" and "female" readings of the Apocalypse. By examining the Lady's textual strategies more closely, and then drawing connections between them and those used in women's devotional texts on the Apocalypse, I shall now examine devotional writers' attempts to create an authoritative female Christian voice.

IDENTIFYING A "FEMALE" HERMENEUTIC OF THE APOCALYPSE

Orb's exegesis displays at least three qualities which make it stand apart from traditional, "male" historical readings of the last book of the Bible: an affirmation of the Apocalypse's accessibility to ordinary readers who have no formal theological training; an emphasis on Apocalyptic allegory's fundamentally open-ended quality; and an insistence on the Apocalypse's allegorical significance for the exegete's immediate and future circumstances. Examining women's devotional texts written between 1845 and 1900 suggests that these three qualities, far from signifying one author's idiosyncrasies, are defining characteristics of a larger group of "female" readings of Apocalyptic allegory -- readings which implicitly and often explicitly advance a critique of strictures on women within the church and society. By focusing attention on the open-endedness, universal accessibility, and immediate relevance of Apocalyptic allegory, the authors of these readings not only re-interpret the Apocalypse, but re-envision Christian women as Readers of the primary biblical text, rather than merely readers of others' interpretations of it. By doing this, they are able to weave strands of an emergent feminist theology into the Apocalypse itself.

Gaining access to the Apocalypse: the threat of the ordinary and unlearned reader.

Given strictures against women preaching, writing sermons, or interpreting the Bible in mainline churches during the second half of the nineteenth century, the anxiety that the *Orb* Lady expresses about being "accused of dogmatism and presumption" because she offers an original interpretation of Scripture is understandable. It is even more understandable, however, in light of concern being registered among contemporary male exegetes about the Apocalypse falling into the wrong hands. Because the last book of the Bible is so enigmatic, it might be interpreted to mean anything -- and had been, by radical Socialists and feminists, in recent history.

"Male" interpreters of the Apocalypse registered tremendous anxiety about the socially subversive potential of allowing interpretations of the book to proliferate. Many of these writers explicitly emphasized the need to keep "ordinary and unlearned" readers from taking the Apocalypse into their own hands. Rev. Richard Chester's prefatory remarks to the literal-eschatological work entitled *The Revelation Unravelled* (1867) are typical:

> No portion of Holy Writ has had more of various commentary, or of multiplied and diversified interpretation expended upon it than the Book of Revelation. Yet there is unquestionably no so great desideratum just at present in religious literature as a clear, concise, consistent, intelligible guide to the Apocalypse, such as may assist the ordinary and unlearned reader to arrive at a definite conclusion concerning...the appalling judgments which are ere long to burst upon nominal, apostate Christendom. (v)

That an Anglican cleric (strongly believing, most likely, in the need for ecclesiastical authorities to guide believers in spiritual matters) would be concerned about false doctrine spreading through the church is in itself not unusual. What is surprising is that proliferating readings of the Apocalypse should pose a concern in this regard. Although any book of the Bible could, obviously, be used to support some theological doctrines, the Apocalypse has provided theologians with little material for doctrine per se. As Adela Yarbro Collins has pointed out, the Apocalypse has had little part in theologians' making sense of Christianity's central tenets -- sin, salvation, and so forth. Rather, the Apocalypse has exerted its greatest influence as a socio-political document fueling revolutionary and counterrevolutionary movements (369). The concern that Rev. Chester and others share over the Apocalypse's proliferating meanings is clearly tied to their socio-political, rather than strictly doctrinal, ramifications.

Chester's comments are also important in the way they illuminate the perceived magnitude of the socio-political threat posed by proliferating readings of the Apocalypse during the mid-Victorian period. Text after popular text share the urgent tenor of Chester's remarks: *No portion of Holy Writ has been as diversely interpreted; there is unquestionably no so great desideratum* in all religious literature at present as a document that pins down the Apocalypse's meaning *clearly and concisely*, once and for all. Significantly, Chester is not so much worried about biblical scholars such as himself, but "ordinary and unlearned" readers -- that is, Christian laypeople, a majority of whom would have been women -- who need to be led to "a definite conclusion" about the Apocalypse's meaning.

In contrast to "male" readings of the Apocalypse which express anxiety over the reading activity of the "ordinary and unlearned," devotional texts almost uniformly stress the value of such readers engaging with the Apocalypse for themselves. L.B., the author of the devotional text *Short Notes on the Revelation* (1886), begins her exegesis by glossing Revelation 1:3 -- "Blessed is he that readeth and they that hear the words of this prophecy, and keep those things which are written therein" -- to mean that "those who are unlearned, as well as those who are learned, may study it" (2). In the second edition of *His Last Word: Bible Readings in Revelation* (1896), Mrs. M. (Elizabeth) Baxter goes a step further, suggesting that denying ordinary readers access to the Apocalypse is actually hindering the Bible's final prophetic book from being fulfilled:

> It has pleased Him who hath chosen the weak things of this world to use the first Edition of this little book of suggestions, so that a second Edition has been called for....I have learned from many readers that they have been led to study the Book of Revelation very thoroughly for themselves. O that the coming of our expected Lord may no longer be unhindered by our unreadiness. (ii)

Ostensibly, devotional Scripture reading by women is non-threatening because it is restricted to meditating on how established interpretations of Scripture should be applied in everyday life and how they can stir affective response. The nagging threat that women might be overstepping their bounds as biblical readers in devotional texts, however, often announces itself in prefatory disclaimers. M.S.'s *Songs of the Apocalypse* (1887), for example, begins with a male clergyman's assurance that the female author stays within conventional bounds as a reader:

> I would earnestly commend to the Lord's people the following series of meditations on the Seven Songs of the Apocalypse, assured that it is the prayerful desire of the author that the Holy Ghost may "stir up the wills" of God's faithful people in more true exercise of the "new creature" life, to "wait for His Son from heaven" (I Thess. i 10)...(ii)

The minister's phrases "stir up the wills," "more true exercise," and "new creature life" build on each other to emphasize, strongly, the practical nature of M.S.'s text. Even more interesting, however, is the way his attempt to downplay her agency as a woman writer subtly turns in on itself. He quotes the author using biblical language twice to make her desire to focus on Christian practice feel more authentic and immediate ("stir up the wills," "new creature"); but in doing so he actually reminds us of her distinct presence as a biblical reader who uses biblical language to express her own desires. This suggestive subtext is reinforced by his decision to quote the Bible directly in the same breath that he quotes her ("wait for His Son from heaven"). Not only are both voices given the same weight in this small paragraph, but the biblical "voice" appears to be brought in to articulate what the woman's voice will not: a desire to "wait" passively, rather than act, until the Second Coming.

Although M.S. and other female devotional writers are clearly concerned with drawing out implications of Apocalyptic exegesis for everyday life and worship, their texts deliver more actual intepretive maneuvering than their prefaces and title pages promise. *Songs of the Apocalypse* is a case in point. Its title suggests that the book's primary purpose will be to help readers worship by focusing on the Apocalypse's hymns of praise. In reality, however, the "songs" of the Apocalypse do not provide the core content of M.S.'s text at all: they (and M.S.'s affective musings about them) make up less than half of *Songs*' 104 pages. What the songs do provide is a way for M.S. to restructure the Apocalypse. Eschewing the chapter-by-chapter analysis that dominates "male" exegesis of the Apocalypse, she groups the book's content into seven sections of "songs" which enable her to manipulate which aspects of the text should be emphasized. That she identifies seven songs -- some of which are not clearly songs of praise at all in the Apocalyptic text itself -- is particularly significant. Among allegorical exegetes, seven was (and still is) commonly accepted as a number denoting perfection; and it has long been commonplace in commentaries to remark upon the recurrence of sevens (seven vials, seven trumpets, seven churches, and so forth) in the Apocalypse. By reorganizing the biblical text itself into seven sections, M.S. suggests that she has found a more perfect way of examining the test as a whole.

Allegorical instability and the possibility of social critique.

Historically, Apocalypse has only become available as a vehicle of social critique when it has been approached as an allegorically unstable document -- unstable in the sense that the allegory's meaning needs to be interpreted and reinterpreted in light of present circumstances. Significantly, dominant "male" exegetical methodologies during the second half of the nineteenth century inherently defused the potential power of the Apocalypse's unstable allegory. Literal-eschatological exegetical systems did this by entirely dismissing the Apocalypse's allegorical level of meaning. Historiocritical and historical-allegorical exegetes did this by arguing that Apocalyptic allegory refers to a fixed and objectively verifiable series of past events. Spiritual-allegorical exegetes did this by insisting that the Apocalypse's allegory, although open to multiple interpretations, referred to timeless, spiritual realities, rather than contemporary events. In a fundamental way, then, "male" hermeneutical approaches to the Apocalypse during the Victorian era were ideologically conservative, denying the book's relevance as a basis for political or social action.

Unlike historiocritical and literalistic exegetes, historical-allegorical exegetes not only tended to dismiss the Apocalypse's value as a foundation for social activism, but went so far as to use the Apocalypse to oppose social change. Although they were primarily concerned with the Apocalypse as a description of past events, their belief that Apocalyptic allegory describes historical realities which still existed in Victorian society (such as the Roman Catholic church) gave them opportunities for contemporary social commentary. They too tended to deny the Apocalypse's relevance as a basis for political or social action: typically they interpreted the forces threatening church and society as decidedly "other" and beyond the Protestant Christian's direct ability to control: no one can hope to stop the Pope's devilry, for example, except God himself.

Again and again, historical-allegorical texts vilify agents of change within church and society -- movements associated with female autonomy, universal suffrage, socialism and organized labor -- by directly or indirectly identifying them with the coming Roman Catholic antichrist's world order. No wonder, then, that the author of *Orb* feels such anxiety in offering a new allegorical-historical reading of the Apocalypse. Consider the comments she makes immediately after suggesting that the "falling star" of Revelation 16 represents not just the historical "fall" of the Roman Church after the Reformation (a widely accepted historical interpretation), but the present decline of the increasingly "Romish" High Church of England:

> My mission is not to fulminate anathemas;...My mission is neither to take away from the words of this book [of Revelation], nor to add thereto....[Yet] I have been told I am calling down a curse upon my people. Did I write the Apocalypse? Did I write the things of the third vial and trumpet? No. All that I would say is, that this coming judgment [it describes] is in the hand of God, and not in the hand of the enemy. (*Orb* 222)

The moment the *Orb* Lady's allegorical-historical exegesis condemning the Catholic church turns toward contemporary critique of the Anglican church, she experiences the conflict inherent in using a "male" hermeneutic to make a critique intended to foster change. She must defend her interpretation of Apocalyptic allegory as not "taking away" or "adding" to the Apocalypse -- as if established historical interpretations of its allegory were transparent and not in need of defense. As a consequence of both taking agency as a female exegete and locating the social threat mentioned in this chapter of Revelation *within* the Protestant church, the Lady fears that her readers will categorize her in the only cultural role available for women who use the divine Word in a transgressive way: a sorceress "calling down a curse upon [her] people."

This insistence on Apocalyptic allegory's open-ended nature is a theme that runs strongly through devotional texts on the Apocalypse. A careful reading of M.S.'s *Songs of the Apocalypse* suggests how female devotional writers justified taking exegetical control over such open-ended Apocalyptic allegory. Building on the widely accepted notion of progressive revelation -- the idea that God continues to reveal Himself more and more clearly as time unfolds -- she argues that new readings need to be made of the Apocalypse continually. Much as a Christian's understanding of the Old Testament would be incomplete without the New, or a Protestant's understanding of the New Testament incomplete without the teaching of the Reformers, existing readings of the Bible's last, future-oriented book remain inevitably incomplete. Mrs. Baxter's appropriation of this doctrinal tenet in *His Last Word* is particularly explicit:

> We must not forget that prophecy in Scripture has a law of development....We need the constant and ever new light of the Holy Spirit that we may compare Scripture with Scripture, not in the light of human wisdom or intelligence, but as being really and immediately taught by God. (359-60)

Other women appeal more directly to the closely related Christian tenet that the gulf which exists between the essence of the divine and the essence of the human is only bridged by Christ: God is perfect in his moral understanding of spiritual realities, while humans (with the exception of Christ) are not. The New Testament's promise is that "the creature itself also *shall be* delivered from the bondage of corruption" (Romans 8:21; emphasis added). As the fullness of that transformation remains future, however, human understandings of God gained by reading Scripture must continually be revised. In her lengthy devotional poem "The Divine and Human in the Book of Revelation: An Attempt to Realize the Conditions of Feeling and Circumstance under which St. John Wrote His Vision" (1863), author C.J.A. focuses on the idea that the gulf between human and divine capabilities renders a complete reading of the Apocalypse impossible:

But how declare the vision? who shall tell / With common lips of the ineffable? / How shall the finite limn the infinite? / Yea, even thou, Apostle, e'en *thy* speech -- / Though the fresh fervours of no earthly fire / Glowed in thy breast, and each astonied sense / Were scarce yet wakened from its ecstasy -- / Yet e'en *thy* speech must fail, and loftiest words / Be but as feeble ministers, when truth / Transcends the power of human utterance.

In the above passage, C.J.A. suggests that the problem of Apocalyptic interpretationn can be traced all the way back to the first human who tried to articulate the vision: John. Though inspired by the Holy Spirit himself, John is limited the very moment his humanness manifests itself in his dependence on human language. How then are we to expect human exegetes to offer a complete reading of the Apocalypse, even if their interpretations were, in some sense, completely accurate?

Similarly, M.S. ironically alludes to the writings of that quintessential patriarch, Paul, to argue against the notion that even a learned man could offer a reading of the Apocalypse which puts its confusing allegory to rest:

> Let us contemplate the vision God vouchsafed to His servant...remembering that we read "as children"; we write "as children," we understand "as children," for we have the promise -- very precious, is it not? -- that God the Holy Spirit shall "show us things to come." (28)

Whereas Paul repeats the phrase "as a child" in 1 Corinthians 13:11 to emphasize his point that everything in this world except love will pass away, M.S. does so to emphasize that contemporary understandings of Scripture are inadequate. M.S. goes on to use the Apocalypse itself to argue that God does not intend believers to come to a completed reading of it until the end of time: "'But in the days of the voice of the seventh angel, when he shall begin to sound, the mystery of God should be finished.' In that day, there should be the complete unfolding of the purposes of grace. We shall understand our Bibles then" (69). Other devotional writers go further, explicitly denouncing approaches which claim to offer a definitive interpretation of the Apocalypse. L.B. does so by appealing to Jesus' own activity as a biblical reader within John's vision. Glossing Revelation 1:20, in which Jesus himself interprets the allegorical meaning of the seven stars and the seven candlesticks which John describes in verses 12 and 16, L.B. argues that He divinely ordains reading the Apocalypse as open-ended allegory: "[Here Jesus] gives authority to a mystical interpretation of this book, and would appear to be the one which would exclude all those narrow interpretations, the tying down the meaning to particular Churches and towns, thus erring for want of charity" (4). Although L.B. implies that she and Jesus share the same interpretive approach to John's vision, she actually goes one step further than Jesus in stressing the especially open-ended nature of the Apocalypse's images. Whereas Jesus interprets the seven candlesticks to be "seven churches" -- which in Revelation 2 and 3 he seems to identify with seven specific churches in Asia Minor -- L.B. (using the accepted interpretation of "seven" as indicating completion) adds a new level of meaning to them, finding in the seven churches "a type of the universal church" (4).

In *The Book of the Unveiling: Studies in the Revelation of St. John the Divine* (1892), Mrs. Rundle Charles even more strongly argues that narrow interpretations which try to impose clarity on the Apocalypse are, ironically, the very source of the confusion and controversy surrounding it:

> [T]he unseen world of the Apocalypse can never be thus sharply divided into sections...Its scenery dissolves as we look at it....it cannot be cribbed, cabined and confined into any picture, in words, form or colour. From the vain efforts so to define and confine it has doubtless arisen much of the perplexity which estranges some of us from this book which we are especially encouraged and commanded to read. (72-73)

Charles's neo-Platonic perspective that ineffable realities escape our vision and speech -- that words and symbols and visual images are mere shadows which dissolve as we use them -- resembles other spiritual-allegorical approaches to the Apocalypse, which posit that the book concerns timeless, spiritual realities. Charles's text is distinct, however, in the association it makes between *defining* and *confining*. Whereas most spiritual-allegorical exegetes freely define Apocalyptic allegory in terms of universal, spiritual struggles and triumphs, she implies that to define Apocalyptic allegory with any sense of finality or completeness at all smacks of an unseemly attempt to make it say what the exegete wants it to say. Hence Charles's devotional emphasis on approaching the Apocalypse as an aid to worship: its language, for her, is about escaping language in favor of a more complete and real transcendental experience.

Charles's conviction that attempts to define the Apocalypse are cloaked attempts to confine (and thus harness) its power is further developed in the following passage, in which she ultimately associates attempts to fix Apocalyptic allegory's meaning with oppressive social and ecclesiastical movements:

> Gazing on...the self-sacrifice of the Self-Existent,...the problems of social life,...the perplexities of our own little wars, are not indeed so

much solved as dissolved in light. Taking up this as our standard of *action*, the disorders, the chaos, the tumult and the void of our social state would glide into order and beauty, the true objects of the most sanguine revolutions would be evolved, *the objects of ambition being themselves revolutionised*; the glory and wealth and might of love being felt to be always in the services it can render, not in the services it can claim...This is no unattainable far-off ideal. It is, according to the Apocalypse, an actual fact, as sure and as present as the existence of the sun in our material heavens....[N]ever lost, from the days of that Apocalypse to these, [Christ's] ideal and pattern of love and sacrifice has...burned and shone through all [Christendom's] confusions and crusts, consuming wrong after wrong in nations; penetrating with its vivifying light through the ice-crusts or lava-ashes which gather round every form of Christian doctrine or ecclesiastical organization;...(27-28)

In this passage Charles suggests that the "light" of spiritual reality defies translation into language; it can only find articulation on the human plane through *action* -- repeated *acts* of Christlike self-sacrifice in which believers progressively become like the Word rather than just becoming speakers or writers of words. Using this notion of light-as-dynamism, Charles constructs a binary in which light is not opposed to darkness, but to stasis. Charles's light/stasis binary calls attention to itself because it intentionally undermines readers' expectations. Readers would have expected her to oppose "light" to "darkness": not merely because it intuitively makes sense, but because John (assumed by non-academics to be the same John of the Gospel and the epistles) elsewhere in the Bible often describes God as "light" opposing darkness.[14] By opposing the light of biblical truth not with the darkness of unbelief, but with Christians' petrifying attempts to define and confine the Apocalypse's meaning, Charles suggests that the motives of exegetes who attempt to translate the Apocalypse into precise language are inherently suspect: "[The Apocalypse] is, indeed, not a map of events, but a revelation of persons, and of principles which can only live in persons" (39). Two of the oppressive systems which result from defining/confining the light of biblical truth by interpreting it too rigidly are "Christian doctrine" and "ecclesiastical organization." They are static, oppressive constructs built on the "crusts," "ice-crusts" and "lava-ashes" of dead language which contains only a trace of the dynamic biblical reality (analogous here with volcanic lava and freely flowing water) that exegetes try to capture and control.

Thus, to read the Apocalypse in a fixed, "male" way controls how others experience (or, more accurately, don't experience) the Apocalypse -- and the Christian faith as a whole. Such oppressive approaches to the Apocalypse, according to Charles, have larger repercussions within a widely "Christian" society such as England. They result not only in the interpretive "confusions" we might expect among the faithful, but in social and political oppression and conflict: "the problems of social life," "our own little wars," "the disorders, the chaos, the tumult and the void of our social state," "revolutions," and "wrong after wrong in nations." Clearly, attempts to define/confine Apocalyptic allegory are the tools of those who seek to consolidate power through biblical language. Charles contrasts this intellectual approach to the Apocalypse, which limits readers' experiences of the book, with a devotional approach which encourages readers to experience the book's open allegory again and again, with the goal of embodying biblical truth through action. Those who would do the latter must emulate Christ's "pattern of love and sacrifice" which "dissolves" rather than "solves" social/material problems by making the pursuit of oppressive power through intellectual activity unthinkable.

After this pivotal passage introducing the subject of social and political oppression, Charles's text repeatedly uses the Apocalypse as a launching point to denounce various forms of this oppression. What is distinctive about Charles's text is not that she uses the Apocalypse to denounce contemporary economic and political oppression, however; after all, the Apocalypse had been used that way for centuries. Nor is it that she raises the problem of how Apocalyptic language should be interpreted: as we have seen, many Victorian exegetes did that at the outset of their texts. What is distinctive, rather, is that she posits a relationship between systemic oppression and dominant exegetical approaches to the Apocalypse which prevent the individual reader from becoming her own exegetical Reader. She not only problematizes the meaning of the text, in other words, but the meaning of exegetical approaches to the text. She makes explicit what other devotional writers implicitly affirm: that Apocalyptic allegory only becomes a vehicle for resisting oppression when it is approached with a devotional hermeneutic -- one emphasizing the open-ended and experiential nature of the text in the individual reader's hands. It is important to emphasize here that although Charles is critiquing how many do Apocalyptic exegesis, her devotional text is itself exegetical. She suggests that reading the Apocalypse experientially, as an inspiration for worship and everyday living isn't a secondary way to read the Apocalypse which complements "male" exegesis, but the primary way it should be read, a way *at odds* with "male" exegesis.

The devotional mode and the possibility of feminist critique.

It was this concern with having an immediate, experiential encounter with the Apocalypse which made the devotional mode such an appropriate vehicle for critiquing injustices felt by the biblical reader herself. To illustrate how central this sense of the present moment is to female exegesis of the Apocalypse, let us return momentarily to the woman's non-devotional text which has served as our point of departure for examining devotional texts: *The Orb of Light.* Unlike most of her contemporaries, *Orb*'s author argues that the Victorian era falls near the beginning (rather than near the very end) of the Apocalypse's narrative of events. Thus, although she spends some time writing about how the Apocalypse has already been fulfilled in history, a far greater portion of her text comments on the Apocalypse's relevance to the immediate future. Her desire to focus on present-day events, far from being a peripheral issue in *Orb*, is the fundamental effect of her radical restructuring of accepted historical-allegorical timelines of the Apocalypse's events.

In devotional texts, Victorian women used the Apocalypse to further a critique of their position within church and society in several different ways. Before identifying these strategies, it is important to locate all of them within the context of the common hermeneutical practice of typology. In *Victorian Types, Victorian Shadows*, George P. Landow describes typology as the belief that Old Testament figures and events, call "types," foreshadow corresponding New Testament figures and events, called "antitypes." Like the doctrine of progressive revelation discussed above, typological interpretation posits that God's method of revealing Himself and His intentions becomes clearer as time passes. Thus "types" of Christ in the Old Testament -- King David, for example -- are necessarily imperfect, while the antitype Christ is perfect. The Israelites passed through the Red Sea in a type of baptism which foreshadowed the more perfect baptism with water and the Holy Spirit experienced by God's people in the New Testament.

Although Landow's discussion of Victorian typology does not specifically mention the Apocalypse, Apocalyptic readers often incorporate typology into their readings. Most commonly, Victorian exegetes who did not entirely disqualify the future import of the Apocalypse believed that "types" of evil in the Bible (from Cain to Herod) would not become fully meanifest in an antitype until the Apocalyptic antichrist. Current events and persons, from the French Revolution to Queen Victoria herself, were thus often referenced as types of some greater evil or good to come, without necessarily being identified as the ultimate referent of an Apocalyptic image.

For Apocalyptic exegetes, viewing present-day realities as imperfect types of antitypes represented in the Apocalypse provided an avenue for contemporary critique. On one hand, "unchristian" movements (such as socialism, trade unions, and revolutionary fanaticism) could be cast as sinister foreshadowings of worse things to come; on the other, the Christian church could be measured against its perfect antitype -- the purified Bride introduced at the end of the Apocalypse -- and found lacking. Although women engaged in both kinds of critique, the devotional writers examined here primarily engaged in the latter. And when they did, they tended to critique the Church in terms of their immediate experience as Christian women -- women prevented by ecclesiastical organization and doctrinal systems from realizing their full potential as God's servants.

Victorian women approaching the Apocalypse from a "female" hermeneutic critique the Church's devaluation of women in three broad ways, each of which will now be discussed in turn.

Revising the misogynist tone of the Apocalypse.

As noted earlier in this chapter, feminist biblical scholars have repeatedly pointed out the misogynist tone of the Apocalypse. The last book of the Bible excludes and commits violence against women in a number of ways; its misogynist impulse finds fullest expression, however, in the highly sexual and autonomous Whore of Babylon figure, who is beaten, killed, stripped, burned and eaten in Revelation 17. She is contrasted with both the Woman Clothed with the Sun of Revelation 12 and the Bride of Revelation 19; the piety and motherhood of the former and the chaste virginity of the latter make them the Whore's antitheses. This dichotomous categorization of women into mothers and chaste virgins on one hand and whores on the other was implicitly or explicitly affirmed by the majority of Victorian exegetes, who found in it a reaffirmation of similar cultural categorizations of woman.

Although it is only within the last several decades that feminist biblical scholars have explicitly debated whether the Apocalypse can be recuperated for women, problems posed by the Apocalypse's misogynist elements were not lost on female devotional writers trying to use the book to imagine new possibilities for themselves. The rhetorical moves they make when faced with the Whore of Babylon figure are especially revealing. Many go to great lengths to "masculinize" the Whore: rather than using her to meditate on their own position as women, as they tend to do with the more positive female figures of the Woman Clothed with the Sun or the Bride, they use the Whore as a launching point to discuss men and male-dominated institutions.

The most commonplace interpretation of the Whore, made by M.S. as well as many non-devotional exegetes, is that she represents "Popery." Although the Roman Catholic church is, of course, a patriarchal institution, it is figured in feminine terms, as seducing men with aesthetic allure. More interesting for the purposes of this essay, therefore, are interpretations of the Whore by Victorian women who break away from misogynist interpretations which reaffirm the Whore as representing grotesque "feminine" error or excess. In *Short Notes on the Revelation*, L.B. does this by interpreting the Whore not in terms of female excess, but male lack. In her text, the Whore represents the "spirit of modern civilization" which "denies Christianity"; in her introductory remarks to Revelation 17, she figures infidel "civilization" as a male phenomenon, an outgrowth of the kinds of academic, intellectual activity only men are allowed to pursue. She does this by interpreting the alternately scorching and darkened sun which causes suffering in Revelation 16:8-11 as representing "the intellect and those who misuse the intellect suffer[ing] through the intellect, the means of light bringing darkness" (58).[15]

In *His Last Word*, Mrs. Baxter pushes this strategy of masculinizing the Whore further in significant ways. Although she condemns male intellectualism earlier, in her exegesis of the great earthquake described in Revelation 6:12-17 ("the great men of the earth -- given over, as they are, to the worship of the intellect, the exalting of the natural law above the Creator of the world -- will also be convulsed") she uses the Whore to indict the male-dominated world of commerce for its distinctly "male" excesses and shortcomings (88). She does this by shifting attention away from the description of the Whore in Revelation 17, on whom she dwells for about a page, to the description of "the merchants of the earth [who have] waxed rich through the abundance of her delicacies," on whom she dwells for four pages (Revelation 18:3). By shifting her emphasis this way, Baxter ends up depersonalizing the Whore and personalizing the merchants: the Whore, in other words, is primarily treated in terms of what she symbolizes (Catholic error), while the merchants are treated as real men -- the men, no less, who are running Victorian England. The way these men do business in England, in fact, is the primary manifestation of Romish spiritual errors introduced by the High Church movement:

> Why should mystic Babylon and commercial Babylon be called by the same name, and spoken of as one? In point of fact, both are one. Unreality in religion leads to commercial corruption....[O]ne of the terrible marks of the present day is the ease with which the devil enables men to put on the semblance of true religion as a cloak for the darkest deeds in commercial life. Babylon in the Church and Babylon in the Exchange go hand in hand. The mad rage for gambling in this day permeates all branches of business; the excitement of running tremendous risks is part of the intoxication of the great harlot....trade will become one huge gambling concern, and multitudes will be ruined...(276-77, 280)

The "unreality" Baxter mentions here is described elsewhere as an Anglo-Catholic tendency to advocate moral laxity in business in return for church patronage from businessmen. Although the harlot is acknowledged as a source of intoxication, Baxter's critique repeatedly falls on her male contemporaries, who merely find themselves able to do what is commonplace in the male world of commerce without having to hide it from the church. To accentuate *their* responsibility, she argues that this "male" way of doing business in England is practiced, clandestinely, even by men in low churches where the harlot is absent:

> [T]here are men, and men professing to be religious, who possess three consciences -- a business conscience, a church conscience, and a family conscience. They do in business what they would not do in the family, and in the family what they would not do in the church; and this is abominable in the sight of a holy God. (281)

The word "abominable" here is carefully chosen. In Revelation 17:5 it is associated with the harlot, who has the phrase "MOTHER OF HARLOTS AND ABOMINATIONS OF THE EARTH" written on her forehead. By using it only to describe the men who actually carry out abominable deeds, Baxter reinforces that the function of the Whore of Babylon in the Apocalypse is to condemn male practices. It is the way men have conducted business, in fact, which will cause the economic aspect of the Apocalypse: the fact that "multitudes will be ruined" facilitates the antichrist's accession to total power.

Revising cultural valuations of men and masculinity.
Closely related to Victorian women's attempts to revise the misogynist nature of the Apocalypse by drawing attention to its representations of male lack and excess are their attempts to use the Apocalypse to question the high value placed on "masculine" qualities and men's achievements -- in the church as well as within society at large. Significantly, this revaluation was occurring while ideas which have loosely been dubbed as "muscular Christianity" were being put forth by Charles Kingsley and others who were wary of the softening "feminine" influence that the Anglo-Catholic movement and other social forces had had on the Christian faith.[16] In *Short Notes on the Revelation*, L.B.'s meditation on the Woman Clothed with the Sun opposes the values of muscular Christianity by suggesting that the church has long needed a feminizing influence:

> The Church is here personified, a *Sign* is seen in Heaven. Note that the chosen type of the Church is a woman, that we may have at once brought to our thoughts the loveliness and the peace, the tender protecting care for the weak, that should be the characteristic of the Church, rather than the harsh, aggressive, domineering *masculine* character, which alas! has been too often a truer likeness of her, whom we call our Mother church. (41)

What L.B. does with the familiar representation of the church as a woman is significant. Rather than stressing her submissive quality (which is analogous to the church's submission to Christ), she stresses other qualities Woman has to offer, which are undervalued in "masculine," muscular church circles. The two words L.B. emphasizes in this passage (in addition to "masculine") are also revealing. By italicizing and capitalizing the word "sign" used in Revelation 12:1, where John calls the Woman a "sign in heaven," L.B. suggests that John is receiving both prophetic knowledge and divine authorization of the Church's destiny as a "feminine" institution -- one shaped by women and their values. By ending the paragraph with a similar emphasis on the word "Mother," L.B. seeks to reframe the threatening prospect of women becoming authorities within a "feminized" church. During the Victorian era, the cultural construct of "Mother" brought the notions of "Woman" and "spiritual authority" together in a domesticized, non-threatening way. Although most Victorians would not be able to accept the notion that Christian men should place themselves under the authority of women within an intentionally "feminized" church, they could, perhaps, accept the notion of women as spiritual "Mothers" -- Mothers with a spiritual authority within church families analogous to the spiritual authority they exercised in so many Victorian homes.

Whereas L.B. questions the validity of a masculine church and asserts that it needs to become more feminized, other devotional writers use the Apocalypse to critique the value placed on men's achievements in society at large. In *Songs of the Apocalypse*, for example, M.S. interprets the Apocalypse's unholy trinity of devil, antichrist and false prophet in radically allegorical terms which allow her to critique three types of achievement usually associated with men. For M.S. the unholy trinity represents the "three forms of evil with which the church is ever at war": intellectual sin, brute force, and the world ("world" used in a Johannine sense to represent earthly systems which elevate the physical/sensual and deny the spiritual). Thus, M.S. broadens what could merely be an indictment of the devil and two men who serve him into an indictment of men at large.

Closely related to M.S.'s critique of intellectual activity, brute force, and worldly systems is the critique of industry and imperialism made in the tract entitled *The End of the World and the Truthfulness of Revelation* (1870). Rather than providing an exegesis of Revelation per se, the author uses Revelation to attempt to prove that "we are in the afternoon of the world's history, and...the end draweth near"; to do so, she must convince her readers that British men's achievements in industry at home and abroad, which give the illusion of endlessly increasing prosperity, are actually hastening the depletion of the earth's resources foretold in the Apocalypse (13). Men's industrial achievements, in other words, are sinister harbingers of an end filled with suffering. By exposing them as such, and using them as a launching point to urge readers to prepare themselves for the End, the female reader of the Apocalypse achieves something spiritual and lasting, beside which the temporal achievements of men pale. Although the gendered binary of male dominion over the physical world and female dominion over the spiritual world is affirmed in a distinctly conservative way, it is also revalued in a manner which suggests the inferiority of "male" accomplishments.

Revising cultural valuations of women and femininity.
The flip side of the revaluation of men and masculinity discussed above, of course, is an implicit revaluation of women and femininity. In Victorian women's texts on the Apocalypse, however, this revaluation goes far beyond implication: the most frequent type of feminist assertions being made are explicit affirmations of women's strengths and their untapped potential as leaders and doers within the church. As we shall now examine, women typically make such assertions by reading the New Earth the Apocalypse describes in two seemingly contradictory ways: as an egalitarian utopia that will be realized in the future, and as an already present spiritual reality that Christians should be striving to realize now.

Taken out of their devotional context, with its experiential focus on the present moment, some of these women's texts appear to support, or at least be resigned to, the status quo by deferring the Apocalypse's egalitarian implications to the future. These meditations from Mrs. Charles's *The Book of the Unveiling*, for example, seem to emphasize the gulf between the oppressive world Victorian women inhabit and the egalitarian world described at the end of the Apocalypse:

> *Healing*, and *reigning*; what meaning those words give to the sufferings...of the past...; what a golden chain they make between the long, sometimes inexplicable, and unfruitful trials of this earthly life and the beautiful ministries of the future! Every faculty trained...through the...servings and subjections of earth, to be fulfilled and employed in the glorious offices of that eternal world, in the planting and tilling of that Paradise, in the reigning and healing of that Holy City, the Mother-city of the worlds, whose gates are not shut at all. (127)

These passages identify Charles's world not only as a place of "trials" and "sufferings" -- a common complaint in Apocalyptic writing -- but more specifically of "unfruitful" trials and sufferings experienced in the context of the "servings and subjections of earth." The carefully chosen word "unfruitful" suggests the gender-specific nature of the trials Charles writes about here. Readers familiar with the New Testament would expect a

Christian writer to stress the *fruitful* nature of earthly trials, which is repeatedly taught in passages such as 2 Corinthians 12, in which Paul asks God to remove a "thorn in the flesh," but is told that God's strength "is made perfect in weakness" (v.9). Thus the specific kind of trials she speaks of are peculiar or unnatural precisely because they produce nothing. Indeed, she soon makes clear that producing nothing is the essence of the trials to which she refers: they emanate from the experience of being kept from productive spiritual employment within the Christian community. In the above passage, her unfruitful trials are opposed to fulfilling employment: "beautiful ministries" and "glorious offices" in which she is allowed to use her talents to plant, till, reign and heal. This visualization of life in Paradise is reinforced later in her texxt, when she offers her own "dream vision" of what life there looks like: men and women are not freed from the obligation to work, but toil side by side (140). Not coincidentally, the four work tasks she envisions being able to pursue in Paradise -- planting, tilling, reigning and healing -- can be used to describe the sum of an Anglican cleric's duties: Jesus and many after him used the metaphors of tilling and planting to refer to the proclamation of the Word, while healing and reigning suggest the priestly duties of providing leadership and administering the sacraments.

Though foregrounding the unfair limitations placed on Christian women, the author seems conservative in her apparent willingness to defer her hopes of becoming a Christian "minister" until the world to come -- a world described in terms distinctly feminine ("Mother-City") and inclusive ("whose gates are not shut at all"). This passage describing the world to come must be read, however, within the larger experiential, present-focused devotional context that Charles establishes throughout her book. Although she believes that a huge gulf exists between the perfect, eternal, egalitarian state described in the Apocalypse and the imperfect, temporal state of suffering experienced on earth, she also holds the neo-Platonic conviction that the two states exist concurrently, and that it is when we experience the Real made manifest on earth that life is most worth living:

> The unseen Universe is not revealed as a place or places apart from our visible world, but as a society, a condition, a world (or rather many worlds) touching and interpenetrating ours at all points, around us, close to us, with us always; which gives a far more awful and beautiful and tender significance to our everyday natural life, as well as to our eternal supernatural faith. (107)

Thus, for Charles, the Christian woman can experience the liberating reality of the Apocalypse's New Earth now by becoming spiritually aware of its manifestations in the world around her. This ability to access the "unseen Universe" through a spiritual, affective experience altering perceptions of life on earth does not make Charles content to wait, passively, for the New Earth to become fully manifest, however. Rather than merely pointing out that heavenly and earthly realities exist concurrently, she emphasizes that they are *converging*, and calls her readers to become involved in the conflict being felt within our world as a result. Her conviction that tensions between the two worlds are building toward the final conflict between good and evil described in the Apocalypse undergirds her decision to describe the Christian life in terms of a battle:

> Despondency comes when...we look on ourselves as in an era of universal peace, in the best of all possible worlds, and start at injustices, wrongs, misunderstandings, as some unforeseen, unforetold, quite irregular and accidental disturbances of our optimistic calm, to be ignored or evaded if possible, or if this is not possible to be smoothed over and compromised as soon as may be. What the Apocalypse unveils, we dare never for a moment forget, is that we are living in a time and a world of ceaseless war. (110)

Although the metaphor of Christian life as a battle is as old as the New Testament itself, Charles's use of it to describe the Christian life does not represent the norm in devotional literature as a whole; as religious historian Margaret Miles observes, "the three metphors for Christian life most frequently developed in devotional literature [are] Christian life as the imitation of Christ, as pilgrimage, and as ascent" (14). The decision to interpret the Apocalypse's battles as a metaphor for Christian life in these texts is a significant one. Although the metaphor of battle, like the metaphors of pilgrimage and ascent, suggests exertion, it suggests a different kind of exertion: exertion against evil forces opposed to the Christian making spiritual progress, rather than self-exertion toward spiritual progress. Thus the Christian's duty is to oppose every earthly force that sets itself up against the kind of self-exertion Scripture calls for. For the Christian woman, this includes restrictions on their service within the church community.

Charles's text is hardly an explicit feminist manifesto, of course; it like the other devotional texts examined in this chapter shies away from issuing an explicit call for action by women. It does, however, keep attention focused on how the flawed current social order keeps women from realizing their innate potential as Christian workers:

> Imagine a community, a world, consisting of the best and brightest, the wisest and tenderest men and women we have ever known, at their best and brightest, "at home," and therefore free to bring out

their best and highest gifts, their most individual and characteristic qualities, all that made them what they really were, what we loved in them....It is what is unnatural that is uninteresting, the echo, the repetition, the imitation, the efforts even of good people from good motives to seem and to be what they are not and were never intended to be. (122-23)

In the church, women are forced to become uninteresting imitators of men, which denies their "highest gifts" of creativity and leadership. This is especially apparent in the way that women's devotional writing is expected to echo men's biblical exegesis in "practical" and "feminine" ways. If the Christian woman dares to challenge this "unnatural" arrangement, she will inevitably come in conflict with "good people [who] from good motives" perpetuate it.

A number of devotional writers similarly suggest that the revaluation of women as equals which is foreshadowed in the Apocalypse should affect how Christian women are positioned in the immediate present. In *Songs of the Apocalypse*, M.S. repeatedly insists that ambiguously gendered actors in the Apocalyptic narrative represent women as well as men. After suggesting that the "Elders" who first appear in Revelation 4 symbolize highly committed believers of both sexes, M.S. challenges readers who would object to her depiction of women as agents and leaders to consider whether their gender ideology is biblical:

> This honor have all His saints [:...] they obediently occupy their assigned position in the overthrow of Antichrist. We, perhaps, cannot understand this now, but shall we therefore hesitate to believe the "sure word of prophecy?" Shall we not rather, as we read the prophetic Word and, under the Spirit's teaching, compare spiritual things with spiritual, earnestly desire that "imaginations" or "reasonings" may be cast down and every thought brought into captivity to the obedience of Christ? (2 Cor.x.5). (M.S. 91)

Using human imagination or reason without the help of the prophetic Word and the guidance of the Holy Spirit, M.S. suggests, people are not apt to see beyond the cultural horizon of mainstream gender ideology.

Ultimately, devotional writing on the last book of the Bible gave Victorian women who appealed to the doctrine of progressive revelation a chance to challenge gender ideologies which were commonly supported by other books of the Bible, without actually challenging the authority of those books. Most commonly, they revisit the Genesis story of Eve's disobedience and curse. Baxter jumps from the observation that Eve was initially created as Adam's equal to the observation that male and female Christians, since the Pentecost, have both shared in the promise to be remade as jointly equal to Christ (8-9). Similarly, after describing the person of Christ in terms of his relationship with Eve and other women ("Christ is...the Hope given of old to broken-hearted Eve, 'mother of all the living;'...Redeemer and Restorer of all womanhood..."), Charles emphasizes that woman's position at the end of the Apocalypse makes her position at the beginning of Genesis irrelevant: "The Apocalypse is the new Genesis of the new heavens and the new earth. There is a new book of Origins begun, a new "Let there be light," a new "God saw all He had made, and it was good" (21-22, 116-17). Charles's more famous contemporary, Christina Rossetti, also envisions a new beginning for the Christian woman in her devotional commentary on the Apocalypse, *The Face of the Deep* (1892). In her interpretive eye, Revelation 12's "woman clothed with the sun" represents a new Eve who portends new possibilities for Christian women:

> [As] instinctively we personify the sun and moon as *he* and *she*, I trust there is no harm in my considering that her sun-clothing indicates how in that heaven where St. John in vision beheld her, she will be made equal with men and angels; arrayed in all human virtues, and decked with communicable Divine graces: whilst the moon under her feet portends that her sometime infirmity of purpose and changeableness of mood have, by preventing, assisting, final grace, become immutable; she has done all and stands; from the lowest place she has gone up higher. (310)

In envisioning the Apocalyptic destination of the female Christian, Rossetti, like the other devotional writers examined in this essay, found a way to inscribe feminist impulses onto the authoritative Christian text. From our vantage point a century later, women writing devotional Apocalyptic prose appear not only to have accomplished a measure of integration of their feminist and Christian selves, but also to have provided a formative context for the feminist, biblically-centered theologies that continue to redefine Christian faith and practice.

NOTES

1. Although Catholics tend to call the last book of the Bible the Apocalypse and Protestants tend to call it the Book of Revelation, the names are interchangeable. "Apocalypse" comes from the Greek verb "to reveal." See *The Catholic Encyclopedia*, p.594.

2. This profusion of writing for religious edification was mirrored in the literary publishing market: the Apocalypse's cultural accessibility led many authors to "salt their prose with heavy allusion to [it]" during this time (Carpenter 300).

3. In *Eve and the New Jerusalem*, Barbara Taylor writes: "Female preachers were unknown in the Established church and most of the old Dissenting congregations. In its early years, Methodism sponsored women preachers..., but by the early nineteenth century they had been suppressed in the main Methodist organization... By the second quarter of the nineteenth century the Word had few spokeswomen within the larger churches, despite the bitter battles waged by some of these women to retain their right to speak. As the claims for women's spiritual knowledge became more extravagant, so the curbs on their right to speak this knowledge (except to their children and, if they were leisured ladies, the poor) became much tighter" (127-8). Taylor goes on to trace how the mainline churches' opposition to female leadership resulted in some women's gravitation toward more radical and heretical religious and social movements.

4. Betty Flower thus explains the Protestant church's conflicted stance regarding the sacred relationship between the Bible and the individual believer when that believer happens to be a woman: "The close study of Scripture was one form of intellectual work which women were encouraged to undertake. They were, however, to study 'to obey' rather than to question" (164). As a result, most of the biblically-centered texts women published were, at least ostensibly, devotional or evangelistic adaptations of biblical exegesis done by men.

5. See Carpenter and Landow, pp.304-307.

6. For a contemporary feminist reading of the Woman Clothed with the Sun of Revelation 12 and the Bride of Revelation 21, see Tina Pippen, *Death and Desire*.

7. Even the book's inclusion in the canon was fraught with an unusual amount of controversy. For an overview, see *The International Standard Bible Encyclopaedia*, pp. 582-85.

8. See Barbara Taylor, *Eve and the New Jerusalem*, pp.118-182.

9. For more information about these female "messiahs," see Taylor, pp.118-182.

10. For more on pre-twentieth century attempts to envision a Christian feminism, see "The Past: Does It Hold a Future for Women?" in *Womanspirit Rising: A Feminist Reader in Religion*, pp.63-130.

11. Although no women during the mid- to late-Victorian period seem to have undertaken a historiocritical approach to the book (understandably, given that it required training which only all-male colleges and seminaries offered), a small but significant number wrote texts echoing the prominent popular approaches published by men: historical-allegorical, literal-eschatological, and spiritual-allegorical. In addition to the openly exegetical texts by women discussed in this essay, Mrs. J.C. Martin's *The Revelation of St. John Briefly Explained* (1851), Catherine Gauntlett's *The Sevenfold Book* (1853), and *The Orb of Light* (1860), at least four other such Apocalyptic texts by women have been preserved in the British Library: the anonymously authored *Conversations on the Revelation: Being a Simple Exposition for the Young* (1868), Helen Maclachlan's *Notes on the Book of Revelation* (1869), Gracilla Boddington's *The Revelation of St. John the Divine, Practically Considered in Simple and Familiar Language* (1881), and the anonymously authored *The Great Roman Eclipse: with the Visions of Locusts and Horsemen* (1882).

12. The frequency with which male clerics and theologians praise the spiritual benefits to be gleaned from devotional texts attests to their wide-ranging audience. See, for example, the Preface to M.S.'s *Songs of the Apocalypse*, quoted on page 15 of this essay.

13. Although other such texts may exist, *The Orb of Light* is the only one in the British Library's extensive holdings.

14. See, for example, 1 John 1:5.

15. Obviously, such critiques of "masculine" qualities such as the tendency to rely on intellect rather than the Spirit for guidance reinscribe essentialed notions about men and women. Nevertheless, they represent one conflicted way Victorian women attempted to revaluate "feminine" qualities.

16. For detailed accounts of how "muscular Christianity" evolved as a response to the feminization of Anglicanism during and after the Oxford Movement, see *Muscular Christianity: Embodying the Victorian Age*, edited by Donald E. Hall.

WORKS CITED

A., C.J. *The Divine and Human in the Book of Revelation. At Attempt to Realize the Conditions and Circumstance under which St. John Wrote His Vision.* Oxford and London: John Henry and James Parker, 1863.

Anderson, Bernhard W. *The Books of the Bible. Vol. 2: The Apocrypha and the New Testament.* New York: Scribner's, 1989.

B., L. *Short Notes on the Revelation.* London: J. Masters & Co., 1886.

Bakhtin, Mikhail M. *The Dialogic Imagination: Four Essays.* Ed. Michael Holquist. Austin: U of Texas P, 1981.

Baxter, Mrs. M. [Elizabeth]. *His Last Word: Bible Readings in Revelation.* 2nd ed. London: Christian Herald, 1896.

B[oddington], G[racilla]. *The Revelation of St.John the Divine, Practically Considered in Simple and Familiar Language.* London: James Nisbet & Co., 1881.

Carpenter, Mary Wilson, and George P. Landow. "The Apocalypse and Victorian Literature." *The Apocalypse in English Renaissance Thought and Literature.* Eds. C.A. Patrides and Joseph Wittreich. Ithaca: Cornell UP, 1984.

Catholic U. of America, eds. *New Catholic Encyclopedia.* Vol.1. New York: McGraw-Hill, 1967.

Charles, R.H. *Studies in the Apocalypse: Being Lectures Delivered Before the University of London.* Edinburgh: T.& T. Clark, 1913.

Charles, Mrs.[Elizabeth] Rundle. *The Book of the Unveiling. Studies in the Revelation of St.John the Divine.* London: Society for Promoting Christian Knowledge, 1892.

Christ, Carol P., and Judith Plaskow, eds. *Womanspirit Rising: A Feminist Reader in Religion.* San Francisco: Harper & Row, 1979.

Conversations on the Revelation: Being a Simple Exposition for the Young. London: Hall and Co., 1868.

The End of the World and the Truthfulness of Revelation. Manchester, England: John Heywood, 1870.

Fiorenza, Elisabeth Schussler. "Revelation." *The Books of the Bible.* Ed. Bernhard W. Anderson. Vol.2. New York: Charles Scribner's Sons, 1989.

Flowers, Betty S. "The Kingly Self: Rossetti as Woman Artist." *The Achievement of Christina Rossetti.* Ed. David A. Kent. Ithaca: Cornell UP, 1987. 159-74.

Gauntlett, Catherine. *The Sevenfold Book. Hints on the Revelation.* London: Seeleys, 1853.

The Great Roman Eclipse: with the Visions of Locusts and Horsemen. London: Elliot Stock, 1882.

Greenwell, Thomas William. *The Illustrated Apocalypse. Being a Complete Series of Cartoons Explanatory of the Past and Future Fulfilments of the Revelation of St.John the Divine.* London: W. Ridgway, 1884.

Hall, Donald E., ed. *Muscular Christianity: Embodying the Victorian Age.* New York: Cambridge UP, 1994.

Hebermann, Alex, Charles George, et al., eds. *The Catholic Encyclopedia.* Vol.1. New York: The Encyclopedia Press and the Gilmary Society, 1907-1958.

Landow, George P. *Victorian Types, Victorian Shadows: Biblical Typology in Victorian Literature, Art and Thought.* Boston: Routledge & K. Paul, 1980.

Maclachlan, Helen. *Notes on the Book of Revelation.* London: James Nisbet & Co., 1869.

Martin, Mrs. J.C. *The Revelation of St.John Briefly Explained.* Dublin: James McGlashan, 1851.

Miles, Margaret Ruth. *The Image and Practice of Holiness: A Critique of the Classic Manuals of Devotion.* London: SCM Press, 1989.

The Orb of Light; or, The Apocalyptic Vision, by a Lady. London: Wertheim, Macintosh, and Hunt, 1860.

Orr, James, ed. *The International Standard Bible Encyclopaedia.* Chicago: The Howard-Severance Co., 1915.

Pippin, Tina. *Death and Desire: The Rhetoric of Gender in the Apocalypse of John.* Louisville, KY: Westminster/John Knox Press, 1992.

The Revelation Unravelled: An Outline Exposition on a New Plan. London: S.W. Partridge and Co., 1867.

Rossetti, Christina G. *The Face of the Deep: A Devotional Commentary on the Apocalypse.* London: Society for Promoting Christian Knowledge, 1892.

S., M. *Songs of the Apocalypse.* London: James Nisbet, 1887.

Seigman, E.F. "Book of Apocalypse." *The New Catholic Encyclopedia.* Vol I. Eds. Catholic University of America. New York: McGraw-Hill, 1967.

Taylor, Barbara. *Eve and the New Jerusalem.* New York: Pantheon Books, 1983.

Yarbro Collins, Adela. *Crisis and Catharsis: The Power of the Apocalypse.* Philadelphia: Westminster, 1984.

The Kiss of the Soul:
The Mystical Theology of Christina Rossetti's Devotional Prose

Frederick S. Roden
New York University

"The flowers planted in Paradise
Are budding now for me.
Red roses like love visible
Are blowing on their tree,
Or white like virgin purity."
                    - Christina Rossetti, *Maude*

"We are his bliss, we are his reward, we are his honour, we are his crown."
                    - Julian of Norwich, *Showings*

In recent years, feminist theology has sought to reclaim women's voices in speaking of -- and from -- the Divine. Historical theologians and literary scholars have looked to the works of medieval women mystics to understand the ways which, within a hegemonic, patriarchal culture, women have striven and succeeded in finding a voice to speak with authority on matters of the spiritual life. Our present age is enjoying a revival of interest in women such as Hildegard of Bingen -- whether viewed as sapiential theologian in religious and literary studies or prototypical Earth Mother in the New Age Movement and practical mysticism.[1] Concurrent with these developments have been inquiries as to the place and space of what might be called the "feminine" aspect of the Divine. Several theologians in the past decade have looked to Biblical Wisdom, Sophia, and sapiential tradition through late antiquity to trace the development, perhaps arrested development, of this phenomenon.[2] Such theological inquiries have indeed changed the ways in which the body -- both spiritual and corporeal -- is viewed. By the late 1980's, theologians such as Carter Heyward and James Nelson were developing practical "body theologies," attempting to reconcile the many scholarly projects on gender and sexuality with contemporary social issues.[3]

In this paper, I wish to examine Christina Rossetti's devotional prose in the context of the Victorian medieval revival, while seeking to understand the place of gender and the body in mysticism. With few exceptions, Rossetti's prose works have received scant critical attention.[4] The six volumes include *Annus Domini: a Prayer for each Day of the Year* (1874), *Seek and Find: a Double Series of Short Studies of the Benedicite* (1879), *Called to Be Saints: the Minor Festivals Devotionally Studied* (1881), *Letter and Spirit: Notes on the Commandments* (1883), *Time Flies: A Reading Diary* (1886), and *The Face of the Deep: a Devotional Commentary on the Apocalypse* (1892). Their more than 2000 pages provide insight into the theologian that was Rossetti the poet.

With the revival of interest in incarnational theology through the Oxford Movement in the early nineteenth century, the relationship between religion and sexuality, spirituality and gender, began to be re-examined. In glorifying the beautiful body of Christ in the Real Presence, religious discourse took on a more body-centered voice. It is significant to note, however, that this phenomenon cannot be labeled "new." Striking "namings" of the body in devotional and visionary writing may be found in the late medieval period. In a far different time and place, the relationship between body and spirit, sexuality and spirituality, was spoken in a similarly religious voice. This voice began to be heard again in nineteenth-century England, for during the 1840's, works such as the fourteenth-century *Showings of Divine Love* of Julian of Norwich were reprinted for the first time in three hundred years. Richard Rolle's writings also became available during the mid-century. Christina Rossetti prays in *Annus Domini* that Christ may be a "Fire of Love," which is the title of the Hampole hermit's most famous work (16). The return to England of the Church Catholic, with its mystical heritage, in both Anglican and Roman forms, contributed to later emerging discourses of gender and sexuality through the re-introduction of spiritual bodies into this culture.

In reading a mystical theologian such as Rossetti, it is important to consider medieval resonances. My analysis here focuses primarily upon comparisons between the nineteenth-century writer, Hildegard, and Julian. Approaching Rossetti's works from this perspective requires a knowledge of her reading history. Rossetti clearly had access to medieval material. Her sister Maria, an Anglican nun, translated early Church works. The study of the relationship between Rossetti's writings and medieval texts may be placed under the general theoretical/thematic rubric of "women writing theology." Within different cultural frames, religious women have come to some of the same answers to their theological inquiries. Furthermore, they have hence succeeded in their searches to validate themselves and the life-experiences of other women. I do not maintain that Rossetti knew of Hildegard, for that would be virtually impossible. Nevertheless, direct knowledge is not crucial to make such a comparison.

The resonances shared by these theologians may be demonstrated by examining two short excerpts. In one of Hildegard's sacred songs, the "Sibyl of the Rhine" writes, "O feminea forma, soror Sapientiae, quam gloriosa es" (O feminine form, sister of Wisdom, / How glorious you are!) (*Symphonia* 264). Rossetti observes in *Seek and Find*: "And well may she glory, inasmuch as one of the tenderest of divine promises takes (so to say) the feminine form: 'As one whom his mother comforteth, so will I comfort you'" (31). Beyond the similarity of the language these two women used in writing theology, we may also explore the similarity of their works' content. Hildegard's song is entitled "O magna res" (O greatness). The work praises Divinity within all material creation. "O greatness that lay hidden in nothing created, so that it was neither made nor created by anyone but abides in itself" (*Symphonia* 265). The song laments that through the female death came into the world. However, Woman is finally exalted as the form that gave shape to eternal Life, providing God with human flesh. *Seek and Find* is also concerned with the order of natural creation. In this volume, the theologian comments on the Benedicite, exaltations of God's works. Rossetti's fierce incarnationalism, locating the Divine in the material world, evokes Hildegard's earlier theology, at the heart of which lies a creation-centered, Sapiential embodiment of God.

In analyzing Rossetti's prose here, I wish therefore to locate the spiritual lives of nineteenth-century women with respect to hegemonic patriarchal and heterosexist religious frameworks. I am interested in the ways in which religious discourse may function as an alternative avenue to power for those who might otherwise be disenfranchised: namely women in Victorian culture by virtue of their gender, and men of same-sex desire, whose identity was named at the *fin-de-siècle*. In both the medieval and Victorian periods, religious literature served to empower those who did not identify as "male" or "heterosexual" in their relationships to a divine, fostering the creation of religiosities which simultaneously satisfied the spiritual needs of the individual and offered a voice from which to speak with authority. The flesh of medieval woman -- empowered through her humility, her likeness to Christ -- commanded her to "cry out... and write" (Hildegard *Scivias* 59). Bernard of Clairvaux preached on the Song of Songs passage, "Let Him kiss me with the kiss of His mouth," situating the Christian soul in a "feminized," passive relationship with the Divine. Voices such as these, which demonstrate non-dominant positions of gender identification in devotion, have the potential to call forth reconciling perspectives for the lost physical body in spirit-centered Christian theology.

In the Victorian period, such reconciliation incited much cultural anxiety. There were accusations of "effeminacy" among men of High Church, which perhaps were not unfounded, as the Ritualist churches may have fostered the development of emergent urban male homosexual cultures. The secular culture also expressed fears about a single woman's renunciation of her procreative duties in taking the convent veil.[5] H. W. Burrows, in his foreword to Christina Rossetti's *Annus Domini*, observes that all of the 366 prayers in the volume were "addressed to the Second Person of the Blessed Trinity, and are intended therefore to be used as supplementary to other devotions" (n.p.). Burrows' commentary seems to be somewhat of a warning, reflecting cultural discomfort about the over-emphasis of Divine Embodiment.

Like Chaucer's Wife of Bath, Rossetti establishes her authority to speak in a religious voice by means of and because of her body. She begins in *Seek and Find*: "I, being a woman, will copy St. Paul's example and 'magnify mine office'" (30). Rossetti continues: "In many points the feminine lot copies very closely the voluntarily assumed position of our Lord and pattern" (30). She utilizes the strategy of many female theologians before her, associating her humanity and humility with Christ's. Julian of Norwich wrote in her *Showings*:

> But God forbid that you should say or assume that I am a teacher, for that is not and never was my intention; for I am a woman, ignorant, weak, and frail. But I know very well that what I am saying I have received by the revelation of him who is the sovereign teacher…All this blessed teaching of our Lord was shown to me in three parts, that is by bodily vision and by words formed in my understanding and by spiritual vision (135).

These women simultaneously denigrate their identities as females and claim to have received Divine revelation. Julian is especially clear in stating that revelation was received through her *body*. Rossetti further claims equality of both genders before God, in spite of enforced submission in this world:

> But if our proud waves will after all not be stayed, or at any rate not be allayed (for stayed they must be) by the limit of God's ordinance concerning our sex, one final consolation yet remains to careful and troubled hearts: in Christ there is neither male nor female, for we are all one (Gal. iii 28) (*SF* 32).

Rossetti's point is complex and subtle in alluding to the Pauline Christ that is neither male nor female. In exegesis, this statement may be read that "among the faithful, gender is not a category fit to separate one believer from another." However, the statement also may be interpreted that "within the body of Christ, the Church, gender as a category does not exist as we think of it." This issue raises the important question of the gender inflection of the literal human body of Christ, Jesus, who may "perform" in "masculine" and "feminine" roles, an issue which Rossetti pursues further in her later works. She gives several Biblical examples of Jesus teaching humility to both men and women. Defeating pride is not easy, but "our Master first performs the task He is about to set us" (*SF* 322). Christ-like humility is associated with femaleness in *Time Flies*, where Rossetti speaks about a saint, "If she was a weak maid, who of us cannot by Divine Grace become as strong as a weak maid?" (194).

Rossetti forcefully likens woman to God Incarnate throughout her prose. She looks to Christ's maternal behavior. This concept is ultimately fleshed out in *Face of the Deep*. "O Christ our God, remember Thy strong and weak ones, great and small, men and women for good. Remember the nursing Fathers and nursing Mothers of Holy Church" (*FD* 434-435). In *Annus Domini*, the earliest of the devotionals, Rossetti's prayer to Christ was to "make the wise and prudent of the world as babes, that they may desire the sincere milk of Thy Word" (7). All of these metaphors recall monastic culture of the High Middle Ages, which Caroline Walker Bynum discusses extensively in *Jesus As Mother*. In his *Prayers*, St. Anselm addressed both St. Paul and Christ as nursing mothers.[6] Christ's feminine "behavior" is also described by Julian of Norwich in the fourteenth century:

> The mother can give her child to suck of her milk, but our precious Mother Jesus can feed us with himself, and does, most courteously and most tenderly, with the blessed sacrament, which is the precious food of true life (298).

Julian's association of Christ with mother elevates the status of woman. In turn, her use of this strategy as a woman writing theology gives added authority to her voice. In appropriating the motherhood trope, Rossetti places herself within a tradition. The metonymic employment of "motherhood" to represent femaleness emphasizes the fecundity of woman's nature. Writing thus demonstrates feminine productivity: the effusion of the female religious voice at once recapitulates and is justified by the maternal image of Christ.

As women speaking about religion, whether in the twelfth, fourteenth, or nineteenth century, theologians such as Hildegard, Julian, and Rossetti were forced to justify their acts of speech, often bringing their female bodies into their texts. Rossetti is anxious about practicing exegesis in all of her theological writings. She formally fashions herself as simultaneously a religious woman and a contemplative theologian in *Letter and Spirit*. In this work, a commentary on the Ten Commandments, Rossetti asserts that if all women are not intended to be contemplatives, certainly some are. She includes herself among the elect.

> Our study of Martha and Mary (St. Luke x. 38-42) assures us that the former was not wrong in the main, the latter setting an example to be followed cautiously because (we flatter ourselves) not applicable to all persons (28).

Earlier in *Annus Domini*, Rossetti had prayed, "Give us grace to choose the good part which shall not be taken away from us" (92). The "good part" is, of course, to be Christ's chosen one. While the female contemplative is particularly elevated, all women are given dignity in *Letter and Spirit*. "Our 'Lord God, merciful and gracious,' has been pleased to give honour unto the weaker vessel" (*LS* 37). Greatness is claimed for women through their secondary status:

> The rule is prominence for the husband, retiredness for the wife; nevertheless, the Source and Author of all rule once emphatically declared, 'Many that are first shall be last; and the last first,' which authoritative declaration has already even in this world oftentimes been verified (*LS* 57).

The road to power through Christ-like humility is demonstrated by the place of the sisterhoods in Victorian -- as well as medieval -- culture. The nineteenth century in England was a period when many women found empowerment through the "secondary status" of religious life. Some of these women took vows and joined Anglican religious orders, re-instituted in the Church at the time of the Oxford Movement. Abolished at the time of the Reformation, this "career" that had given many intelligent women the opportunity to find fulfillment outside of married life returned to English culture after a three-century absence.[7] During the Victorian period, taking the veil was a radical act. To reject the "law of the father" or husband in this world in favor of the authority of a Father in heaven and live in a community of non-biologically-procreative women was seen as subversive to reproductive patriarchy. In addition to formal sisterhoods, many British women in the nineteenth century found niches for useful work, whether "active" in charity positions or "contemplative" in writing and lay Church involvement.

Rossetti contrasts the contemplative virgin with the active wife extensively in *Letter and Spirit*.

She whose heart is virginal abides aloft and aloof in spirit. In spirit she oftentimes kneels rather than sits, or prostrates herself more readily than she kneels, associated by love with Seraphim, and echoing and swelling the 'Holy, Holy, Holy,' of their perpetual adoration. Her spiritual eyes behold the king in his beauty; wherefore she forgets, by comparison, her own people and her father's house. Her Maker is her Husband, endowing her with a name better than of sons and of daughters. His Presence and His right hand are more to her than that fulness of joy and those pleasures which flow from them. For His sake rather than for its own she longs for Paradise; she craves the gold of that land less because it is good than that it is His promised gift to her. She loves Him with all her heart and soul and mind and strength; she is jealous that she cannot love him more; her desire to love Him outruns her possibility, yet by outrunning enlarges it. She contemplates Him, and abhors herself in dust and ashes. She contemplates Him, and forgets herself in Him. If she rejoices, it is on spiritual heights, with Blessed Mary magnifying the Lord; if she laments, it is still on spiritual mountain-tops, making with Jephthah's daughter a pure oblation of unflinching self-sacrifice. The air she breathes is too rare and keen for grosser persons; they mark the clouds which involve her feet, but discern not those early and late sunbeams which turn her mists to rainbows and kindle her veiled head to a golden glory. Her heart talks of God; 'Seek ye my Face -- Thy Face, Lord, will I seek;' until truly her danger in the Day of Judgment would rather seem that she should not have recognized Christ's brethren to whom she ministered, than that she should have overlooked Him in them (*LS* 91-2).

This excerpt explains in vivid detail the heart of Rossetti's spirituality, the life of the mystic seeking Divine Love, absorbed in God and herself. Extraordinarily carnal, the contemplative enters into a marriage with the Heavenly Spouse. The wife's state is contrasted:

The Wife's case, not in unison with that other, yet makes a gracious harmony with it. She sees not face to face, but as it were in a glass darkly. Every thing, and more than all every person, and most of all the one best beloved person, becomes her mirror wherein she beholds Christ and her shrine wherein she serves Him. Her vocation is composed of indulgences and privileges as well as duties; yet being her vocation, she religiously fulfills it 'as to the Lord, and not unto men.' Her earthly love and obedience express to her a mystery; she takes heed to reverence her husband, as seeing Him who is invisible; her children are the children whom God has given her, the children whom she nurses for God. She sits down in the lowest place, and is thankful there. She is faithful over the few things, and not impatient to rule over the many things; she is faithful in that which is another man's, and can wait patiently for that which is her own. As the Cloudy Pillar deigned indifferently to head the Exodus on to bring up the rear of the children of Israel, so she leads or follows; and is made all things to all her own, if by any means she may save some; while like that sacred Symbol she also veils her perfections from alien eyes, reserving the luminous fire of her gifts and graces to him most of all whose due they are, and in him to the maker of them both (see Ex. xiv. 19,20) (*LS* 92-3).

To turn oneself over to the omnipotent Lord of the universe as his special spouse would seem to entice much more than the quotidian responsibilities of another fallen mortal. In this context, the "secondary status" as contemplative is much more empowering than the forced servitude of earthly marriage. The wife's duty is submission; the single woman follows her own heart's desires. The simple dichotomy between the "empowered" celibate and "enslaved" wife is complicated, however, by Rossetti's Biblical image. Her comparison of the wife to the pillar of cloud questions the "powerless" obedience of the active woman. Jehovah himself is led or follows within the cloud, hence identifying the wife with signs of God's favor or guidance.

Nevertheless, the solitary woman is led only by a celestial Jehovah, not by God's human representative on earth, a husband. This distinction is evident in Rossetti's emphasis upon mystical experience. Individuals who have chosen the solitary life in devotion consistently glorify the *via mystica*. "In her spiritual marriage she despises [the idea of] a fleshly husband...she is [God's] Bride and He is her Bridegroom" (Hildegard *Scivias* 178). The Bride/Bridegroom imagery of the Song of Songs is utilized by Rossetti in all of her devotionals. In renunciation, the Spiritual Companion, the great lover of the soul, is embraced. In *Annus Domini*, Rossetti's prayer to Christ was that He might show "loving kindness" to the neglected, "little loved," forgotten (*AD* 56). "Be Thou their beloved Companion, and let communion with Thee be to them more dear than tenderest earthly intercourse. Teach them to seek Thee in prayer, and to find Thee in Thy Blessed Sacrament" (*AD* 56).

It is significant to note, in comparing "active" and "contemplative" lives, that in *Letter and Spirit* Rossetti also manipulates gender politics, making men and women equal before God. Male or female may be embraced by the Lover of the Soul; worldly persons may likewise stand before God with no distinction by gender. Rossetti analyzes the commandment against coveting another's wife. She takes this further, commodifying husbands' bodies as well as wives':

> Thus obviously [the wife] ranks with the man himself, being constituted equally with him an informing presence of a forbidden house. Besides this she takes her place as first, nearest, dearest, most precious and altogether unique among his possessions: as indeed he ranks among hers (*LS* 191).

Women's bodies, are, however, located in a revered place:

> [Woman] appears to stand as the connecting link, akin to both, between what the man is and what he has; even as Christ's sacred humanity, bridging over the severing gulf, unites the Godhead to the Church (*LS* 193).

Woman's body is hence associated with Christ's body, and not only in His humility. Through Rossetti's metaphor, woman's body is sculpted into the trope of the Incarnation. The female body is simultaneously associated with the material world in its alignment with property and raised above the mundane by being compared to Christ.

Here it is useful to consider the doctrine of the Real Presence at the Eucharist and the association of woman with carnality. C. W. Bynum has observed the medieval association of Christ's body with female bodies, both giving nourishment at table.[8] An illustration from the manuscript of Hildegard's *Scivias* depicts the female figure of Ecclesia, the Church, in two poses. She simultaneously catches Christ's blood in a chalice, while He hangs on the cross, and awaits Him at the altar, bearing a cup. Therefore, marriage to the Divine Lover is linked with consuming His flesh and blood, underscoring the carnal aspects of the mystical union. In *Annus Domini*, one of Rossetti's prayers to Christ likewise petitions:

> God that hidest Thyself, give us grace, I implore Thee, to discern Thee spiritually in the most Blessed Sacrament of Thy Body and Blood; to receive Thee into souls prostrate in adoration, to entertain Thee with our utmost love (133).

To delve into questions about spiritual and carnal bodies (of Christ) is to consider more closely Rossetti's development of her theology of mystical love found in both her devotional and secular poetry.[9] As early as *Seek and Find*, Rossetti wrote about the mystical marriage between Christ and the

Church in a manner akin to Hildegard's visions of the Eucharistic feast/marriage.

> Yet so long as each of us gives all diligence to make her own personal calling and election sure (2 St Peter i.10), it will do us no harm to recognize in this saintly spouse a figure of the Church: that great Mother and Mistress (Gal. iv.26) who because her whole family is washed and beautified in the Blood of Christ (Rev. vii.13,14) has no need to fear any transitory creature; who through the burden of her day of probation looks forward to the day of praise; who even now amid many sins and many shortcomings, knows that less for her love's sake than for His own the heart of her Divine Husband safely trusts in her and accounts that she doth Him good and not evil all the days of her life (see 2 Cor. xii.9; Rev. iii.7-13) (224).

The Bride finds her love in the communion cup, in consuming her spiritual husband through their lovemaking at the altar. Woman as Church looks forward to final union with Him in Paradise. For Rossetti, the relationship with the Divine -- what we might call "faith" -- must be mediated by the trope of human relationship. This perspective is necessary for comprehension and contemplation of God. Hence in her theology, love leads to faith. Rossetti's singular emphasis upon love, like that of Julian, creates an affective, sentimental piety in harmony with Victorian culture.

> When all due weight has been conceded to secondary motives, the paramount motive for what we do or leave undone -- if, that is, we aim at either acting or forbearing worthily -- is love: not fear, or self-interest, or even hatred of sin, or sense of duty, but direct, filial love to God (*LS* 35).

Mystical loves always keep the soul attached to its body. The Bride/Bridegroom language of mystical love pervades *Face of the Deep*, manifested in a way that may surprise modern readers. Christ desires the Bride, a concept crucial in understanding the mystic's spirituality.

> The All-Holy desires to sanctify us, the All-Pure to purge us, that in the end He may set us up on high and satisfy us with long life, and show us His salvation. Love desires the beloved; Christ desires us: shall Love desire us, Christ desire us in vain? God forbid (*FD* 236).

Rossetti prays: "O Lord Jesus, Who hast called the Church Thy sister, love, dove, spouse: Abide close to us, our Brother, our Friend, and prepare us" (*FD* 248). Christ's love for the Bride, the Church, is not one of spousal chastity. Rather, it is passionate ecstasy. Exuberant love poetry has been written by travelers of the *via mystica*, who cultivate Love Divine.

Rossetti's perspective is not far from Julian of Norwich's celebration of Christ's love for us: "We are his bliss, we are his reward, we are his honour, we are his crown" (Julian 145). The anchoress writes:

> For truly our lover desires the soul to adhere to him with all its power, and us always to adhere to his goodness. For of all the things that the heart can think, this pleases God most and soonest profits the soul...

> That is to say, there is no created being who can know how much and how sweetly and how tenderly the Creator loves us. And therefore we can with his grace and his help persevere in spiritual contemplation, with endless wonder at this high, surpassing, immeasurable love which our Lord in his goodness has for us; and therefore we may with reverence ask from our lover all that we will, for our natural will is to have God, and God's good will is to have us, and we can never stop willing or loving until we possess him in the fulness of joy (Julian 186).

Rossetti also wrote emphatically about Christ's love: "In heaven all the redeemed are to be made like unto their Redeemer; and I know, and am sure that Christ Who loves us all, loves us each" (*FD* 234). In one of the poems included in the commentary, she expands her amatory theology:

> What is the beginning? Love. What the course? Love still.
> What the goal? The goal is Love on the happy hill.
> Is there nothing then but Love, search we sky or earth?
> There is nothing out of Love hath perpetual worth:
> All things flag but only Love, all things fail or flee;
> There is nothing left but Love worthy you and me (*FD* 75).

Rossetti's personification of love suggests the presence of the Divine Incarnate: the "happy hill" may be read as Calvary. Even in a work such as *Face of the Deep* which focuses ultimately on vivid transcendence, Christ's carnality and humanity are underscored. Rossetti strikingly privileges the body and elevates humankind:

> The Godhead was not converted into flesh, but the manhood was taken into God...in our Lord Himself Very Man dwells the Fulness of Godhead bodily. Further we are reminded that Christ as Man,

over and beyond the Indivisible Unity of the Divine Trinity, became a Temple of the Holy Ghost (*FD* 153).

Within this body-centered paradigm, the Eucharist as Christ's body may be read as an eternal Presence, a replicating performance of the Incarnation. Receiving Him is hence a profoundly erotic act. "In the Blessed Sacrament of His Body and Blood [He] left to His Church a perpetual memorial of His sole sufficient Sacrifice" (*FD* 245). For Rossetti, taking the Word of God into one's body by mouth at the Eucharist is also associated with devouring the Word in scriptural sight. She gives the example of a dying woman, probably her sister Maria, who desperately wanted to read only Holy Scripture. "She fed on the Word of Life, being evidently fed with food convenient for her. Thus she prepared for death: thus went out to meet the Bridegroom, having oil in her lamp" (*FD* 534). The image of oil to sustain a fire (of love) emphasizes the erotic passion of the mystic. Medieval theories of reading advocate the "mastication" and "digestion" of Scripture, part of monastic study of the Word.[10] The body of the text is associated with the Body of Christ as *Logos*, both as He is eaten in the Eucharist and as one prepares for final reunion with Him as Bridegroom after death. Woman's eating of Christ -- her participation in his eucharistic Incarnation -- serves to recapitulate both her role in his first carnal birth in the world through Mary, and matter's reception of the original breath of Divine Wisdom which created humanity. Above all, it manifests their love relationship. For their Ultimate Union, the Bride awaits the Bridegroom in what may be described as a [sexually] receptive state:

> **Opening** is suggestive of mercy; of Christ's arms spread wide to draw all men unto Him, of His Heart pierced to shelter us. **Shutting** suggests (though not always does it imply) durance or exclusion (*FD* 110).

After death, the Bride will receive her glory. This grand moment explains Rossetti's obsession with the life beyond the grave. God "becamest Man thereby to become One of twain, Thyself and Thy Bride the Church. Thou hast laboured for her; and labourest with her, and sharest with her Thy reward" (*FD* 278). Rossetti exalts the Bride in a poem in *Face of the Deep*:

> Who sits with the King in His Throne? Not a slave but a Bride, With this King of all Greatness and Grace Who reigns not alone; His Glory her glory (145).

Earlier in *Letter and Spirit*, Rossetti had similarly maintained that

God in Christ reconciles the world unto Himself...not that she should thenceforth abide afar off as a trembling slave...but that as a beloved bride she should sit down with Him in His Throne (308).

Since prostrating oneself before the Immortal Beloved is subjugation worthy of both genders, passionate physical relationships between bodies need not fall strictly along heterosexual lines in mystical theology. In *Letter and Spirit*, Rossetti writes of several same-sex affectional pairings that eventually lead to Christ in the New Testament. "Still, we are bound to esteem the tie which united Ruth to Naomi as sacred and stringent in a very high degree, even if not equalling the birth-tie of blood" (*LS* 53). Rossetti also considers a male pairing of the Old Testament that foreshadows the New:

At the noble name of Friend we recall Jonathan, more than royal in his disregard of that throne on which he delighted to install one whom he loved with a love wonderful, passing the love of women... Thus centuries later St. John Baptist claimed for himself no title nobler or dearer than that of Friend of the Bridegroom, to hear whose voice was the fulfillment of his joy (*LS* 62).

Although Rossetti mentions John the Baptist here, the more famous John is the Beloved, "the Divine."[11] Rossetti quotes scripture about Jesus's love for John in *Called to Be Saints*, her volume on the special holy days of the Church year. "We may hope that he whom beholding 'Jesus loved' may, although sorrowfully, still have relinquished all, taken up his cross and followed Him Who loved him" (*LS* 32-3).

Appropriate to the mystical nature of the devotional, the love between Christ and John the Beloved is discussed extensively in *Face of the Deep*. Rossetti writes:

"Come up hither." -- Thus was St. John brought into the haven where he would be: but not to abide there. It was as when he leaned on His Master's Bosom, and after a while had to arise; as when he set off to follow, and after a while had to pause and tarry. Love laid him on his Master's Breast, love sped him along that blessed Foot-track; and equally it was love which constrained him to arise and depart from that Rest which was not at once to be his final rest, and to turn back from that 'Way' which vouchsafed not yet to lead him home (*FD* 148).

Elsewhere Rossetti compares her love to St. John's. Speaking to Christ, she writes, "Thou hast not ceased to be my Wise Master and my Gracious Lord; Thou lovest as Thou hast ever loved; alas, it is I who have not loved as St. John loved" (*FD* 193). "Perhaps it may comfort some to think that St. John had a share in the common trial: much more would it comfort us all to undergo it in his spirit. And wherefore not? The disciple whom Jesus loved was not loved to our exclusion" (*FD* 256).

Rossetti locates both the saint and the individual believer in marital relationships with Christ. Although this image is common in mystical theology, the emerging discourses of gender and sexuality in the late nineteenth century coupled with the more Protestant nature of English culture make these depictions of Jesus and John's friendship significant. Whereas in a Catholic country they might be deemed excessive devotional piety, within the Victorian church where Popery was associated with sexual perversion, Rossetti's writing of male friendship is noteworthy.[12] Perhaps her "female audience" was composed of enough passionate, homosocial Tractarian men to make the deployment of the Jesus/John relationship added spiritual titillation.[13]

Rossetti's elaboration of spiritual friendship in the devotionals may certainly be set within the context of Victorian sentimental friendship. On the other hand, "spiritual friendships" have a long history in western monasticism: Aelred of Rievaulx's twelfth-century tract of that name attests to the place of affectional bonds within the religious community.[14] The Victorian re-invention of "Jesus our friend" underscores the Incarnate aspect of the Divine emphasized during this period.[15] Physical bodies are not forgotten in spiritual relationships. Even if she may be left out, existing in a somewhat Sedgwickean triangle between Christ and His Beloved, Rossetti proclaims, "To be excluded with St. John surely excludes not from the innermost blessedness, from the deepest heart of Divine Love" (*FD* 461).

In *Called To Be Saints*, Rossetti's scripture quotations for the feast of St. John include two passionate examples of affective piety from the Gospels.

St John xiii.23. "There was leaning on Jesus' Bosom one of His disciples, whom Jesus loved. Simon Peter therefore beckoned to him, that he should ask who it should be of whom He spake. He then lying on Jesus's Breast saith unto Him, Lord, who is it?" (*CS* 65).

St John xix.25. "Now there stood by the cross of Jesus His Mother. When Jesus therefore saw His Mother, and the disciple standing by, whom He loved, He saith unto His mother, woman, behold thy son!

Then saith He to the disciple, Behold thy mother! And from that hour the disciple took her into his own home." (*CS* 66).

Such Biblical passages underscore the "non-traditional" nature of the "Christian family." Contemporary theologians have cited Jesus' act of entrusting Mary to John as evidence of the significance of His love for him. Many locate the deep friendship within the homosocial patriarchal culture of the period. Others even speculate about same-sex eroticism between Jesus and John.[16] Rossetti celebrates the friends' union:

> Thus does Holy Scripture draw for us the portrait of him who beloved, loving, lovely, forsook not his Lord along the way of sorrows, and has for his eternal reward to follow the Lamb whithersoever He goeth...

> Centuries before, a meeting of consecrated human loves faithful and tender, the welcome of a most noble bridegroom to a veiled bride, had typified the union of Christ with each individual beloved soul, no less than His espousals to His universal Church (*CS* 70-1).

She concludes:

> St. John has moreover been called the Apostle of Love: a designation justly his, whether we trace it to his words or to his works:--
> "Beloved, let us love one another: for love is of God; and everyone that loveth is born of God, and knoweth God." -1 St. John iv.7.
> While he himself draws his own title not from love preached or love proferred, but from love received: --
> "That disciple whom Jesus loved" - St. John xxi.7. (*CS* 74).

The fact that Christ's love is *for* John is crucial in understanding mystical union. As in His kenosis, the Divine is fluid and the human receptive here. However much we may emphasize the Immaterial/material nature of their encounter, the fact that Christ is also human defines the relationship between these men. Rossetti's prayer for John's feast day is "for union with Christ" (*CS* 76).

> O God, of Whose free gracious bounty Thy holy Apostle and Evangelist St. John was specially beloved; -- whom Christ chose and who chose Christ; -- whom Christ loved and who loved Christ; --

who forsaking his father preferred Christ; who leaving all that he had followed Christ; -- who on the Mount of Transfiguration beheld the glory of his Lord; -- who in the upper chamber leaned on the Bosom of his Beloved; -- who in the High Priest's palace clave unto His Friend (*CS* 76).

In her final prose text, *Face of the Deep*, Rossetti fleshes out the soul's kiss, crossing this [mystical] bar between body and spirit, as well as life and death. Christ's love for John was the mystic's model. Rossetti prefigures "the kiss" in *Time Flies*, published six years earlier:

> The "kiss" enjoined being a spiritual kiss of loving fealty, we of this nineteenth century, while still on earth, can as readily and can truly offer it to Christ in heaven, as could St. Peter and St. John to that same Divine Master when on Blessed Feet he trod the weary ways of Palestine.
> For the literal kiss is the symbol, the spiritual kiss the reality... the spiritual embrace excels the literal embrace; this being but the symbol, that the reality (261).

Published two years before her death in 1894, during the "apocalyptic" *fin-de-siècle*, *Face of the Deep* is a lengthy and detailed exegesis of the Biblical book of Revelation. It anticipates the world beyond as it is prepared for Brides of Christ. Toward the end of the work, Rossetti gives an extensive commentary on the new Jerusalem, coming down out of heaven as a bride adorned for her husband. She concludes:

> Behold her! yea, also, and behold thyself, O thou called to be a saint. Her perfections are thy birthright; thou are what she was, what she is thou mayest become...To-day put on the garments of salvation prepared for thee, that tomorrow thou mayest be promoted to wear the garments of praise (*FD* 480-1).

Rossetti's prose works were indeed written for those who are "called to be saints:" all humanity, the many incarnations that comprise the heavenly Jerusalem and the Church catholic. However, the devotionals were written especially for those virgins in Christ who strive to find empowerment by accepting "the lowest place," flourishing in their secondary status. The title "*Time Flies*" reminds the reader of the transitory nature of creation. Seen in this light, Rossetti's sensual devotion is difficult to reconcile with her transcendental theology:

A sensual Christian resembles a sea anemone. In the nobler element, air, it exists as a sluggish unbeautiful excrescence. In the lower element, water, it grows, blows, and thrives. The food it assimilates is derived not from the height, but from the depth. It possesses neither eyes nor ears, but a multitude of feelers. It squats on a tenacious base, gulps all acquisitions into a capacious chasm, and harmonises with the weeds it dwells amongst. But what will become of it in a world where there shall be no more sea? (*TF* 198)

"Sensuality," perhaps, is the sole root/route for the female theologian to cultivate and follow. Like Hildegard and Julian before her, Rossetti looks to her carnal female body, her "feminine form" as her avenue to salvation. Nevertheless, her writing -- secular and religious, poetry and prose -- demonstrates an unquestionable awareness of and search for the substance that lies behind all "forms." Rossetti elucidates the ways in which the Divine Transcendent may be achieved through relationships with and within this material creation. The role of humanity -- particular female humanity -- in the continuum of cosmic creation redeems the flesh and makes it holy. For these female theologians, Woman's relation to transcendent Wisdom negates the limitations of material creation.

Stylizing oneself as a Bride of Christ was one highly effective means of attaining a voice within Rossetti's culture, as it was for Hildegard and Julian before her. Just as medieval religious writing cannot be read outside of its context, let us neither impose our own *fin-de-siècle*'s paradigms upon nineteenth-century English culture. For Rossetti, in renunciation was found liberation. The many life-affirming and body-affirming gestures which develop out of her theology of "hope deferred" recapitulate the ultimate Christian paradox of life through death.

NOTES

1. See, for example, Barbara Newman's *Sister of Wisdom: St. Hildegard's Theology of the Feminine* (Berkeley: U California P, 1987) for a scholarly study of the abbess. There are numerous New Age interpretations of Hildegard, all of them received with high degrees of skepticism in the academy. Matthew Fox's *Illuminations of Hildegard of Bingen* text (Santa Fe: Bear, 1985) provides some interesting translations of the abbess which work within a certain creation-centered paradigm appropriate to contemporary mysticism.

2. An early readable work on this subject is *Sophia: The Future of Feminist Spirituality* by Susan Cady, Marian Ronan, and Hal Taussig (San Francisco: Harper & Row, 1986). Numerous feminist theologians have written on Sophia. A recent work is *Jesus: Miriam's Child, Sophia's Prophet: Critical Issues in Feminist Christology* (New York: Continuum, 1995) by Elisabeth Schussler Fiorenza.

3. See Carter Heyward's *Touching Our Strength: The Erotic as Power and the Love of God* (New York: HarperCollins, 1989). See also James Nelson, *Body Theology* (Louisville: Westminster John Knox P, 1992), and with Sandra P. Longfellow, eds.

Sexuality and the Sacred: Sources for Theological Reflection (Louisville: Westminster John Knox P, 1994).

4. Recent studies of the prose are few: Joel Westerholm, "'I Magnify Mine Office': Christina Rossetti's Authoritative Voice in Her Devotional Prose" (*Victorian Newsletter* 84(1993): 11-17); Colleen Hobbs, "A View from "The Lowest Place": Christina Rossetti's Devotional Prose" (*Victorian Poetry* 32(1994): 407-28); and two essays in David A. Kent's 1987 anthology, *The Achievement of Christina Rossetti* (Ithaca: Cornell U P): Diane D'Amico, "Eve, Mary, and Mary Magdalene: Christina Rossetti's Feminine Triptych" (175-91); and P.G. Stanwood's "Christina Rossetti's Devotional Prose" (231-49). Most book-length studies treat Rossetti's prose only in passing. Jan Marsh's recent biography is an exception (*Christina Rossetti: A Writer's Life*. New York: Viking, 1994)

5. For a discussion of the former topic, see David Hilliard, "'Unenglish and Unmanly': Anglo-Catholicism and Homosexuality." *Victorian Studies* 25(1982): 181-210. On the latter, see Susan Casteras, "Virgin Vows: The Early Victorian Artists' Portrayal of Nuns and Novices." *Victorian Studies* 23(1981): 157-83

6. Rossetti mentions Anselm in her reflection on St. Alphage in *Time Flies*. The work is a reading diary for the Church year. Rossetti's emphases in *Time Flies* are comparable to her other devotional prose: she pays special attention to women saints, particularly virgin martyrs, and stresses a strongly incarnational theology. In the volume, Rossetti states that she quotes "second hand from the Golden Legend," a huge medieval compendium of hagiography (*TF* 169). She also acknowledges her debt to S. Baring-Gould's *Lives of the Saints*, a seventeen-volume work published in the 1870's.

7. See Michael Hill, *The Religious Order* (London: Heinemann, 1973) and Martha Vicinus, *Independent Women: Work and Community for Single Women, 1850-1920* (Chicago: U Chicago P, 1985) for two different perspectives on the sisterhoods in Victorian England.
See also Peter Anson, *The Call of the Cloister: Religious Communities and Kindred Bodies in the Anglican Communion* (London: SPCK, 1955); Brian Heeney, *The Women's Movement in the Church of England , 1850-1930* (Oxford: Clarendon P, 1988); John Shelton Reed, "'A Female Movement': The Feminization of Nineteenth Century Anglo-Catholicism" (*Anglican & Episcopal History* 57(1988): 199-238; and, especially, Diane D'Amico, "'Choose the Stairs That Mount Above': Christina Rossetti and the Anglican Sisterhoods." *Essays in Literature* 17(1990): 204-21.

8. See *Holy Feast, Holy Fast: The Religious Significance of Food to Medieval Women* (Berkeley: U California P, 1987).

9. Given Rossetti's incarnational theology, it is difficult to think of any of her works as secular. We must expand the definition of the term "religious": the dichotomy of "body and spirit" as it is aligned with "profane and sacred" is useless when we consider examples of sensual religiosity, which clearly encompasses the *via mystica*.

10. See Jean LeClercq, *The Love of Learning and the Desire for God*, 3rd ed., trans. Catherine Misrahi (New York: Fordham U P, 1982).

11. In *Letter and Spirit*, Rossetti recalls the story of the rich young man who asked Jesus's advice. He is the third beloved John of the New Testament, and sometimes is thought to be the same individual as John the Divine.

12. For a reading of Christina Rossetti within the context of the Oxford Movement which preceded her, see G. B. Tennyson, *Victorian Devotional Poetry: The Tractarian Mode* (Cambridge: Harvard U P, 1981). For other perspectives on gender at Oxford appropriate to the consideration of male friendship, see Linda Dowling, *Hellenism and Homosexuality in Victorian Oxford* (Ithaca: Cornell U P, 1994) and Oliver Buckton, "'An Unnatural State': Gender, Perversion, and Newman's *Apologia Pro Vita Sua*." *Victorian Studies* 35(1992): 359-83.

Rossetti also dramatically demonstrates same-sex spiritual alliances in her entry for the dual feast of Sts. Philip and James in *Time Flies*:

On their Feast Day they stand before us as it were hand in hand: "Behold, how good and joyful a thing is, brethren, to dwell together in unity."

Whatever remains uncertain about them, of two facts we rest assured: they loved God, and therefore cannot but have loved one another (83).

13. The question of male reader of Rossetti is significant. Victorian devotional prose written by women is usually assumed to be addressed to a female audience.

14. A book-length biography of Aelred written by John Dobree Dalgairns in 1844 was included in Newman's *Lives of the English Saints*. A number of later Anglo-Catholic monks took the name Aelred, honoring this Saxon forefather who stressed the Gospel of Love.

John Boswell's *Christianity, Social Tolerance and Homosexuality: Gay People in Western Europe from the Beginning of the Christian Era through the Fourteenth Century* (Chicago: U Chicago P, 1980) was perhaps the first of early "gay studies" work to discuss Aelred's possible violation of norms of gender behavior. See more recently Brian Patrick McGuire, "Sexual Awareness and Identity in Aelred of Rievaulx (1110-67)." *American Benedictine Review* 45(1994): 184-226.

15. Consider nineteenth-century Protestant hymns of sentimental piety, such as Joseph Scriven's 1855 "What A Friend We Have in Jesus" or Joseph Small's 1863 "I've Found a Friend, O Such a Friend."

16. A number of works of gay theology have been written in the past ten years which discuss this issue with varying degrees of academic rigor. See Richard Cleaver, *Know My Name: A Gay Liberation Theology* (Louisville: Westminster John Knox, 1995); Gary Comstock, *Gay Theology Without Apology* (Cleveland: Pilgrim P, 1993); John McNeill, *Freedom, Glorious Freedom: The Spiritual Journey to the Fullness of Life for Gays, Lesbians, and Everybody Else* (Boston: Beacon P, 1995) and *Taking a Chance on God: Liberating Theology for Gays, Lesbians, and Their Lovers, Families, and Friends* (Boston: Beacon P, 1995); and Robert Williams, *Just As I Am: A Practical Guide to Being Out, Proud, and Christian* (New York: HarperPerennial, 1992).

WORKS CITED

Anson, Peter. *The Call of the Cloister: Religious Communities and Kindred Bodies in the Anglican Communion.* London: SPCK, 1955.

Boswell, John. *Christianity, Social Tolerance, and Homosexuality: Gay People in Western Europe from the Beginning of the Christian Era through the Fourteenth Century.* Chicago: U Chicago P, 1980.

Buckton, Oliver. "'An Unnatural State': Gender, Perversion, and Newman's *Apologia Pro Vita Sua.*" *Victorian Studies* 35(1992): 359-83.

Bynum, Caroline Walker. *Holy Feast, Holy Fast: The Religious Significance of Food to Medieval Women.* Berkeley: U California P, 1987.

---. *Jesus As Mother: Studies in the Spirituality of the High Middle Ages.* Berkeley: U California P, 1982.

Cady, Susan, Marian Ronan, and Hal Taussig. *Sophia: The Future of Feminist Spirituality.* San Francisco: Harper & Row, 1986.

Casteras, Susan. "Virgin Vows: The Early Victorian Artists' Portrayal of Nuns and Novices." *Victorian Studies* 23(1981): 157-83.

Cleaver, Richard. *Know My Name: A Gay Liberation Theology.* Louisville: Westminster John Knox P, 1995.

Comstock, Gary David. *Gay Theology Without Apology.* Cleveland: Pilgrim Press, 1993.

D'Amico, Diane. "'Choose the Stairs That Mount Above': Christina Rossetti and the Anglican Sisterhoods." *Essays in Literature* 17(1990): 204-21.

---. "Eve, Mary, and Mary Magdalene: Christina Rossetti's Feminine Triptych." *The Achievement of Christina Rossetti.* Ed. David A. Kent. Ithaca: Cornell U P, 1987. 175-91.

Dowling, Linda. *Hellenism and Homosexuality in Victorian Oxford.* Ithaca: Cornell U P, 1994.

Fox, Matthew. *The Illuminations of Hildegard of Bingen.* Santa Fe: Bear, 1985.

Heeney, Brian. *The Women's Movement in the Church of England 1850-1930.* Oxford: Clarendon P, 1988.

Heyward, Carter. *Touching Our Strength: The Erotic as Power and the Love of God.* New York: HarperCollins, 1989.

Hill, Michael. *The Religious Order.* London: Heinemann, 1973.

Hilliard, David. "Unenglish and Unmanly: Anglo-Catholicism and Homosexuality." *Victorian Studies* 25(1982): 181-210.

Hobbs, Colleen. "A View from 'The Lowest Place': Christina Rossetti's Devotional Prose." *Victorian Poetry* 32(1994): 407-28.

Hildegard, of Bingen. *Scivias.* Trans. Columba Hart and Jane Bishop. New York: Paulist P, 1990.

---. *Symphonia: A Critical Edition of the Symphonia armonie celestium revelationum.* Trans. Barbara Newman. Ithaca: Cornell U P, 1988.

Julian, of Norwich. *Showings.* Trans. Edmund Colledge and James Walsh. New York: Paulist P, 1978.

Krueger, Christine L. *The Reader's Repentance: Women Preachers, Women Writers and Nineteenth Century Social Discourse.* Chicago: U Chicago P, 1992.

LeClercq, Jean. *The Love of Learning and the Desire for God: A Study of Monastic Culture.* 3rd ed. Trans. Catherine Misrahi. New York: Fordham U P, 1982.

Marsh, Jan. *Christina Rossetti: A Writer's Life.* New York: Viking, 1994.

McGuire, Brian Patrick. "Sexual Awareness and Identity in Aelred of Rievaulx." *American Benedictine Review* 45(1994): 184-226.

McNeill, John. *Freedom, Glorious Freedom: The Spiritual Journey To the Fullness of Life for Gays, Lesbians, and Everybody Else.* Boston: Beacon P, 1995.

---. *Taking a Chance on God: Liberating Theology for Gays, Lesbians, and Their Lovers, Families and Friends.* Boston: Beacon, 1988.

Nelson, James P. *Body Theology.* Louisville: Westminster John Knox P, 1992.

--- and Sandra P. Longfellow, eds. *Sexuality and the Sacred: Sources for Theological Reflection*. Louisville: Westminster John Knox P, 1994.

Newman, Barbara. *Sister of Wisdom: Hildegard's Theology of the Feminine*. Berkeley: U California P, 1987.

Reed, John Shelton. "'A Female Movement': The Feminization of Nineteenth Century Anglo-Catholicism." *Anglican & Episcopal History* 57(1988): 199-238.

Rossetti, Christina G. *Annus Domini: A Prayer for Each Day of the Year, Founded on a Text of Holy Scripture*. Oxford: James Parker & Co., 1874.

---. *Called To Be Saints: The Minor Festivals Devotionally Studied*. 1881. New York: E. & J.B. Young, 1902.

---. *The Face of the Deep: A Devotional Commentary on the Apocalypse*. 1892. New York: E. & J.B. Young, 1895.

---. *Letter and Spirit: Notes on the Commandments*. London: SPCK, 1883.

---. *Maude. Maude, On Sisterhoods, A Woman's Thoughts About Women*. Ed. Elaine Showalter. New York: New York U P, 1993.

---. *Seek and Find: A Double Series of Short Studies of the Benedicite*. 1879. New York: Pott, Young, & Co., n.d.

---. *Time Flies: A Reading Diary*. 1886. New York: E. & J.B. Young, 1902.

Schussler Fiorenza, Elisabeth. *Jesus: Miriam's Child, Sophia's Prophet: Critical Issues in Feminist Christology*. New York: Continuum, 1995.

Sedgwick, Eve Kosofsky. *Between Men: English Literature and Male Homosocial Desire*. New York: Columbia U P, 1985.

Stanwood, P. G. "Christina Rossetti's Devotional Prose." *The Achievement of Christina Rossetti*. Ed. David A. Kent. Ithaca: Cornell U P, 1987. 231-49.

Tennyson, G. B. *Victorian Devotional Poetry: The Tractarian Mode*. Cambridge: Harvard U P, 1981.

Vicinus, Martha. *Independent Women: Work and Community for Single Women, 1850-1920*. Chicago: U Chicago P, 1985.

Westerholm, Joel. "'I Magnify Mine Office': Christina Rossetti's Authoritative Voice in Her Devotional Prose." *Victorian Newsletter* 84(1993): 11-7.

Williams, Robert. *Just As I Am: A Practical Guide to Being Out, Proud, and Christian*. New York: HarperPerennial, 1992.

The Madonna and Anna Jameson

Kimberly VanEsveld Adams
Rutgers University

Anna Brownell Murphy Jameson (1794-1860) was in her century an influential practitioner of feminist scholarship and a respected and versatile professional writer, whose works were reviewed in the major British periodicals. An Irish-born Englishwoman, she was best known for her history and criticism of medieval and Renaissance art, but she also wrote popular lives of queens and the consorts of poets, Shakespeare criticism, and accounts of her travels in France, Italy, Germany, and North America. Jameson was an honored adviser to the Langham Place feminists, a London-based group led by Barbara Bodichon, Bessie Parkes, and Emily Faithfull. She was active in their campaign for married women's property rights, she lectured and wrote in favor of better education and job opportunities for women, and her art-historical scholarship was used as testimony of the high abilities of women.

Jameson's major work is the multi-volume series *Sacred and Legendary Art*, which was designed to help Britons and Americans (particularly Protestants) touring the galleries and churches of Europe to understand what they saw.[1] In *Legends of the Madonna* (1852), the third title in the series, Jameson categorizes and explains the various representations of Mary found in medieval and Renaissance art. She also uses this art to support high claims for Mary as Christ's equal or near-equal. For example, she calls Mary the goddess-figure of Christianity, "a new type of womanly perfection," as Christ is the model of manly perfection (*Madonna* xx). She even claims that Mary, like Jesus, is in orthodox Christian thought fully human and fully divine. My argument is that such statements reflect painstaking historical scholarship, but they are hardly disinterested. They instead mirror the author's own feminist and religious beliefs.

In a credo that appears several times in her writings, Jameson expresses her relational-feminist belief in the fundamental equality of men and women, while admitting certain essential and enduring differences, such as woman's physical and psychic capacity for motherhood. As I will show, Jameson sees Mary's place in Christianity as an important sign of male-female equality -- an acknowledgment that female nature is represented by the blessed Virgin Mother rather than by the fallen Eve, and that female as well as male nature can be made radiant, perfect, divine. God, in her argument, has a feminine as well as a masculine face. Mary's roles, moreover, show that woman's destiny is not merely to be a man's dependant and a mother devoted only to her own family. She is also Queen of Heaven and "Mother of All Humanity," and as the solitary, self-sufficient Virgin is "complete in her own perfections."

Jameson's use of the Madonna in feminist arguments sets her apart from other advocates of women's rights in England and America. She was not the only nineteenth-century practitioner of a feminist biblical hermeneutics; the American abolitionist Sarah Grimke published *Letters on the Equality of the Sexes* in 1838, and Elizabeth Cady Stanton's notorious *The Woman's Bible* appeared in 1895-98. But while Grimke and Stanton single out certain biblical women as role models (Grimke favors the female prophets, Stanton the rebellious Eve), neither has any use for the Virgin Mary. I will briefly compare Jameson with her American counterparts in order to suggest that the British writer's high regard for church tradition and her knowledge of European art and culture are what enable her to use the Madonna as an empowering figure for women. My analysis of Jameson will qualify the view of many twentieth-century scholars, in the fields of religion, history, and literature, that the figure of Mary has until recently been controlled by men rather than by women and thus has only impeded liberatory movements for women.

LEGENDS OF THE MADONNA

In *Legends of the Madonna*, Jameson divides her discussion of artistic representations of Mary into two parts -- first, Devotional Subjects, which illustrate a dogma, such as the Coronation of the Virgin, the Mater Dolorosa, or the Immaculate Conception, and appeal to the "faith and piety" of the viewer; and second, Historical Subjects, which are dramatic treatments of biblical and legendary incidents from the life of the Virgin (liii-lv). It is primarily in the devotional section of *Legends of the Madonna* that we see Mary as Jameson describes her in the general introduction to the book: "an impersonation in the feminine character of beneficence, purity, and power, standing between an offended Deity and poor, sinning, suffering humanity..." (xvii). "Beneficence, purity, and power": the key word in this phrase is the last. Even allowing for the extravagances of late-medieval Mariology, we can see that Jameson selects and praises devotional images of the Madonna that emphasize her spiritual power, which is often exercised independently of her Son's. For instance, Jameson in her opening chapter on the Virgin without the Child describes the earliest representations of the solitary Virgin as "female figure[s] of colossal dimensions,...stand[ing] immediately beneath some figure or emblem representing almighty power," "grand and mysterious," "wonderfully majestic and simple" (4). Mary is here "not merely the mother of Christ" but also "the second Eve, the mother of all suffering humanity; THE WOMAN of the primaeval prophecy whose issue was to bruise the head of the Serpent"; the type of the Church triumphant and crowned in heaven; "the most glorious, most pure, most pious, most clement, most sacred Queen and Mother, Virgin of Virgins" (*Madonna* 4). These titles for Mary come from patristic and medieval Mariology; yet, as I will show, Jameson's emotional responses to the heavenly Queen and Virgin go far beyond mere reporting.

Jameson describes numerous examples of the Coronation of the Virgin (*Madonna* 13-26), but she provides sketches of the images that maximize the Virgin's power and status. Four of her six sketches are of the Virgin seated on the same throne as Christ receiving her crown (see figures 13 and 15, both fourteenth century, and plate IV.1). In Jameson's first, admittedly singular example, a twelfth-century mosaic, the Virgin is "seated at [Christ's] right hand, at the same elevation, and altogether as his equal" (figure 12). In Jameson's two sketches of the Virgin kneeling rather than sitting on the throne, she is being crowned by the Father himself and the other members of the Trinity (see figure 14 and plate IV.2).

Jameson also chooses to emphasize Mary's equality or near-equality with Christ in her discussions of the Virgin of Mercy, "the most powerful of intercessors," who is frequently shown in late-medieval art pleading for sinners before Christ the stern judge. Jameson observes that the Virgin of Mercy is usually seated on the same level as Christ or at least at his right hand (*Madonna* 26-27). In a painting by Martin Schoen (or Schoengauer, fifteenth century), which shows the Father as judge, armed with a sword and javelins, and the Son standing beside him, the Virgin is in the foreground, "looking up to her Son with an expression of tender supplication," while the "imploring looks" of sinners "are directed to *her*" (28). The Virgin as dispenser of mercy on earth, in Jameson's description, is a huge figure who can protect with the folds of her robe men, women, and children, kings, nobles, and priests -- in other words, all of Christendom (29-30).

Jameson emphasizes the Virgin's independence as well as her power. One of the last devotional images of the Virgin without the Child that she analyzes is the Immaculate Conception, a favorite subject of the seventeenth-century painters Guido and Murillo. While the Virgin's mercy toward suffering humanity, as Jameson notes, is thought to be an expression of her maternal character, in the Immaculate Conception "the maternal character is set aside, and she stands alone, absolute in herself, and complete in her own perfections" (*Madonna* xxxvi).

On turning to devotional images of the Virgin *with* the Child, Jameson herself seems frequently moved to worship:

> When the glorified type of what is purest, loftiest, holiest in womanhood, stands before us, arrayed in all the majesty and beauty that accomplished Art, inspired by faith and love, could lend her, and bearing her divine Son, rather enthroned than sustained on her maternal bosom, "we look, and the heart is in heaven!" and it is difficult, very difficult, to refrain from an *Ora pro Nobis*. (*Madonna* 58; see also 73-76)

The Madonna who worships her Son is herself his throne, and she is adored by attendant angels, saints, and men and women crying "Salve Regina!" to the being "so human, so maternal, and yet so unearthly" (73, 102-3). Jameson here celebrates the maternal character, which she sees as present in all women (*Letters to Ottilie von Goethe* 234). Fathers, divine and human, are unnecessary in these paintings; God is not shown, and Jameson notes that Mary's father Joachim and Joseph are often omitted from votive groups that include Mary's mother Anna (*Madonna* 80). Even the Son may be overlooked in the exaltation of the divine mother:

> ...the Virgins of the old Italians....look so divinely ethereal that they seem uplifted by their own spirituality: not even the air-borne clouds are needed to sustain them. They have no touch of earth or earth's material beyond the human form; their proper place is the seventh heaven; and there they repose, a presence and a power -- a personification of infinite mercy sublimated by innocence and purity; and thence they look down on their worshippers and attendants, while these gaze upwards "with looks commercing with the skies." (*Madonna* 76)

It is with reluctance that Jameson moves on from the devotional representations of the Madonna in the first part of *Legends of the Madonna* to the historical subjects, those drawn from the Gospel stories and legends about her life (*Madonna* 133-34). One reason for Jameson's comparative lack of enthusiasm seems to be that the historical paintings are generally not by her favorite "old Italians" but by late sixteenth- and seventeenth-century artists -- Titian, Tintoretto, Correggio, Poussin, Rubens, Vandyck, Rembrandt -- whom she sometimes discerningly praises but more often criticizes as coarse, violent, showy, materialistic, and lacking in religious feeling.[2] But a more important reason is that Jameson clearly prefers the devotional images of "the sovereign lady of Christendom" to the historical representations of Mary as "mere woman" (133-34). It is also the case that

Mary is no longer the primary focus of the historical paintings, which instead depict *events* in which she, usually Jesus, and others are involved (e.g., the marriage at Cana). Jameson consequently must spend less time contemplating and praising Mary and more time explaining the legends and the theological points behind the paintings (e.g., the nativity of the Virgin, the death of Joseph), many of which would be unfamiliar to her Protestant and Bible-centered readers.

But the "mere woman" is a useful figure nonetheless. Jameson argues that our humanity is reflected in the earthly Mary of the Gospels and legends: our maternal experiences are made sacred by her loving gaze at her first-born son, our losses are solaced by her grief over the death of her husband and child, and our work is given value when Jesus' mother is shown cooking, spinning, sewing, and washing the holy family's clothes.[3] Mary also has an important function in Jameson's brief social commentaries on the condition of women and children -- for example, their victimization by men. Jameson says of the Magi:

> They had come, perhaps, from some far-distant savage land, or from some nation calling itself civilised, where innocence had never been accounted sacred, where society had as yet taken no heed of the defenceless woman, no care for the helpless child; where the one was enslaved, and the other perverted: and here, under the form of womanhood and childhood, they were called upon to worship the promise of that brighter future, when peace should inherit the earth, and righteousness prevail over deceit, and gentleness with wisdom reign for ever and ever! (*Madonna* 212)

The nations purporting to be civilized are here the ancient pagan East but could also include the American South, in this book written by an anti-slavery sympathizer, or the England of the factory slaves, some so young, or Jameson's mother-country Ireland, suffering from famine and political oppression and so often on her mind (see "Woman's Mission," 196-207; Clara Thomas, 183-86). (Jameson's linkage of the status of women to the progress of Christianity and of civilization, which is an important element in her thought, will be discussed below.) Jameson later, in her discussion of the outpouring of the Holy Spirit at Pentecost, argues that as this divine and empowering gift descended upon both men and women, the sexes are equally called upon to do the Lord's work of loving, serving, acting, and suffering (*Madonna* 304; similarly, Sarah Grimke, *Letters* 89-92).

Jameson, then, is generally calmly approving rather than enthusiastic in her analyses of the humanized mother of Jesus. But her commentaries on the various biblical and legendary images strengthen the links she establishes between Mary and ordinary women. In the devotional section, the

Madonna is a divinized representative of womankind. In the historical section, she experiences all women's earthly joys and sorrows. Both linkages, as I will show, have political resonances and feminist implications.

It could be said -- indeed, the art historian Adele Holcomb has said -- that Jameson is merely *describing* the religious art of the Middle Ages and Renaissance, without indicating her own artistic preferences or religious views ("Sacred Art," 111). But internal evidence from *Legends of the Madonna* and other volumes in the series *Sacred and Legendary Art* calls this view into question. Jameson carefully selects *powerful* representations of Mary to discuss in *Madonna*, as I have just shown. And her approach to religious subjects and paintings is often far from neutral. Jameson is quite ready to criticize even the greatest of painters and paintings -- for example, Rubens for his "daring bad taste" in a Last Judgment, and Michelangelo for his degraded Christology (*Madonna* 29). She also singles out works for praise on both artistic and religious grounds -- the Transfiguration of Raphael, for example, the often-criticized but to her mind the only gloriously successful representation of this most difficult subject (*The History of Our Lord* I:341-46). Jameson, moreover, does not distance herself or her readers from the Marian representations she describes by citing Protestant doctrinal differences. For example, she says of the various titles given to Mary -- such as Our Lady of Mercy, Refuge of Sinners, Our Lady of Wisdom, Our Lady of the Rosary -- that they express the wants and sorrows of "poor suffering humanity" or the "divine attributes from which they hope to find aid and consolation" (*Madonna* lxiv-v). She does not note that "humanity" here includes very few Protestants, who are usually taught to abhor such names and claims for Mary. Jameson's inclusiveness in *Legends of the Madonna* contrasts with her practice in the earlier *Legends of the Monastic Orders* (1850), where she proclaims in her preface that she is no Roman Catholic and describes ascetic monachism as "the apotheosis of deformity and suffering" (*Monastic Orders* xiv, xviii). Jameson's reluctance to articulate Protestant doctrinal positions in *Madonna* is significant, because it implies that the Madonna in her full historical development -- the physical and moral and theological type -- is a figure all can receive. This point is reinforced by the verses of English poets -- Wordsworth, Shelley, and Browning -- which Jameson cites as addressed to or evocative of the celestial Virgin Mother worthy of worship (*Madonna* xlii-xliii).

The arrangement of *Legends of the Madonna* is also evidence that Jameson is not merely describing Marian art but advancing an argument of her own. The organization is primarily artistic and topical: Jameson begins with devotional subjects -- the Virgin without the Child, the Virgin with the Child, Votive Images, and so on -- and then presents the biblical and legendary scenes of Mary's life, from the Immaculate Conception and the Annunciation to her Assumption into heaven. Jameson's discussion only roughly follows the history of Christian doctrine, although doctrinal changes lead to the emergence of new Marian images. For example, by treating the Virgin without the Son first, Jameson discusses both the earliest and late (seventeenth-century) images of Mary, and she analyzes the solitary Queen of Heaven (the Assumption, seventh and eighth centuries) before rather than after the Theotokos (fifth century). Jameson's plan of organization means she begins with representations of Mary at her most powerful and independent: "Queen of Heaven, Virgin of Virgins!" She thus reinforces the message of the general introduction, that Mary is the goddess of Christianity, powerful, solitary, and divine, rather than just the simple maid of Galilee.

The significance of Jameson's organization also becomes clear when one compares *Legends of the Madonna* to the final title in the series *Sacred and Legendary Art*, *The History of Our Lord* (1864), which was begun by Jameson and completed after her death by Elizabeth Eastlake.[4] Eastlake notes that Jameson (as in *Legends of the Madonna*) planned to begin with ideal and devotional subjects -- here the Good Shepherd, the Lamb, and the Second Person of the Trinity -- and then treat the biblical history of Jesus' life; the final section was to have been types from the Old Testament. Eastlake instead has a chronological organization which incorporates the material Jameson had completed: she begins with the Fall of Lucifer and the Angels, the Creation, and the Fall of Adam and Eve, discusses Old Testament types (for example, Abraham, Samson, and Jonah) and prophets, and then treats the scenes of Jesus' life, from his birth and ministry to the Last Judgment (*History of Our Lord* I:v-xi). Eastlake's *History of Our Lord* is a decidedly Protestant work. It reflects the Protestant understanding of providential history -- the Fall, the foreshadowings of the Redemption, the Redemption, the Last Judgment -- and it makes a Protestant discrimination between Holy Scripture, which is thought to provide inspired information about Jesus, and the apocryphal and legendary sources, which are considered far less worthy and reliable. For example, Eastlake rejects as "spurious" and "puerile" the legendary accounts of Jesus' childhood that Jameson planned to discuss in the book, because represented in art (*Our Lord* I:276). Eastlake goes so far as to criticize paintings of the Passion that show Mary swooning (rather than quietly standing) by the cross "and thus diverting the attention both of the actors in the scene and the spectators of the picture from the one awful object" (*Our Lord* I:6). The author of *Legends of the Madonna* would not have concurred in this reading of the Blessed Virgin's attention-getting behavior and inappropriate centrality to the scene (see *Madonna* 284, 289-96).

Eastlake's evaluations of religious art seem ultimately based on sectarian rather than aesthetic criteria. When she states that the purpose of art is to instruct and edify believers with materials derivable from Scripture, and then notes that Southern artists after Raphael (that is, Tridentine artists) failed to have this aim, and when she argues that the art of some German painters of the fifteenth and sixteenth centuries is debased because it predates the Reformation, which "unlock[ed] the Bible itself," one sees that Eastlake considers art good if it is acceptable to the heirs of the Reformation (*Our Lord* I:3,9; II:3-4). Jameson, in contrast, thinks that historians' and critics' sympathy with earlier minds should guide their evaluations. Human fears and human longings that gave rise to divine attitudes and sacred legends, and beliefs that modern viewers may understand but do not share: these to Jameson are the key to unlocking the secrets of religious art. Even though Jameson's artistic preferences are often similar to Eastlake's, she provides aesthetic rather than primarily theological criteria for her judgments, and she usually suggests some religious common ground for early and modern viewers of the paintings.

If Jameson had done an "Eastlake" version of *Legends of the Madonna*, an obviously Protestant version, the Mary of the Gospels would be presented as the true Mary, and the biblical account of her life, from the Annunciation through Cana and the Cross, would receive the greatest emphasis. The Queen of Heaven would probably be treated because of the number of examples, but likely in the back, under "Post-biblical Developments." She would not be the type that informs the whole.

JAMESON'S FEMINIST AND RELIGIOUS VIEWS

Jameson's high claims for Mary, found through the series *Sacred and Legendary Art*, are integrally related to her feminist and religious understanding of the essential equality of men and women. An appropriate starting point for an examination of these views is an 1847 "credo" that appears several times in her writings and contains ideas reiterated throughout her work. Here Jameson states her fundamental belief: that God created man and woman equal in reason, in freedom, in their responsibility to develop their God-given capacities, and in their immortal destiny.[5] There is no difference in the virtues and vices of the sexes -- "whatever is morally wrong, is equally wrong in men and in women and no virtue is to be cultivated in one sex that is not equally required by the other" -- nor in their marital responsibilities of "mutual truth" and fidelity to the sacred vow, "self-controul," and "purity of heart" (*Letters to Ottilie von Goethe* 233-34). Jameson does, however, see certain essential differences in men's and women's "endowments," specifying the "maternal organisation" common to all women, whether or not they are mothers. Women's "sacred province" is consequently the home, while men administer the affairs of the larger community (234).

This statement of beliefs is significant, first, for its form, the credo. Although much of Jameson's work deals with Christian doctrine as represented in art, she nowhere in her public or private writings has a lengthy discussion of the creeds of the Church and only once states her own agreement or disagreement with them (*Sacred and Legendary Art* I:339). Instead, she writes her own creed, showing which belief is most important to her -- male-female equality. Yet Jameson bases her claims on the highest religious authorities: the creation order of God as described in Genesis, "the Gospel of Christ," "the eternal law of justice," and natural law (*Letters to Ottilie von Goethe* 233-34). Like her predecessors Mary Wollstonecraft, author of *Vindication of the Rights of Woman* (1792), and Sarah and Angelina Grimke, Jameson makes her starting point the sameness of men and women as "souls" or "moral natures," in order to demonstrate that her feminist beliefs are not contradictory to but founded on religious beliefs, specifically those of Christianity. And like her younger friend, the women's-rights activist Barbara Leigh Smith Bodichon, Jameson utilizes the traditional form of the credo to give her statements religious authority and power.[6]

Jameson's reference in her creed to women's domestic role -- "the ordering of domestic life is our sacred province indissolubly linked with the privileges, pleasures, and duties of maternity" -- may seem to twentieth-century feminists to be a troubling slip into "True Woman" mode (*Letters to Ottilie von Goethe* 234). But one must remember that for Jameson, as for many single or separated women of her day, home was a *privilege*. She left the house her husband Robert Jameson built for her in Toronto because of the impossibility of living in Canada -- to her, the North Pole -- or of sharing the place with him. For years she kept her invalid father, her mother, and her unmarried sisters in a tiny "nest" only by writing and traveling incessantly, gathering material for her books. One should also note that Jameson's compressed statement about women's domestic responsibilities is developed and clarified in her essays on women's work, written about the same time. In "'Woman's Mission,' and Woman's Position" (1846), Jameson points out the contradiction between the "assumed condition" of women -- all happy in their domestic sphere -- and the real conditions of working women's lives. After describing the value of the work women do at home, she notes the cost to working-class families of the loss of home -- for when a wife and mother is turned into a wage slave, she often does not have the energy after her hard day's labor, or the skills ordinarily learned in girlhood, to make the family's lodging a safe, clean, and welcoming place, where children are nurtured and cherished, and men are "refine[d] and comforte[d]" ("Woman's Mission," 196-207). Jameson is somewhat patronizing in her middle-class expectations for working-class women, but she does offer perhaps compensatory sympathy for the working women who, then as now, struggle under the double burden of paid work and housework. Jameson insists that both working-class and middle-class women take jobs out of necessity, to support themselves and feed their families. They are impeded by the reluctance of men to open more positions to them, to pay them adequately, and to allow them appropriate training. One of Jameson's examples is male opposition to a female School of Design that the government recently opened at Somerset-house:

> The first expression of opinion which this just and benevolent project elicited, was a petition drawn up by the artists employed in wood engraving, praying that the women might not be taught, at the expense of the government, arts which would "interfere with the employment of men, and take the bread out of their mouths"; and further "tempt the women to forego those household employments more befitting their sex." (No petitions were presented on the part of men against young women let out in gangs to break stones and dig potatoes.) ("Woman's Mission" 221-22)

Jameson concludes that either men should live up to their rhetoric about "woman's sphere" and protect and fully provide for women, or else they should "play fair" and get out of the way ("Woman's Mission" 223-24).

In *Sisters of Charity* and *The Communion of Labor*, two lectures that Jameson delivered and then published in the mid-1850's, she more positively emphasizes the common obligation of men and women to *work* and contribute to the welfare of the community, and she uses this obligation (which, like the earlier creed, draws on the "creation order" of Genesis 1-3) to authorize new roles for women (*Sisters of Charity* 26-31). Jameson argues that men and women are by nature "mutually dependent, mutually helpful," and this "communion" extends to every possible relationship between the sexes:

> Thus, for instance, a man, in the first place, merely sustains and defends his home; then he works to sustain and defend the community or the nation he belongs to: and so of woman; she begins by being the nurse, the teacher, the cherisher of her home, through her greater tenderness and purer moral sentiments; then she uses these qualities and sympathies on a larger scale, to cherish and purify society. (*Sisters of Charity* 26-29)

The idea of "communion" has practical consequences for this writer. She demands the public recognition of "the woman's privilege to share in the communion of labor at her own free choice, and the foundation of institutions which shall train her to do her work well" (*Sisters of Charity* 32). Women have the energy, intelligence, and natural capabilities to work alongside men in improving their society; it is the cowardice and short-sightedness of legislators that has prevented them (*Sisters of Charity* 30-32). What makes Jameson's moderate proposals feminist is her assertion of male-female equality in the areas that really matter: reason and strength of character; social rights and responsibilities; the right to education and employment; and legal protections, especially of women's property. The mid-century campaigns of British and American feminists for married women's property rights show these women's concern to improve the domestic position of their sex even as they pushed for increased opportunities in the areas of education and employment.[7] For Jameson, as for other nineteenth-century feminists, the household is not the border for woman's ambition, but first base.

Jameson's feminism informs and reinforces her Mariology in several significant ways. I will focus on her treatment of women's maternal and non-maternal roles; her interest in inclusiveness and diversity; and the historical connections she sees between the changing representations and worship of Mary and the status of ordinary women.

As a feminist Jameson calls attention to the importance of woman's maternal role. As an art historian she admires representations of the *Mater Amabilis*, who is not shown as a goddess but simply as the loving earthly mother of the Redeemer and, like many young mothers, is occupied only by her first-born child, caressing him, gazing fondly on him, hanging in adoration over his cradle (*Madonna* 114-15, 200). But woman's contributions to the "communion of labor" must not be limited to her at-home services as a wife and mother, Jameson says (*Sisters of Charity* 26-29). And accordingly, Mary's "maternal character" is sometimes set aside, and she appears in other roles -- which have obvious though unstated relevance for nineteenth-century women. She is "poetess and prophetess." She is shown with a book as the *Virgo Sapientissima*, "the Most Wise Virgin." She represents perfect purity as the Immaculate Conception. And she exercises spiritual power as the "empress of heaven" (*Madonna* xxxvi, xli, 69-70, 134; Holcomb, "Sacred Art" 114).

Jameson's feminism is also reflected in the inclusiveness of her Mariology. Throughout her well-traveled life she shows a keen interest in the condition of women of different classes and races (though rarely without the comfortable conclusion that Englishwomen of her class are the best off, although their position still requires improvement). For example, she reports on the benefits of active religious sisterhoods -- especially the Sisters of Charity -- for the women involved and the sick and poor people they help, and she analyzes the ways that contact with European settlers has lowered the status of Indian women in North America.[8] Jameson's art histories have a comparable emphasis on Mary as a symbol not just of Woman but of women in all their diversity. She notes the national variations in Marian portraiture -- there are Madonnas with the features of Greek, Florentine, Milanese, Venetian, Spanish, and Flemish women -- and she adds, "I never looked round me in a roomful of German girls without thinking of Albert Dürer's Virgins" (*Madonna* xxxviii). Jameson's taste is not for representations of Mary with peasant features (e.g., *Madonna* 115), though she can recognize the power of the great Northern painters. But in her discussions of historical subjects, she considers both accurate and moving many of the paintings and legends that emphasize Mary's humble social status. Mary is shown giving birth in a "poor stable" or "rough rocky cave," and she is serenaded, in paintings from the Campagna and Calabria, by piping shepherds with sheepskin jackets and ragged hats (*Madonna* 200, 209). During her flight into Egypt, a refugee from political violence, Mary greets a Gypsy fortuneteller as "Sister" (*Madonna* 242-45). As the wife of a carpenter and housebuilder who trains their son in his craft, Mary is appropriately shown with her own tools, the work basket and distaff. She is not only the symbol of female industry but also a figure with whom the "poor artisan" can identify (*Madonna* 177-78, 193, 267-69).

Jameson also insists on a Madonna who ages. Criticizing the inappropriate youthfulness that sometimes afflicts Marian images -- a young sentimental Mater Dolorosa whose mourning over her dead Son seems to be what a dead sparrow would elicit (*Madonna* 36) -- she says Mary should be a young woman from fifteen to seventeen in the subjects preceding her return from Egypt, but "a matron between forty and fifty,...still of a sweet and gracious aspect," during her Son's ministry and Passion (*Madonna* l). And on the authority of "all the most ancient effigies" in the catacombs and early mosaics, Jameson indicates that the Virgin after the Resurrection should be shown alone as "a majestic woman of mature age" -- much like the author herself, a stout woman in her late fifties at the time of *Legends of the Madonna*. Such responses from a woman who was early separated from her husband and never had children of her own are not dispassionate scholarship, but are consistent with the author's feminism. The Madonna should represent all women -- single, widowed, grieving, glorified in old age -- and not just the Victorian ideal of that "'holiest thing alive,'" a young mother adoring her baby (*Madonna* 115).

Finally, Jameson on historical in addition to aesthetic grounds links the status of Mary to the status of actual women. Jameson's preference for the "chaste and sacred" Madonnas of the Middle Ages, which she considers reverently drawn and conducive to worship, over the more skillfully drawn but often sensual and secular Madonnas of the Renaissance is typical of Romantic taste.[9] But it is also closely linked to her understanding of the historical condition of women. In her lecture *The Communion of Labor*, she notes that the early and medieval Church adored the Virgin and canonized superior women as saints. In contrast, the misogynistic Reformers "had repudiated angels and saints, but...still devoutly believed in devils and witches"; they attributed showings of female superiority not to God but to

Satan and burned women at the stake. "All the women who perished by judicial condemnation for heresy in the days of the inquisition," Jameson says, "did not equal the number of women condemned judicially as witches, -- hanged, tortured, burned, drowned like mad dogs..." (*Communion of Labor* 282-83). Jameson's conclusion is that medieval societies, which reverently and appropriately honored the Madonna, also honored female nature and female accomplishments. She often associates the Renaissance (in its Catholic and classical as well as Protestant aspects) with images of women that are "secularised, materialised, and shockingly degraded," not to mention deadly (*Madonna* 165-66; see also xxx-xxxv; 183-84).

This Victorian art critic, by reevaluating European history from the perspective of women, interestingly anticipates modern feminist historians such as Joan Kelly, Margaret King, and Merry Wiesner. King, like Jameson, argues that the conventual life of celibacy and productive work "offered the greatest scope for autonomy and dignity to the women of Christian Europe" during the Middle Ages and early Renaissance, though she adds that this life was only available for the privileged. King also shows that devotion to the Virgin and female saints increased along with the power of female religious leaders until the eve of the Reformation. Wiesner in her study of witchcraft in the sixteenth and seventeenth centuries contends that women accused of witchcraft were treated much more harshly in the Protestant North than under the Roman and Spanish Inquisitions, which rarely burned witches. Wiesner's explanation has parallels to Jameson's argument about the Reformation: in the North, accused witches were punished for who they were rather than for what they did, and therefore "witch" was an ontological category attached to the category of "woman."[10]

Jameson's highest claim for Mary is that the Mother, as the representative of woman, is equal to the Son, the representative of man. As I have shown, Jameson as a feminist writer generally emphasizes the sameness of the sexes, but she does posit some enduring differences. It is the essentialist emphasis on *difference* that will enable her to make her most radical statements about the Virgin Mother.

At the start of *Legends of the Madonna*, Jameson explains the history of Marian thought in this way:

> With Christianity came the want of a new type of womanly perfection, combining all the attributes of the ancient female divinities with others altogether new. Christ, as the model man, united the virtues of the two sexes, till the idea that there are essentially masculine and feminine virtues intruded itself on the higher Christian conception, and seems to have necessitated the female type. (*Madonna* xx)

Jameson here claims that Christian thought began with *sameness*: since virtues and vices were considered the same for men and women, Christ served as the model of moral perfection for both sexes. But in time Christians began to want a female divinity, because they desired a successor to the mother-goddesses of the ancient world, and because they began to believe that men and women have different virtues and therefore need different moral representatives, i.e., Jesus and Mary. Jameson, as shown earlier, disagrees with this idea and considers it a step down from the "higher Christian conception" of moral sameness. Nonetheless, she presents *difference* as the initial reason for the emergence of Mary in Christianity. What happened next, according to Jameson, is that as Christian ideas about Jesus began to develop, Mary was raised with him: she became the Theotokos, the Queen of Heaven, and so on. *Sameness* again became predominant -- Mary and Jesus must have the same status, similar powers -- and sameness makes the Mother and Son equals or near-equals. Jameson does, however, note some enduring measure of complementarity or difference: for example, when in the Middle Ages Jesus was characterized as the avenging Judge, Mary became the Mother of Mercy, pleading with him for sinners (*Madonna* 27).

This, then, is Jameson's *historical* argument. Her own views, as presented in her *Commonplace Book* (5, 77-78, 83), are strikingly parallel.[11] Jameson again begins with *sameness* -- i.e., with claims that the virtues and vices for the two sexes, and the moral standards, are the same. Jesus is the moral exemplar for both men and women, and individual characters approximate perfection as they approach his (*Commonplace Book* 77-78). Yet Jameson also admits *difference* into this argument. She says the two sexes do not differ in the "quality" of their virtues and vices, but in "the modification of the quality" (*Commonplace Book* 77-78). An example might be gentleness and affectionateness. Jameson thinks that these qualities should be considered *human* virtues, not just feminine ones (78). Yet she elsewhere argues for woman's essential maternal role as the cherisher, nourisher, teacher, and refiner of her family and household ("'Woman's Mission,' and Woman's Position" 196-97; *Sisters of Charity* 26-29). One might conclude that gentleness and affectionateness are virtues for both sexes but are appropriately more dominant in woman than in man because of her maternal role.[12]

By extending this argument about *difference*, Jameson posits a role for Mary. She writes:

> It might seem, that where we reject the distinction between masculine and feminine virtue, one and the same type of perfection

should suffice for the two sexes; yet it is clear that the moment we come to consider the personality, the same type will not suffice: and it is worth consideration that when we place before us the highest type of manhood, as exemplified in Christ, we do not imagine him as the father, but as the son; and if we think of the most perfect type of womanhood, we never can exclude the mother. (*Commonplace Book* 83)

"Personality" here seems to mean "person-ness" or "individual nature" -- i.e., the qualities that make up one person; the individuating traits of a human being plus the traits he or she shares with other members of the same sex. Woman's maternal personality -- her psychical and physical capacity for motherhood -- means her model for perfection cannot be Jesus, but must be a woman, specifically a mother. And who but Mary is Jameson's "most perfect type of womanhood"? Reinforcement for this reading is Jameson's claim that "the highest type of manhood" is Jesus, in his role as Son (*Commonplace Book* 83).

Jameson's emphasis on the *Son* rather than the Father as the perfect type of manhood allows two inferences. First, a son, in contrast to a father, presumably resembles his mother, physically as well as psychologically, and is guided by her. And as Jameson points out, Mary's son must have borne the likeness of his mother, his only human parent (*Madonna* xl-xli; Elizabeth Cady Stanton also makes this point). Thus even though in the history of doctrine Christology defines Mariology (the doctrinal characterization of Jesus determines that of Mary), Jameson suggests that in the Holy Family the Mother has certain kinds of priority, bearing and caring for a Son in *her* image. The second inference is that the Son represents perfect manhood because in him the masculine capacity for violence is not fully developed, as it is in the Father. Support for this interpretation is Jameson's close association of Christianity and the feminine character with peace, the secular power and masculinity with violence. She writes in *Legends of the Madonna*, for example:

[Some say ideas represented by earlier goddesses] which were afterwards gathered into the pure, dignified, tender image of the Madonna, were but as the voice of a mighty prophecy, sounded through all the generations of men, even from the beginning of time, of the coming moral regeneration, and complete and harmonious development of the whole human race, by the establishment, on a higher basis, of what has been called the "feminine element" in society. And let me at least speak for myself. In the perpetual iteration of that beautiful image of THE WOMAN highly blessed -- *there*, where others saw only pictures or statues, I have seen this great hope standing like a spirit beside the visible form: in the fervent worship once universally given to that gracious presence, I have beheld an acknowledgment of a higher as well as gentler power than that of the strong hand and the might that makes the right, -- and in every earnest votary, one who, as he knelt, was in this sense pious beyond the reach of his own thought, and "devout beyond the meaning of his will."[13]

In this quotation, the phrase "a higher as well as gentler power than that of the strong hand and the might that makes the right" seems to refer to the power of women ("the feminine element in society"), as represented by Mary, and also to the power of Christianity. Both these forces for good can transform a world where (one infers) a "masculine element" is responsible for the domination of the violent and the strong. The implication of this remarkable statement is that the spirit of Christianity is best represented by the feminine form of the Virgin Mother, the Queen of Peace, who gave her likeness to the Prince of Peace, and women rather than men will bring about the "moral regeneration" of the race.

JAMESON, SARAH GRIMKE, AND ELIZABETH CADY STANTON
Jameson was quite unusual among nineteenth-century Anglo-American feminists for her ability to see liberatory potential in the figure of the Madonna.[14] Of her contemporaries, the Americans Sarah Grimke (1792-1873) and Elizabeth Cady Stanton (1815-1902) were the most notable feminist interpreters of the Bible, but neither shared Jameson's high regard for the Virgin Mary. Sarah Grimke, the Quaker author of *Letters on the Equality of the Sexes and the Condition of Woman* (1838), was an abolitionist speaker for a short time in the 1830's; she and her sister Angelina were the first abolitionists to link the issues of slaves' rights and women's rights (Lerner 165-204; Ceplair 135-41). Elizabeth Cady Stanton was a freethinker who identified male-controlled religion as the root of female oppression (*Woman's Bible* xix-xxvii). She became the instigator and principal contributor to *The Woman's Bible* (1895-98), an often caustic commentary on important biblical passages concerning women.[15]

Sarah Grimke in her *Letters on the Equality of the Sexes* celebrates the female prophets of the Old and New Testaments in order to argue that women like herself, the present-day "prophetic daughters," should be allowed to preach and teach (*Letters* 85-95). Yet the Virgin Mary is excluded from Grimke's gallery of heroic women -- biblical prophets and ministers, secular queens and intellectuals -- although, as Jameson points out, the

Church has historically represented Mary as "poetess and prophetess," the divine Mother of Wisdom, and Queen of Heaven (see *Madonna* xli, 69-70, 134, 303-4; Pelikan IV:38-50). Grimke in a later unpublished essay, "Sisters of Charity" (the title taken from Jameson), offers a powerful vision of what woman should be: "Hitherto...the majesty of her being has been obscured, and the uprising of her nature is but the effort to give to her whole being the opportunity to expand into all its essential nobility."[16] But it is Jameson, not Grimke, who sees this hope already embodied in a woman, who gives this majestic figure the name of Mary.

In Elizabeth Cady Stanton's *Woman's Bible*, the New Testament section contains only brief and desacralizing comments on the Virgin Mary, which are credited to Mrs. Stanton and Anonymous (who may conceal her identity because she sounds so much like the notorious Mrs. S). Both Stanton and her collaborator reject the Virgin Birth (which they sometimes confuse with the Immaculate Conception). Anonymous adds that the Virgin Birth is a slur on "natural motherhood," and her own mother was as holy as Mary (*Woman's Bible* II:113-14; similarly, Stanton, *Eighty Years* 230). Stanton's hostility toward Marian doctrines extends to all aspects of Catholicism; in her account of her travels in southern France, she refers to "the fallacies of Romanism" and describes the Catholic churches and rituals as from the "Dark Ages" (*Eighty Years* 342, 346). Yet Stanton has a high regard for the virgin's state; she says of her unmarried collaborator, Susan B. Anthony:

> The world has ever had its vestal virgins, its holy women, mothers of ideas rather than of men, its Marys as well as its Marthas, who, rather than be busy housewives, preferred to sit at the feet of divine wisdom, and ponder the mysteries of the unknown [Luke 10; John 11]....All honor to the noble women who have devoted earnest lives to the intellectual and moral needs of mankind! (*Eighty Years* 156-57)

The fascinating difference between Stanton and Jameson is that the latter sees the *Madonna* as a powerful symbol of the feminist virgin. Jameson also brings together the roles that Stanton has separated; the Virgin Mother represents a woman's hope of being *both* Mary and Martha, and having intellectual and moral work to do while also enjoying a family and household of her own (see the discussion of *Madonna* above; *Sisters of Charity* 26-32).

Why is it that Jameson, unlike Grimke and Stanton, can develop a feminist Mariology? The differences in their feminist views do not seem striking enough to be the explanation. Although Jameson is less radical as a feminist than Grimke and Stanton, all three agree on the fundamental equality of men and women as rational, moral, and free beings, and there are essentialist elements in Grimke's and Stanton's work, though more in Jameson's.[17] Nor do the religious backgrounds of the three writers sufficiently account for their differences. The Anglican, the Quaker, and the ex-Presbyterian freethinker all believe that the individual has direct access to divine truth, apart from religious institutions, ministers, and sacred writings; Grimke speaks of the "inner light," Jameson of feeling (*Commonplace Book* 26, 46, 57), and all three emphasize the power of reason. Jameson does have a high regard for church tradition and church history unshared by the American Protestants, whose approach to religious argument is *sola Scriptura*, and her Anglicanism definitely fosters her interest in the art and doctrine of the patristic and medieval periods -- interests shared by the Tractarians and the Pre-Raphaelite painters. But Jameson's inclusive attitude toward tradition is not necessarily representative of Victorian Anglicans (who of course included Evangelicals). Elizabeth Eastlake (the co-author of Jameson's *History of Our Lord*), who evaluates religious art according to strict Protestant standards, may well be more mainstream.

The most telling difference between Jameson and her American counterparts, I have found, is her knowledge of European art and culture. Drawn by friendships and the necessity of researching her books on the Madonna and the saints, she spent probably half of her adult life abroad, making numerous trips to Germany, Austria, Italy, and France, as well as to Ireland and North America. In contrast, Sarah Grimke seems never to have been outside the United States. Stanton made three trips to Great Britain, Ireland, and France (in 1840 and the 1880's), but her negative comments on monasticism and the Mass suggest her imperviousness to Catholic culture.

Grimke and Stanton probably had few glimpses of the Madonna, or of any European art, religious or secular, in the United States. Neither Quakerism nor Presbyterianism used visual art in worship; the Quaker meetinghouse where Grimke was a member in the 1830's still stands at Fourth and Arch streets in Philadelphia, and it has bare walls. The major art museums in the East Coast cities where the two women lived were all established after the Civil War, while the earlier Carolina Art Association in Charleston (founded 1858) and the Academy of the Fine Arts in Philadelphia (1805) seem to have been collections of American art -- portraits, American history paintings, and genre scenes.[18] The experience of the American Unitarian Margaret Fuller is also enlightening. Before she went to Europe in 1846, the only art she mentions seeing in her native Boston was the recently acquired plaster casts of Greek and Roman sculptures at the Athenaeum and the engravings of European paintings that a friend brought back from his trip abroad (Dall 6-7; Blanchard 133-34). Until the late nineteenth century, European and European-style religious paintings may have been visible in America only in private collections and Catholic churches. The religious experiences of Grimke and Stanton, then, combined with the aesthetic barrenness of their young country, help explain the almost complete absence of references to visual art in their work.[19] Bible-centered American Protestantism provided them with verbal rather than visual riches.

CONCLUSION

This study of the Madonna and Anna Jameson suggests some new directions for scholarship on women and religion. Because of the predominance of Quaker and Unitarian women in the nineteenth-century women's movement on both sides of the Atlantic, historians have tended to focus on radical Protestantism and also Evangelicalism as the religious ideologies that fostered women's equality.[20] But Jameson, an Anglican writing about the art of Catholic Europe, shows the contribution of hierarchical and traditionalist versions of Christianity to feminist thought. She made her Protestant readers look up from their Bibles to see the Queen of Heaven, and she gave this figure a troubling relevance to their lives, for in her work the Christian goddess replaces the Victorian Angel in the House as the dominant and glorious image of woman.

Jameson's feminist Mariology qualifies the assumption of many feminist scholars in the fields of religion, history, and literature -- for example, Rosemary Radford Ruether, Mary Daly, Elizabeth Johnson, Barbara Pope, Sandra Gilbert and Susan Gubar, and Margaret Homans -- that the Virgin Mary is so closely linked to the misogynistic practices and oppressive politics of the patriarchal Church and male-dominated societies that historically she has served *only* as a distorted and repressive ideal for women.[21] Jameson is able to see the Madonna in new ways because of her Protestantism and her profession. This Victorian writer balances her reverence for what previous generations considered holy and precious with a Protestant's freedom to appropriate or reject the religious past. And like Grimke and Stanton, she has a Protestant's confidence that she may interpret the ancient legends, liturgies, and sacred images for herself, and find what she calls their living spirit. Jameson travels through the art galleries and churches of Europe with the exceptional insight of the professional art historian. But she also reveals herself as a worshipper of the feminine divine: "'she looks, and the heart is in heaven!'" (*Madonna* 58), and she brings the Virgin Mother down to earth, using this powerful image to advance the causes of progressive religion and sexual equality.

NOTES

1. *Sacred and Legendary Art* is the title of both the series and the first volume (which first appeared in 1848 under a longer title, *The Poetry of Sacred and Legendary Art*). The other titles are *Legends of the Monastic Orders* (1850), *Legends of the Madonna* (1852), and *The History of Our Lord* (1864), finished by Elizabeth Lady

Eastlake. The series was popular and went through many editions (see Thomas 176-79).

2. *Madonna* xxxi-xxxviii. On Correggio, 92, 263, 324-25; on Poussin, Vandyck, and Rembrandt, 221; on Rubens, 29, 253, 326. On Jameson's preferences as representative of Romantic taste, see Hugh Witemeyer 21-23.

3. *Madonna* 115, 200, 275, 292-94, 240-41, 263-70. Jameson is not critical of "portrait Madonnas" in the historical scenes, apparently because Mary is not here a divinized figure. The author praises two of Rubens's paintings of the Madonna and the Holy Family in which he reproduces his own family's features (*Madonna* 151, 253).

4. Eastlake carefully distinguishes her contributions from Jameson's, which are marked with the initials *A. J.* (*History of Our Lord* I: vii).
Lady Eastlake was the wife of Charles Eastlake, director of the National Gallery of London and president of the Royal Academy. Before her marriage, as Elizabeth Rigby, she wrote a famous attack on *Jane Eyre* that appeared in the influential *Quarterly Review* (Dec. 1848): "Altogether the auto-biography of Jane Eyre is pre-eminently an anti-Christian composition" (see *Victorian Britain, s.v.* "Eastlake, Elizabeth Rigby" 234-35).

5. *Letters of Anna Jameson to Ottilie von Goethe* 233-34. A very similar statement of beliefs appears in 1847 in Jameson's edition of the dramas of Princess Amalie of Saxony, *Social Life in Germany* (see *Letters to Ottilie von Goethe* 233 n. 1).

6. Wollstonecraft, *Vindication* 118; Sarah and Angelina Grimke, in Rossi, ed., 296-322; Bodichon, *Women and Work*, in Lacey 37-38.

7. In Great Britain, the Langham Place feminists, led by Barbara Bodichon and Bessie Parkes, circulated the first petitions for married women's property rights in the mid-1850's. The petitions were signed by Mary Howitt and Jameson, who presented them to Parliament, as well as by George Eliot (Marian Evans), her friend Sara Hennell, Elizabeth Barrett Browning, and Elizabeth Gaskell (Herstein 80; *Victorian Britain, s.v.* "Bodichon, Barbara Leigh Smith" and "Married Women's Property" 85-86, 478-79). In the United States, the campaigns took place on the state level. Ernestine Rose, soon joined by Elizabeth Cady Stanton and Susan B. Anthony were active in the New York campaign; acts protecting married women's property were passed in 1848 and 1860 (Schneir 72-74, 117-27, 132-33).

8. Jameson, *Sisters of Charity* 49-69; *Winter Studies and Summer Rambles in Canada* 301-4.

9. Jameson, *Madonna* xxx-xxxiv, 183-84; Hugh Witemeyer 21-23.

10. Kelly, "Did Women Have a Renaissance?" 19-50; King, *Women of the Renaissance* 94-101, 130-31; Wiesner, *Women and Gender in Early Modern Europe* 218-33. My thanks to the Renaissance scholar Maryclaire Moroney for helping me make this point.

11. Jameson's *Commonplace Book* is a collection of discrete statements, usually by others but followed by Jameson's commentaries, that "became part of [her] individual mind" (Preface to *Commonplace Book* 3-5).

12. The cited passage reads in full: "[It is a mistake to believe] that there are essential masculine and feminine virtues and vices. It is not, in fact, the quality itself, but the modification of the quality, which is masculine and feminine; and on the manner or degree in which these are balanced and combined in the individual, depends the perfection of that individual character--its approximation to that of Christ. I firmly believe that as the influences of religion are extended, and as civilization advances, those qualities which are now admired as essentially *feminine* will be considered as essentially *human*, such as gentleness, purity, the more unselfish and spiritual sense of duty, and the dominance of the affections over the passions" (*Commonplace Book* 77-78).

13. *Madonna* xix. In her earlier work *Celebrated Female Sovereigns* (1831), Jameson similarly assumes that the feminine character and Christian beliefs are or ought to be allied forces for peace in the world; see her discussions of Queen Elizabeth (I: 222-23); Christina of Sweden (II: 26-27), and Isabella of Castile (I: 111, 120). There are interesting parallels to Jameson in Sarah Grimke's discussions of female leadership (which postdate *Celebrated Female Sovereigns*); see Grimke's *Letters on the Equality of the Sexes* 62-67, 85-95.

14. Two other nineteenth-century writers, the American Transcendentalist Margaret Fuller and the British novelist George Eliot, similarly used the Madonna in feminist arguments. Both were familiar with Jameson's writings, although Fuller died before *Legends of the Madonna* was published. See Adams, "Feminine Godhead, Feminist Symbol"; "The Madonna and Margaret Fuller."

15. A comparison of these three writers proves especially interesting because I have found that Jameson, because of her interest in the American anti-slavery cause, possibly met Grimke and definitely met Stanton. Jameson was in Massachusetts in 1837 during the Grimke sisters' public speaking tour and the publication of their letters in abolitionist newspapers (Thomas 98-125; Macpherson 133-39; Erskine 158-60; Lerner, *Grimke Sisters* 165-204; see Ceplair, ed., Grimke, *Selected Writings* xvii), and she visited two anti-slavery activists, William Ellery Channing in Boston and Catherine Sedgwick in the Berkshires (Sedgwick was a writer cited by Sarah Grimke in her *Letters*, 58 and n. 15). Jameson, moreover, was a friend and admirer of the British writer Harriet Martineau (their travel books were reviewed together), and Martineau was an abolitionist who mentions the Grimkes several times in her writings (see "The Martyr Age of the United States" 13-14, 27; Pichanick 87, 94).

In 1840 Jameson and a number of her friends, including Lady Byron and Mary Howitt, were spectators at the World's Anti-Slavery Convention in London. There the vote against seating the female delegates from the United States so angered Lucretia Mott and Elizabeth Cady Stanton that eight years later (still at a simmer) they organized the first women's-rights convention at Seneca Falls, New York. Jameson may have spent much time in the company of Stanton during the convention, since Jameson's close friend Lady Byron and Stanton were both great admirers of Mott (Stanton, *Eighty Years* 80; Bacon, *Valiant Friend* 91-96). Mott and Stanton noted that the Englishwomen they met were familiar with the writings of their friend Sarah Grimke (Flexner 344 n. 19).

16. *Letters* 154, 163. On Grimke's use of Jameson, see Lerner, "Sarah M. Grimke's 'Sisters of Charity'" and "Comment on Lerner's 'Sarah M. Grimke's "Sisters of Charity."'"

17. Grimke and Stanton argue, for example, that women are more moral and religious than men; see Grimke, *Letters* 126-27; *Woman's Bible* I:86; II:57. Stanton tends to make essentialist arguments when she wants to prove women's superiority rather than mere equality. On Jameson's essentialism, see the discussion of her feminist and religious views above.

18. The Boston Museum of Fine Arts was founded in 1870, with the Athenaeum holdings as the nucleus of the collection. The Metropolitan Museum of Art in New York was founded in 1872, the Philadelphia Museum of Art in 1876 (at the time of the popular Centennial art exhibition), and the National Gallery in Washington not until 1937. See *The New Encyclopaedia Britannica* (Chicago: Fifteenth Edition 1995) 2:404; 3:126-27; 4:780; 8:74-75, 533; Lila Sherman, *Art Museums of America* 300-1, 311-12.

19. The few references are Grimke, "Marriage," in *Letters* 149; *Woman's Bible* I:46; II:158. Stanton mentions visiting art galleries and museums, among other sights, during her trips to Europe. But an anecdote in Margaret Hope Bacon's biography of Lucretia Mott seems more in character: when Stanton was in London in 1840, she kept asking Mott so many questions about abolitionism and women's rights that the two did not get beyond the entrance of the British Museum (Bacon 98).

20. For summaries of the scholarship on American women, see Bartlett, ed., *Letters* 1-29, especially 6-15; Fitzgerald, ed., *Woman's Bible* vii-xxii; Rossi 241-81; Herstein 24-94. A useful barometer in Great Britain is the number of Quaker and Unitarian women signing the 1856 Married Women's Property petition; they included Barbara Bodichon, Bessie Parkes, Mary Howitt, Anna Mary Howitt, Harriet Martineau, Elizabeth Gaskell, and Sara Hennell (Herstein 79-94).

21. Ruether, *Mary* 76-87; *New Woman/New Earth* 36-62; *Sexism* 33-37, 148-52; Daly, *Gyn/ecology* 83-86; *Beyond God the Father* 81-97; Johnson, "Marian Tradition" 129-34; "Mary and the Female Face of God" 511-13; Pope 175, 193-95; Gilbert and Gubar 18-21, 468, 485, 490-501; Homans 156-60, 216.

WORKS CITED

Adams, Kimberly VanEsveld. "Feminine Godhead, Feminist Symbol: The Madonna in George Eliot, Ludwig Feuerbach, Anna Jameson, and Margaret Fuller." *Journal of Feminist Studies in Religion* 12/1 (1996): 37-66.

---. "The Madonna and Margaret Fuller." *Women's Studies* 25 (1996): 385-405.

Bacon, Margaret Hope. *Valiant Friend: The Life of Lucretia Mott.* New York: Walker, 1980.

Blanchard, Paula. *Margaret Fuller: From Transcendentalism to Revolution.* Radcliffe Biography Series. Reading, Mass.: Addison-Wesley, 1987.

Bodichon, Barbara Leigh Smith. *Women and Work* (1857). Excerpts in Candida Lacey, *Barbara Leigh Smith Bodichon and the Langham Place Group.* Women's Source Library. New York and London: Routledge and Kegan Paul, 1987. 36-73.

Dall, Caroline. *Margaret and Her Friends* (1895). New York: Arno Press, 1972.

Daly, Mary. *Beyond God the Father.* Boston: Beacon Press, 1973.

---. *Gyn/ecology.* Boston: Beacon Press, 1978.

Erskine, Beatrice (Mrs. Steuart), ed. *Anna Jameson: Letters & Friendships* (1812-1860). London: T. Fisher Unwin, Ltd., 1916.

Flexner, Eleanor. *Century of Struggle: The Women's Rights Movement in the United States.* New York: Atheneum, 1959.

Gilbert, Sandra and Susan Gubar. *The Madwoman in the Attic.* New Haven: Yale University Press, 1979.

Grimke, Sarah. *Letters on the Equality of the Sexes and Other Essays.* Ed. Elizabeth Ann Bartlett. New Haven and London: Yale University Press, 1988.

Grimke, Sarah, and Angelina Grimke. *The Public Years of Sarah and Angelina Grimke: Selected Writings, 1835-1839.* Ed. Larry Ceplair. New York: Columbia University Press, 1989.

Herstein, Sheila. *A Mid-Victorian Feminist: Barbara Leigh Smith Bodichon.* New Haven: Yale University Press, 1985.

Holcomb, Adele. "Anna Jameson (1794-1860): Sacred Art and Social Vision." In *Women as Interpreters of the Visual Arts.* Ed. Claire Richter Sherman with Adele Holcomb. Westport, Connecticut: Greenwood Press, 1981. 93-121.

Homans, Margaret. *Bearing the Word: Language and Female Experience in Nineteenth-Century Women's Writing.* Chicago and London: University of Chicago Press, 1986, 1989.

Jameson, Anna. *Celebrated Female Sovereigns* (1831). Superior Printing Co., 1916. 2 vols.

---. *A Commonplace Book of Thought.* New York: Appleton and Co., 1855.

---, and Elizabeth Lady Eastlake. *The History of Our Lord* (1864). London: Longmans, Green, and Co., 1864. 2 vols.

---. *Legends of the Madonna* (1852). London: Longmans, Green, and Co., 4th ed. 1867.

---. *Legends of the Monastic Orders* (1850). London: Longmans, Green, and Co., 4th ed. 1867.

---. *Letters of Anna Jameson to Ottilie von Goethe.* Ed. G. H. Needler. Oxford: Oxford University Press, 1939.

---. *Sacred and Legendary Art* (1848). New York: AMS Press, rpt. 1970. 2 vols.

---. *Sisters of Charity and the Communion of Labor.* Boston: Ticknor and Fields, 1857; rpt. Hyperion, 1976.

---. *Winter Studies and Summer Rambles in Canada* (1838). New York: Wiley and Putnam, 1839. 2 vols.

---. "'Woman's Mission,' and Woman's Position." In *Memoirs and Essays* (1846). London: Richard Bentley. 187-224.

Johnson, Elizabeth. "The Marian Tradition and the Reality of Women." *Horizons* (Villanova University) 12 (1985): 116-35.

---. "Mary and the Female Face of God." *Theological Studies* 50 (1989): 500-26.

Kelly, Joan. "Did Women Have a Renaissance?" In *Women, History, and Theory*. *Women in Culture and Society Series*. Chicago and London: University of Chicago Press, 1984. 19-50.

King, Margaret. *Women of the Renaissance*. *Women in Culture and Society Series*. Chicago and London: University of Chicago Press, 1991.

Lacey, Candida Ann. *Barbara Leigh Smith Bodichon and the Langham Place Group*. *Women's Source Library*. New York and London: Routledge and Kegan Paul, 1987.

Lerner, Gerda. "Comment on Lerner's 'Sarah M. Grimke's "Sisters of Charity."'" *Signs* 10/4 (Summer 1985): 811-15.

---. *The Grimke Sisters from South Carolina*. New York: Schocken Books, 1971.

---. "Sarah M. Grimke's 'Sisters of Charity.'" *Signs* 1/1 (Autumn 1975): 246-56.

Macpherson, Gerardine. *Memoirs of the Life of Anna Jameson*. Boston: Roberts Brothers, 1878.

Martineau, Harriet. "The Martyr Age of the United States." *London and Westminster Review* (American Edition) 32 (Dec. 1838): 1-32.

Pelikan, Jaroslav. *Reformation of Church and Dogma* (1300-1700). *The Christian Tradition*, Vol. IV. Chicago and London: University of Chicago Press, 1984.

Pichanick, Valerie K. *Harriet Martineau, the Woman and Her Work*. Ann Arbor: University of Michigan Press, 1980.

Pope, Barbara Corrado. "Immaculate and Powerful: The Marian Revival in the Nineteenth Century." In *Immaculate and Powerful: The Female in Sacred Image and Social Reality*. Ed. C. W. Atkinson, C. H. Buchanan, and M. R. Miles. Boston: Beacon Press, 1985. 173-200.

Rossi, Alice. *The Feminist Papers*. Boston: Northeastern University Press, rpt. 1988.

Ruether, Rosemary Radford. *Mary: The Feminine Face of the Church*. Philadelphia: The Westminster Press, 1977.

---. *New Woman/New Earth*. New York: Seabury Press, 1985. 36-62.

---. *Sexism and God-Talk*. Boston: Beacon Press, 1983.

Schneir, Miriam, ed. *Feminism: The Essential Historical Writings*. New York: Vintage, 1972.

Sherman, Lila. *Art Museums of America: A Guide*. New York: William Morrow, 1980.

Stanton, Elizabeth Cady. *Eighty Years and More: Reminiscences, 1815-1897* (1893). Boston: Northeastern University Press, 1993.

---. *The Woman's Bible* (1895-1898). Boston: Northeastern University Press, 1993. Two volumes in one.

Thomas, Clara. *Love and Work Enough: The Life of Anna Jameson*. University of Toronto Press, 1967.

Victorian Britain. Ed. Sally Mitchell. New York and London: Garland, 1988.

Wiesner, Merry. *Women and Gender in Early Modern Europe*. Cambridge: Cambridge University Press, 1993.

Witemeyer, Hugh. *George Eliot and the Visual Arts*. New Haven: Yale University Press, 1979.

Wollstonecraft, Mary. *A Vindication of the Rights of Woman* (1792). Ed. Miriam Brody Kramnick. Harmondsworth: Penguin, 1983.

Intertextual Constructions of Faith:
Julia Wedgwood (1833-1913)

L. Robert Stevens
University of North Texas

Does a sacred text require a separate and distinct hermeneutical model, a privileged model of interpretation? Or is a sacred text accessible to all of the interpretive methods which can be used to open any other text? If sacred texts will open themselves only before a privileged interpretive theory, then what are the warrants for this privilege? Could a text which depended upon a unique hermeneutic ever "talk to" other texts?

Julia Wedgwood must have thought a good bit about such issues because in a number of essays her method suggests that the Bible illuminates itself most richly in its conversation with other texts of the classical world -- its neighbors. In short, Wedgwood seems to have believed that one effective model of Biblical interpretation requires our overhearing the dialogue between a sacred text and its cultural environs. A great granddaughter of Josiah Wedgwood, founder of the celebrated potteries, Julia wrote 36 articles for the Victorian periodical press, as I count them in *The Wellesley Index to Periodical Literature*. Most of these articles appeared in *Contemporary Review*, although she also published in *British Quarterly Review, Macmillan's Magazine, National Review*, and *Westminster Review*. In these essays Wedgwood addresses a variety of subjects: literary criticism, the woman question, political issues, and the like. In at least six of her articles, however, she addresses explicitly theological subjects: "Plutarch and the Unconscious Christianity of the First Two Centuries," "Male and Female Created He Them," "The Unfaithful Steward," "Greek Mythology and the Bible," "Fiction and Faith," and "Boundaries of Science." In others she addresses ethical or moral questions which at least implicate her theological views. In short, when one considers that for Victorians, periodical journalism was a sort of seminary for middle-class readers, Julia Wedgwood deserves to be considered as an occasional, but -- in some ways -- original theologian.

Wedgwood's own work is little studied at present. Perhaps her intellectual reputation has suffered from her incidental relations with two of the most dominant male voices of nineteenth-century intellectual life. She was Charles Darwin's cousin (and the niece of Emma Darwin); in fact, as a review of *Origin of Species*, she wrote a two-part essay, "Boundaries of Science," which Darwin claimed he did not quite understand. Again, Julia Wedgwood has been remembered as the sometimes impassioned correspondent of Robert Browning in the years following Elizabeth's death (Curle passim). If we did not consider her to be Browning's afterthought, we might be better able to sift her theological work on its own merits; that is, Victorian scholars have generally examined the letters looking for clues to Browning's mind, rather than looking for clues to Wedgwood's mind. It is clear that for a time, Browning himself found her to be a fascinating correspondent, and in their letters we find further important sources from which to construct Julia Wedgwood's theology (Curle 51-54, 149-59, 170-171). In addition to her relation to the most important British scientist of the century and one of the two most important British poets, Julia Wedgwood was also the daughter of a substantially well-known philologist -- Hensleigh Wedgwood, the brother of Emma Darwin.

As a starting point for discussing Wedgwood's theology, I observe that she was severely impatient with the low intellectual expectations which worshipers in the Victorian church brought to the pew: "The Christian leaves attention at the threshold of the church as the Mussulman does his shoes. He does not really believe that anything which he will hear within its walls is meant for intelligent attention" ("Unfaithful Steward" 52). She believed that clergymen responded to these low expectations with sermons that were fully within the grasp of their hearers' lassitude. Lacking a pulpit herself, Wedgwood nonetheless found a way to address this intellectual privation among the faithful. She did what a number of women did by taking up the homiletical pen. The male monopoly of the Anglican pulpit can not be explained in a few brief generalizations, but it is nonetheless true that a woman who used the periodicals for her pulpit had found a way to have a voice without a body. This, after all, is what writing allows. It allows a faceless, disembodied utterance to go forth without a timbre or tone, unaccompanied by braids or bosoms or other enticements to male desire. In "Fiction and Faith" Wedgwood focuses on an orthodoxy which has been severed at the trunk:

> When a tree has been cut down, many green shoots surround the truncated stem, and seem in their...wealth of foliage to replace with richer life the central column....When the central growth of faith is arrested, the rising sap of instinctive trust floods many lesser convictions, which for the same reason seem more real (218).

I believe that Julia Wedgwood's central project is to sift the thought contemporaneous to her, the many shoots clustered around the severed trunk, and to bring the intelligence to bear in such a way as to rediscover what is possible and what is not possible for faith in the late modern world. Her strategy is to bring secular texts to bear upon the Biblical texts in such a way as to identify both the limits of faith and the new possibilities (the "green shoots") of faith. Thus, her theology is marked by four themes of interest to postmodern audiences on the threshold of the twenty-first century. 1) Some secular texts of the first century reflect a moral sensibility akin to that of emerging Christianity; the appearance of these simultaneous impulses marks a revolutionary turn in human moral thought. 2) Through the analysis of narrative form, Wedgwood sifts both the similarities and differences between classical narratives and biblical narratives, each narrative adding its own clue to a larger meaning than either can tell alone. 3) By historicizing the sacred text, Wedgwood reveals new possibilities for interpretation. 4) The argument from first causes can accommodate any scientific narrative. What all of these claims have in common is Wedgwood's habit of reading the Biblical text under the light cast by other, non-Biblical texts.

For the first point, I consider Wedgwood's perception that in the first two centuries of the common era, there is at least one instance of a Roman who is "Christianized," though not Christian. As Augustine "baptizes" Plato, and as Aquinas "baptizes" Aristotle, so Wedgwood "baptizes" Plutarch. She begins her study of Plutarch by drawing an important distinction between antiquity and modernity. Wedgwood quotes Aristotle in defining that distinction -- specifically, Aristotle claims that "The artisan only partakes of virtue so far as he partakes of slavery" while Wedgwood, conversely, believes that "the artisan only partakes of virtue so far as he is emancipated from any remains of slavery" ("Plutarch" 45). For Wedgwood, then, access to personal freedom within the state is the defining theme of modernity. Her notion that this changed relation between slavery and virtue is the watershed between antiquity and modernity is linked also to her view that the meaning of virtue itself changed during the first century and that at just the same historical moment when Christendom was redefining virtue, so was Plutarch redefining it in an unconsciously parallel way.

Up until the first century, Wedgwood observes, the word "virtue" had implied "valour" ("Plutarch" 46). She goes on to observe that valor is the excellence of a man, while the new sense of the word "virtue" -- a sense which is common both to Christian thought and to Plutarch -- is "chastity," "the excellence of a woman" ("Plutarch" 46). The grand scope of this insight can hardly be overstated. In antiquity war (historically thought of as masculine) is viewed as that condition which places humans *in extremis* and thereby calls forth the most fundamental quality of character -- namely, valor. The ethos of Christendom, as Wedgwood would have it, urges that love is the most primitive activity, that love places humans *in extremis* and calls forth the most fundamental quality of character -- namely, chastity (viewed as the appropriate use of the body rather than as simple abstinence). Indeed, in defining this revolution from valor to chastity as the central human ideal, Wedgwood sees a vast turn from a masculine to a feminine ethos. To the extent that Plutarch was sympathetic to this shift, Wedgwood identifies him as the "unconscious preacher of Christian morality" ("Plutarch" 47).

Wedgwood finds Plutarch's views on modesty, conjugal love, animal rights, and immortality all to be conformable to Christian views on the same subjects. What Plutarch brings to these ideals is a thoroughgoing sympathy for all sentient beings, which could be said to be a kind of love for them. Two examples in particular will catch the modern eye; on the subject of women's rights and animal rights, Wedgwood believes that Plutarch is the most enlightened of classical authors. She claims on his behalf that "Plutarch is the first to protest against that theory which in allotting the woman a lower standard than the man, gave her the position of a slave" ("Plutarch" 53). In thus praising Plutarch's liberal view of women she cites his *De Mulierum Virtutibus*: "Virtue differs in man and woman just as it differs in man and man and in no other way. There is not one virtue in woman and another in man. There is but one virtue for all human beings" ("Plutarch" 53-4).

Wedgwood exploits this far-flung sympathy in Plutarch by identifying him at least unconsciously with that Christian thought which was growing in the world around him: "that revolution [shared by Plutarch and Christendom] which has made virtue possible to the weak...has exchanged a merely masculine for a truly human ideal" ("Plutarch" 46). I infer that this "truly human ideal" is very nearly synonymous with "the kingdom of heaven," a kingdom without national boundaries, classes, or genders, without parliaments or prisons.

Still, in spite of the universality of the new idea, Wedgwood herself held that certain attributes accrue to women which are in some measure different from those that accrue to men, and that Christendom actually recognizes a kind of moral primacy in women. Like many contemporaries, she is delicately juggling the "sameness/difference" themes in predicating her thoughts about the "gender" of ethical norms. She asserts her claim based on Darwin's supposition that in the laws of inheritance, some qualities descend only to children of the same sex as that of the parent who transmits them; fathers pass some qualities only to their sons (secondary sex qualities), while mothers pass some qualities only to their daughters. Among these same-sex qualities are behavioral and temperamental attitudes which accompany the physiological differences.   Wedgwood argues that in our remote evolutionary past there must have been "mothers" before there were fathers; that is, mothers were confronted with the necessity of giving birth, of nursing, and of nurturing even before we were human, and therefore before "paternity" became an accessible concept.   Only during an early human period when males became able to conceptualize the link between begetting and fathering did "fatherhood" become real.   Motherhood is an animal condition; "The father is created by civilization" ("Male and Female" 124). Here, while arguing that motherhood is biological, Wedgwood strikingly anticipates postmodern theories in speculating that fatherhood is a social construct.   Hence, Wedgwood believes that

> Woman inherits a longer tradition of moral relation than man does: she in the very dawn of her existence finds herself dowered with a heritage of instincts unknown to him; he passes through a long stage of his education before he knows himself to be a father, but she is, from the first, consciously a mother. He is not more surely stronger in the realm of physical might than she is the elder in that of moral law (125).

Wedgwood sees Plutarch as one of the first to see that this "feminine" morality must become the law of the state before an enlightened civilization may take the stage. It was the great thing lacking in antiquity's struggle to articulate a universal ethos.

Another instance of Wedgwood's linking of Plutarch to first century Christendom is available to her in Plutarch's valuing of animals as sentient beings with their own claims upon our virtue:

> Not a single voice before him [Plutarch], or for all that period after him, was ever raised for those who could not plead for themselves. He considered not only the rights of the weaker half of humanity, but the rights of beings weaker than humanity. Nothing gives us a stronger sense of his moral originality. Think of all the thousands of years during which good men and Christians watched the suffering of animals with absolute indifference, and remember that he was the solitary advocate in the world of Greek civilization for those who could make no appeal for themselves ("Plutarch" 54).

As this quotation shows, Wedgwood even believes that Plutarch is well beyond those Christian multitudes who across the centuries never extended the imperative of the love of God so far as to include the animals; for Wedgwood, however, the indifference of these multitudes does not vitiate a claim that the central ethos of Christendom is universal and embraces all sentient beings.

A second feature of Wedgwood's theology is her tendency to sift the narrative parallels between fictional texts and Biblical texts. Her usual method of analyzing narratives aims at locating the moral themes which can be teased out of the action. The events of the narrative, then, become metaphors for the moral themes. By using this method, Wedgwood is able to find comparisons and contrasts between classical and Biblical narratives which for the rest of us might seem awkward or strained. Still, in speaking of the ancient world which provided the contextual environment for early Christendom, she says "There never was a time when the great masters of fiction were so consciously mediators between philosophy and the world" ("Plutarch" 60). Julia Wedgwood's search for fictive counterpoints between the sacred and the classical tales of antiquity is nothing new in itself, but her boldness in the face of an entrenched orthodoxy makes her account worth our while.

In her essay "Greek Mythology and the Bible," Wedgwood asserts a significant distinction between Greek and Hebrew worldviews; namely, she sees Hebrew morality as marked by the separation of good and evil into distinct categories, but she sees Greek morality as marked by the presence of good and evil upon the same spectrum. Means and extremes occupy the same spectrum and are substantively the same, as good and evil are substantively the same -- one, however, a moderation, the other an extreme. To use Wedgwood's own example, the Greek conceptions of good and evil are variously colored lights on a spectrum. The Hebrew conception is that good and evil are light and darkness.

In the same essay Wedgwood asserts that both the book of Job and the stories of Heracles are moral tragedies, but that Heracles, if anything, "brings forth the problem of suffering more forcibly than even the book of Job does" (381). Heracles' own "bow and his club lay his wife and children at his feet" (380). When Heracles realizes that he is the author of his own tragedy, he simultaneously realizes that God is his foe and not his friend. He contemplates suicide, but his intention is "deferred, and...the hero has to endure more torture and misery before he finds rest on the funeral pyre" (380-1). Wouldn't it have been better, Wedgwood ponders, for Heracles to have committed suicide earlier, rather than later? In Job, on the other hand, the adversary, in the end, is not triumphant but "seems simply forgotten" (380). If Heracles brings forth the problem of suffering more forcibly, Job brings forth a latent response to the problem of suffering. To the Greek spirit, however, "the problem is all that is needed" (381).

Wedgwood concludes her article on "Greek Mythology and the Bible" by observing that

Whenever we suppose that in choosing wrong instead of right we are enriching life with new colouring instead of turning from light to darkness, there, I believe we make the largest error that it is possible for man to commit (381).

Here Wedgwood anticipates precisely the shift from an essentialist to an existential morality which was to characterize modernist thought. I will give citations to suggest that Wedgwood is sympathetic with this notion of good and evil as colors on a single spectrum, but she is also horrified at the possible uses of this metaphor in the private life.

Wedgwood thus tells us something about how far the nineteenth-century was able to tease out its own readings of antiquity, and to what degree this teasing out allowed the century to sustain a faith which had suffered a barrage of attacks from textual criticism.

In "Fiction and Faith," Wedgwood uses the same analytical technique in order to locate the special genius in the novels of Mrs. Humphrey Ward. Namely, Wedgwood believes that Ward's novels celebrate several new modes of postChristian faith -- faith in nature, faith in democratic man -- and that such experiments in alternative faiths are necessary in order for moderns to be able to identify the grounds of their own affirmations. Whatever massive intuitions informed the old Christian religion, those intuitions are still lurking in us and must be addressed. Fiction provides a sort of experimental ground for sifting the options.

A third feature of Wedgwood's theology lies in her willingness to historicize the sacred text. The specific case she presents is the parable of the unfaithful steward found in Luke 16:1-16. The case of the unfaithful steward has often baffled commentators. It describes the servant who believes that he is about to be fired; in order to build alliances with his master's rich customers, the unfaithful steward conspires with each of them to understate the amount of the customer's debt to the master. When the master discovers this conspiracy to defraud him, strangely, he praises the steward for his ingenuity. This parable expressly praises the dishonest steward for cheating his master, it commends friendship with the great figures of the world, and it seems to applaud sharp-dealing -- all in ways that are uncharacteristic of the usual parables of Jesus, and directly contradictory, as Wedgwood points out, to the parables Jesus has just been telling in order to discourage just such conduct, as in Luke 14:1-12, for example. Wedgwood observes that many commentators are baffled by the tale, but that they conceal their bafflement by some trimming of their own -- distorting the story to make it fit their own preconceptions. She cites Richard Trench, who thinks the tale is about "prudence," or using the world's own methods against it. Wedgwood herself believes that such stratagems cater to the low intellectual expectations which most parishioners bring with them to religious discourse. Her own effort to unravel the mystery of the parable which contradicts the other parables hinges upon its own historical context; without its context the story seems to contradict all the wisdom of Jesus. A knowledge of the historical context is central to constructing an intelligible meaning for the tale. Wedgwood herself reads this parable as profoundly ironic. She reminds her readers that the listeners to this parable are those religious leaders of the day who strongly affirmed the sacredness of marriage, but remained silent when John the Baptist had recently been martyred for speaking out against Herod Antipas on this subject. In Wedgwood's reading of the parable, the master becomes a sinister, not a divine person. He is the voice of Herod, who is congratulating his trimming priests for their willingness to strike a bargain with their consciences and keep silent in order to preserve their power base - - just as the unfaithful steward has betrayed his own cause in order to preserve his power base:

> Antipas was but the outrider of Titus, and among his courtiers were doubtless many earnest Jews, filled with deep reverence for the traditions of their race, half submerged as these seemed among the rising tide of Roman dominion, and struggling to justify to themselves the compromise which brought the indispensable support of Rome ("Unfaithful Steward" 57).

It requires only another half-step for Wedgwood to historicize the tale completely: as keepers of a received orthodoxy, the priests of her own Victorian age are challenged not to try to preserve their faith in the manner of the unfaithful steward, not to preserve it at the expense of its own soul, but to let it evolve in the light of a new learning. Her purpose is to stand in the vestibule and mediate a conversation between the texts inside and those outside the chancel.

A fourth theme of Julia Wedgwood's theology lies in her belief that any effectual theology may accommodate any legitimate scientific claim. This theme is seen especially in her two-part essay entitled "Boundaries of Science," a Platonic dialogue intended also as a review of a number of issues raised by her uncle's controversial *Origin of Species*.

The imaginary speakers in Wedgwood's dialogues are Philocalos ("lover of the good" -- the less sympathetic to Darwin) and Philalethes ("lover of the true" -- the more sympathetic to Darwin). They begin with a common assumption. Both resist the most fluent cliche of the age: "I am aware [says Philocalos] that a certain class of thinkers seem to find a charm in the mere division of 'reason and faith'" (II 237). Both of Wedgwood's speakers, however, believe the dispute between faith and reason to be a false dichotomy. The issue between them is to define the boundaries of science.

Philalethes (the more Darwinian), believing that spiritual claims can be made only about the world as we know it in nature, observes that "Every step gained by science is a contraction of the miraculous -- as the one advances, the other must recede" (II 237). But "men of science," as Philocalos observes, are only looking at the window of nature, not through it. If one is studying glass, one looks at the glass in order to learn about glass. If one wants to observe a distant prospect, he or she looks through the glass in order to see what lies beyond. In other words, if one assumes a naturalistic premise, one will end with a naturalistic conclusion.

Charles Darwin read Wedgwood's dialogues and responded in a letter to her:

> I must tell you how much I admire your Article; though at the same time I must confess that I could not clearly follow you in some parts, which probably is in main part due to my not being at all accustomed to metaphysical trains of thought (Darwin 283).

Perhaps there is an element of the disingenuous here. Darwin was certainly practiced in the forms of the Platonic dialogue, having gotten a classical education at Cambridge by translating Greek and Latin daily throughout his university experience. It has also become clear that Darwin thought considerably about metaphysical questions and was by no means the simple positivist he is sometimes said to be (Gruber and Barrett passim). Most likely, Darwin is simply voicing his genuine and habitually modest deference to opinions uttered by others outside of his own domain. Of course, there is also a perfectly true sense in which the metaphysics of origins leave all of us dumbfounded.

Julia Wedgwood's view of the boundaries of science (I tend to identify her own voice with that of Philalethes in the dialogues) is that it is the true business of science to look at the window and the true business of reflective persons to make use of the window for trying to discover what might lie on the horizon.

Finally, by demythologizing the sacred text, Wedgwood makes it accessible to her contemporaries. Indeed, she is adept at finding ways in which the language of a received wisdom and the increasingly secular voices of her own age could interrogate one another.

Consider, for example, her letter of August, 1864 to Robert Browning on the subject of immortality:

> I sometimes fear that the sense of immortality may be the very thing itself -- that those souls which see the future have their inheritance there, but that for others, who merely live on a second hand

investment of those hopes and convictions of others, as they are formalized for us in the deepest words we know, are really deluding themselves with a prospect which is not for them. In other words, that to be immortal is to know it, and then I am sure I am not (Curle 52).

Wedgwood here articulates a sort of demythologized sense of immortality which makes immortality tantamount to the power to live under the aspect of the future -- or, perhaps, what is the same thing -- to live under the aspect of justice actualized in this world, rather than justice deferred. Wedgwood expresses such a notion this way:

> I look to a time when we shall lose sight of the boundary [between good and evil] when this, that we call evil...shall at all events recede and fade, when we shall partake in God's own calm and need no edge of blackness to tell us what is white. But in the meantime, in this world any attempt at rendering this seems to me condemned to hopeless futility (Curle 148-9).

This letter to Browning scolds him for the sheer meanness Wedgwood sees in his Guido in *The Ring and the Book*. She sees Guido as lacking the intelligence and cleverness which make Iago so daunting and Dante's sinners so mournful. Guido, she suggests, is not so evil as he is violent; he merely hacks away stupidly at his victims. Evil is at least interesting -- a color on the spectrum, or a subject of contemplation, while Guido is a mere thug.

Wedgwood's futurist notion of extinguished boundaries and of the absence of those contrasting foils which distinguish between good and evil is reminiscent of her sense that in Greek antiquity good and evil are colors on a spectrum, not a positive and a negative. She seems to be pointing to an order of questions which goes even beyond the demythologizing which has kept us preoccupied for a century and a half. Will generations arise for whom the mythologies have lost all relevance? That is, if the sacred myths are going to be translated into a sort of secular naturalism, will it not be the case that secular naturalism can arrive at the same result without remembering its myths? Does living under the aspect of justice require an authorizing narrative, or only some sort of "gift" -- a grace, perhaps, as inexplicable and unpredictable as terror or tragedy?

Julia Wedgwood spoke quietly and obscurely to an age which was haunted by the disintegration of its master narratives, but to her own satisfaction, she finds a strategy. By allowing the most sacred text of her culture to converse with Plutarch, with the myths of Heracles, with scientific texts, with contemporaneous poetry, she was able to tease out fresh ways of framing the arguments about virtue, gender, and chastity --

about evil and immortality. These intertextual conversations reframe the issues and make them more accessible to a nineteenth-century audience. The consequence is that Julia Wedgwood deserves to be considered as an authentic participant in that long Victorian search for newly possible parameters for belief and doubt; and, if I may extrapolate from her notion of the disappearing boundaries between good and evil, she is searching also for a future when doubt and belief will be colors on a spectrum rather than contrasting foils. Still, her own views are exploratory rather than imperative. Speaking even of the shadows of her own doubts about immortality, she says:

> Perhaps this [doubt of her immortality] is the delusion of the sultry noon, when one is so tired of the journey that one could almost be content, at certain moments, to sit down by the dusty highway and fall asleep, even to wake no more. I saw my stars in the early dawn and perhaps I shall see them again in the twilight (Curle 52).

WORKS CITED

Curle, Richard, ed. *Robert Browning and Julia Wedgwood: A Broken Friendship as Revealed in Their Letters*. London, 1937.

Darwin, Francis, ed. *The Life and Letters of Charles Darwin*. New York: D. Appleton, 1898.

Gruber, Howard and Paul Barrett. *Darwin on Man: A Psychological Study of Scientific Creativity*. New York: E.P. Dutton, 1974.

Wedgwood, Julia. "Boundaries of Science." *Macmillan's Magazine* in two parts, June 1861: 134-38 and July 1861: 237-242.

---. "Fiction and Faith." *Contemporary Review* August 1892: 217-224.

---. "Greek Mythology and the Bible." *Contemporary Review* March 1892: 368-381.

---. "Male and Female Created He Them." *Contemporary Review* July 1889: 120-128.

---. "Plutarch and the Unconscious Christianity of the First Two Centuries." *Contemporary Review* January 1881: 45-60.

---. "The Unfaithful Steward." *Contemporary Review* January 1890: 52-63.

Religion as Contextualized Critique in the Letters of Harriett and Jemima Newman

David Goslee
University of Tennessee

The two sisters, Harriett and Jemima Newman, make up an interesting test case for the power of an extra-canonical genre, letter writing, to constitute a mode of both theological and cultural criticism. Their case is all more significant because of their brother's involvement in the Oxford Movement. Unlike the more radical Methodists, this Movement offered no opportunities for any real-life Dinah Morris to assert herself as a preacher. If religion constitutes the opiate of the masses as a whole, then 19th-century high-Anglicanism might well be considered a dose fatal to its female adherents. Yet just as letter writing comprised women's principal mode of literary production, so religious activity -- decorating the church building, working among the poor and sick of the parish, and teaching Sunday School -- often comprised their principal mode of public activity. Through these sisters, therefore, we can explore how these writings and these activities remained simultaneous vehicles of cultural critique and cultural repression.

As subjects, Harriett and Jemima remain both more individualized and more marginalized than their contemporaries. They grew up among highly quirky siblings and mingled with the intellectual spiritual elite of Oxford; Harriett even established herself as a writer of juvenile fiction. Yet their more famous brother, John Henry, worked systematically to subordinate them and their religious venture to his own. Until the time of his conversion to Catholicism, they willingly supported him, but as he confessed to them his growing doubts about the Church of England, both sisters challenged his unquestioned equation of religious vocation and cultural transcendence. Where Harriett scornfully compared his conversion to a disgraceful marriage, Jemima acknowledged a commitment both to her brother and to the church he was leaving. In their different responses, the two embody the strengths and limitations of what we might call an immanent religious critique, the use of some patriarchal norms to undermine others.

On the surface, it might seem that Harriett and Jemima had the opportunity to formulate a religious position just as autonomous as their brother's. The first four Newman siblings were so strong-willed that fourth-born Frank mused, "we seem to look out on different worlds." After citing Harriett's opinion "that we are all bewitched," second-born Charles, himself in constant danger of being institutionalized, confessed to John that "The family of the Newmans is as mad a family as perhaps can be found in th[is] mad country" (Svaglic 380, 382). Like their brothers, the eldest two sisters reflected John's own nature in ways which impugned some of his cherished opinions. At the age of nine, for example, he had written in a copy-book, "Train up a child in the way he should go, and, when he is old, he will not depart from it." His siblings had the same training which he had -- better, if anything, because he was there to guide them. And yet they all used this training to shape lives different from one another and, worse yet, different from his.

Third-born Harriett in particular had a well earned reputation as a wit; after an early visit to the British Museum, she wrote her sister, "As to the Elgin Marbles, they do not improve by laying by." Yet unlike John, neither she nor her younger sister Jemima will be remembered for leading the Oxford Movement, which reshaped Anglicanism as the high-church denomination we know today; or for writing a classic defense of liberal education in his *Idea of a University*; or for stirring up the religious scandal of his generation by converting to Catholicism; or for then recuperating his lost public stature by defending his life against Kingsley's charges of hypocrisy within his *Apologia pro Vita Sua*.

Harriett *was* acknowledged during her life as a pioneering author of children's novels. Of her four published books, the first, *The Fairy Bower*, is a lively exploration of ethical conflict and growth in a largely unsupervised group of playmates. Among them Maisie Ward finds one modeled on the adolescent John:

> George, aged about thirteen, condescends to play with the younger children, likes to "take off the company" when his parents have visitors, "quizzes" his sisters and cousins. He was a young gentleman who "believed he was clever enough to persuade anybody to do anything he chose."...Compare all this with the living boy...and I think you will see it comes pretty close to a portrait (13-15).

Harriett's second book, *The Lost Brooch*, is an adolescent replay of the Oxford Movement itself, with high- and low-church arguments well articulated by their youthful spokespersons; the third is a less successful adult novel; and the fourth, *Family Adventures*, is again important for its thinly disguised portraits of her siblings as somewhat younger children. Today, however, copies of these novels are almost impossible to obtain outside of the British National Libraries.

If we focus instead on the sisters' letters, we can see the dramatic discrepancy between the forums available to them and to John. Unlike their brother, who often used his correspondents as sounding boards for his latest ideas, the sisters wrote for each other and not for posterity. If their beliefs, their attitudes, even their humor remain embedded within their own social circle and within John's intellectual paradigms, the reasons are not far to seek. As their father became financially ineffectual, John eagerly assumed both that role and his own as eldest brother. He laid out their course of studies, badgered them with moral counsel, married them off to two of his proteges, demanded not just love but complete submission to his changing theological views, defined femininity as restricted to domestic affections, and then defined religious duty as a rejection of these same affections.[1]

John's attempts at appropriation differed from sister to sister. To the more accommodating Jemima, he could afford to be both patronizing and demanding. An early letter to her concludes, "What a gossiping letter this last half has been! It is quite a girl's letter -- ah, I feel ashamed" (*LD* 2: 91). Yet when about to leave the Anglican for the Catholic Church, he turns to Jemima for a sympathetic response to what sounds suspiciously like a mid-life crisis:

> I see men dying who were boys, almost children, when I was born. Pass a very few years, and I am an old man....I have a good name with many; I am deliberately sacrificing it. I have a bad name with more. I am fulfilling all their worst wishes, and giving them their most coveted triumph. I am distressing all I love, unsettling all I have instructed or aided. I am going to those who I do not know, and of whom I expect very little. I am making myself an outcast, and that at my age. Oh, what can it be but a stern necessity which causes this? Pity me, my dear Jemima. (Moz. 2: 411)

Harriett, by contrast, had a reputation for independence; her letters, according to O'Faolain, "are by far the most graphic of all the Newman letters, and the most human. They alone give us hard, bright thumbnails of days and people" (79-80). Glorying in this reputation, she savages one prospective suitor in conversation: "I could hardly keep him down though I several times wounded him enough to extort a cry of 'Miss Newman, you insult me!'; 'Mrs. N., your daughter insults me.'. . . Absurd little person, why did he stay?" (O'Faolain 129). Later, she playfully warns her fiance, Thomas Mozley, of what *he* can expect in marriage: "You don't know perhaps that by some near connexions I have been voted 'a vixen,'...You will have discovered there is something more frightful before you than the long winter evenings -- it is quite cheering to me to think how I might worry and torment you -- you poor dear creature" (D. Mozley 58). Despite John's protestations that "of all my brothers and sisters...you alone know my feelings and respond to them" (*LD* 2: 55), she refused to be convinced: "I hoped you loved me, dear John, whenever I thought of it -- but I could never persuade myself....I cannot persuade myself so now" (*LD* 2: 55-56).

John paid lip-service to this strength: "Harriett thinks and judges much more dispassionately and rationally than I do" (*LD* 2: 6). But long before their father's death, he felt justified, even compelled, to assert a paternal authority, particularly when her attitudes mirrored those he would rather deny in himself. Just after the father's bank had failed and the family had to move, fifteen-year-old John wrote his aunt about his thirteen-year-old sister:

> Why should Harriett be sorry at leaving Norwood?...I hope I shall hear of her with Stoical front disdaining to feel any affection for the place in which she has delighted these last eight years....[John,] when he left Norwood on one Monday morning...must have been conscious to himself, he would never see it (as his home) again; let her ask herself, whether he was in the least unwilling to leave it, tho he liked it; perhaps as much [as] she did. (*LD* 1: 26)

A decade later, his criticisms of her modest social life pass beyond chauvinism into mere crochet: "I meant in my last [letter to warn you against] invitations to places where there will be *many* people, a most irrational mode of spending time. If I had my will, no lady should go where she could not take her work....See as many persons as you can -- though *not all at once*" (*LD* 2: 7). Kathleen Tillotson sums up his attitude with this reported remark: "There is that in Harriett which I will *not* permit" (187).

Harriett tries to take all this hectoring in good humor; in one letter, according to O'Faolain, she makes merry "because John wanted to bury a couple who would have preferred to get married; and then tried to marry the wrong couple, who would thereby have been twice married; and then tried to marry the right couple in the wrong name" (81). Next she tries banter: "your letter...was certainly penned with the quill of a wild goose. I long to expose you, and to read it to some of the sober folk here who are so deluded still with the belief of your wisdom" (Ward 162). Next she is driven to sarcasm: "I wish you had some one with you, poor fellow -- but a monk deserves no compassion. Don't tumble off your horse -- give my love to Klepper [the horse] -- if you see no objection" (*LD* 2: 254).[2] Later she vents more overt hostility: "first, is your own manner, which I am sure you must know is sometimes very trying to me, and which I cannot always understand....Another difficulty I have felt in speaking to you freely, is the great difference I see in our opinions on many points" (*LD* 3: 107). Finally she turns on him: "I wish you would a little more show in your manner towards us the affection and tenderness which I know you feel in your heart....I wish you would open your eyes to your mistakes in this respect" (O'Faolain 206).

Yet from the beginnings of the Oxford Movement in 1833 through John's scandalous attempt to "Romanize" the Thirty-Nine Articles of Anglicanism in his Tract 90 of 1841, both sisters supported his increasingly high-church position. Even during the public outcry over Tract 90, Harriett writes her sister that, John "assures me of his confidence in his cause and seems quite armored." In her brother's defense, she prophesies that his liberal opponents will come to discover that their position has no theological underpinnings: "Our Church cannot stand on that rock of sand. They must go deeper, when they will get nearer than they suspect to the ground they now despise" (D. Mozley 102-03). While John saw his pilgrimage as an individual, even a solitary one, she dramatizes it by pitting his theological integrity against the blandishments of insidious Papists: "My feeling of the matter is that a 'cardinal's hat' or rather more than that has been offered him direct from Rome....[Yet as] simple as a child, and as bold as a lion, he has turned their inconsistency of principle upon themselves" (D. Mozley 101).

Not to be outdone, Jemima attributes to his preaching a Pauline power: "how little you know of the estimation in which [your sermons] are generally held....I am sure it is a great gift, that insight you show into human nature....it is a sort of spiritual perception; and I wonder whether it is anything like the gifts in the Corinthian Church" (Moz. 2: 288). Even when confronting his imminent conversion, she refuses to disown him: "what would become of me if I could not think of you, as I always have thought, with joy and gratitude that I am your sister? Yes, dear John, I feel it cannot be otherwise; whichever way you decide it will be a noble and true part, and not taken up from any impulse, or caprice, or pique" (D. Mozley 139).

Nevertheless, as John becomes increasingly restive with both his church and the constructs he has created to bolster it, the sisters transform their apparent conventionality into an immanent critique of his own claims for spiritual autonomy. Specifically, they challenge his implicit quest for some position -- the "paper church" of the *Via Media*, the Church of the Alexandrian Fathers, or the Catholic Church of his own imagination -- which will let him transcend the moral and spiritual ambiguities of his own world. Ostensibly they use the letter format only to quote John's past views back at him; more fundamentally, however, they create through it a thoroughly English species of Hegel's *Sittlichkeit*, a contextualized ethic which insists that he cannot escape a complicity within it, insists that his affections as a brother, his duties as a priest, and his vision as a theologian can be neither divorced nor ordered within a tidy hierarchy.

Jemima, the only one of John's siblings not to cut him off or be cut off by him, refuses to judge him or his decision. Yet she also refuses to deny that she finds both his reasons and his new faith unconvincing:

> I have so much sanguineness in my composition that I always hope the worst misfortunes may be averted till they are irremediable. And what can be worse than this? It is like hearing that some dear friend must die....Our poor distracted Church seems to me in pieces, and there is no one to help her, and her children's sympathies seem all drawn off another way. And how sad it is to me that I cannot say these things to you without your thinking me in error. (Moz. 2: 409-10)

An early practitioner of Carol Gilligan's ethics of care, Jemima here credits neither the witness of the Patristic Church nor the authority of contemporary Catholicism. What counts as religious evidence is rather her own lived faith as it has shaped her loving relationships with those around her.

Hence when John attempts to back gracefully out of St. Mary's pulpit in 1843, Jemima forwards to him the letter of a woman friend outraged that he is betraying their "mutual sympathy" and insistent that he cannot not so easily divorce person from preacher or auditors from flock:

> [H]e has taught and they have striven to be obedient pupils. He has formed their minds, not accidentally: he has *sought* to do so, and he has succeeded. He has undertaken the charge and cannot now shake them off. His words have been spoken in vain to many, but not to them. He has been the means under Providence of making them what they are....If he was silenced, the blame would rest with others; but, giving them up of his own free will, they will have a sense of abandonment and desertion....our champion has deserted us -- our watchman, whose cry used to cheer us, is heard no more. (Moz. 2: 376)

Two years later, Jemima herself tells John that the circumference of his religious experience must come to include more than the "two and two only absolute and luminously self-evident beings, myself and my Creator," as he would later identify them in his *Apologia* (18). She laments that because his spiritual power remains an interpersonal one, it must fail when he abandons the ties of mutual love, trust, and commitment which his ministry has built up:

> Dear John, when you spoke in the name of our Church your exhortations were all powerful, your voice seemed the voice of an angel, you touched a chord in all our hearts -- you seemed to know our very hearts. Since your new views have gained the ascendancy how great the change!...Your talents, experience, and depth of mind must make your words powerful; but you will not influence the same class of minds that you have in times past. (Moz. 2: 421)

By maintaining their correspondence within this painful yet loving tension, she maintains her own theological commitment to both interpersonal relationship and personal integrity as two pivotal yet often incompatible values within human life: "I know...how little I ought to assume I am right in any one thing. Yet there are some things one dare not doubt, and some things it is one's highest happiness to believe and try to realize. So, however unworthy I am, I feel we must in some measure go by our own faith and our own light, though that light be little better than darkness" (Moz. 2: 414).

Harriett's reaction to the conversion, while far more hostile, is also far more difficult to evaluate. Most Newman scholars find John's outrage over the Protestant Bishopric in Jerusalem more credible than the earlier rationalizations of *Tract 90*. Harriett, however, faithful up to this point, comes to see the Jerusalem issue as part of a pre-scripted scenario:

> It is true that he advances his arguments as from the part of the "certain friends," but they are given too con amore for my taste. I *hope* it is all exaggerated, but I have always noticed things are thought one year, talked over the next and acted upon the third. The arguments throughout seem to me perfectly unsound, childish and pettish....All looks as near like expediency as any thing I can fancy. (D. Mozley 113)

Where Jemima poured coals of fire upon John's head by assuming that he was acting from his own stated ideals, Harriett interprets these same actions from an ironic distance somewhere between Jane Austen and Sigmund Freud. To her, John's motives for converting are not even self-serving but instead regressive, as she states here, or belatedly sexual, as she insinuates five years later when she compares the conversion itself to a bad marriage: "If a man of reason (which J.H.N. especially is) acts against his reason, suffer he must and ought. If he marries so, he does, and J.H.N. has made a most disgraceful match -- the consequences of which he must bear" (D. Mozley 166).

Where Jemima socialized her brother's spiritual quest by detailing its pastoral consequences, Harriett domesticates it by comparing the advent of a new church in the family to the appearance of a new and thoroughly disagreeable in-law. From the fierce individuality she shares with her brother, she predicts accurately that his Catholic career will be just as fraught with controversy as his Anglican one: "I should not wonder if the Church of Rome and he cannot come to terms at the onset. J.H.N. has showed less than ever lately, (less even than I expected) that he can bow to any authority, collected or individual" (165).

Friends of Harriett will praise her criticism as trenchant and fully justified; enemies will dismiss it as her chance to pay back a portion of John's hostility in kind. Efforts to mediate this conflict are hampered by a crucial difference between Jemima's critique and Harriett's. However hesitant its expression, Jemima's theology can appeal with some confidence to personal and ethical norms. Harriett's, by contrast, foreshadows the strengths and weaknesses of some postmodern, post-derridean theologians. Refusing to sanction the institutions or ideologies around her, she also refuses to sanction any alternatives to them. Apart from her brother's case, for example, Harriett's epistolary comments on religion contain remarkably few references to God or Christ. A family friend, Maria Giberne, recollects that while she "called Harriett 'Mother Church,' because she was so strict a Churchwoman,...I was greatly puzzled from not finding [in her any] fervour and readiness to talk on religious subjects" (Ward 123).

Instead of invoking a transcendent but still identifiably male deity, Harriett prefers to expose the self-contradictions within the Victorian religious establishment without pretending that she can stand physically or ideologically outside it. In one witty allusion to the *Tale of a Tub*, she echoes Swift's similarly ambivalent gesture of "civilizing" Christianity by figuring it as a suit of clothes: The new Catholic converts may "fancy they [will] find the other half of the apostolic robes there," but they will "be smothered with the extra garments with which they...find themselves daily encumbered" (D. Mozley 113). In order to delimit her critical distance, she frequently judges the male leaders of one sect with norms championed by the male leaders of another. Besides the adolescent, fuzzy-headed mysticism of the Romeward-drifting Tractarians, her letters pillory the time-serving, Erastian complacency of the Anglican establishment and the narrow, self-righteous provincialism of the Evangelicals: "I...must now go to church and listen to a rhapsody of Mr. Martin's. I hear Mrs. M. will not read his letters on a Sunday, but puts them by as being too profane. I thought it showed sense and wished we could do so by his sermons" (D. Mozley 73).

Amid this satirical brilliance, however, her letters contain one telling admission that the split within her church has torn the fabric of her own life: "I long to be writing again, and yet I feel pretty sure I have lost the power. I believe the Oxford folks have helped to put me in this state, for I feel as if every thing were about to be pulled to pieces and could cry 'cui bono' to every project" (116). Seen together, in fact, Harriett, Jemima, and John Henry Newman define a common dilemma which qualifies their very different, very powerful criticisms of religion within Victorian culture. His sisters succeed in contextualizing and thus qualifying John's individual quest for social transcendence. Yet his quest, in turn, allows a modern reader to see both his sisters trapped within a social context which needs itself to be transcended.

Jemima's consciousness is the more obviously in need of raising; in order to turn John's patriarchal image of divine and human authority back against him, she has to accept it in the first place. The cultural limitations of Harriett's Christianity reveal themselves more subtly. In 1845 she writes Jemima, "There is no party [in Oxford] at present standing up for the truth and those who could have acted, will not" (D. Mozley 155); in 1849 she "heartily wish[es] all the theological books of the last fifteen years behind the fire" (185); in 1846 she justifies her vindictive rejection of John with "*We know* he is wrong" (165). Yet in renouncing her brother, in calling down a plague upon all the houses of her church, in ridiculing their various members, she never articulates her own affiliation, her own position, her own faith. By refusing to identify with the positive qualities in any of the Christian denominations which surround her, Harriett comes close to embodying the most narrow, intolerant, uncharitable qualities in all of them. Jemima, John, and Harriett thus illustrate respectively the rival dangers of grounding religious belief within one's own culture, grounding it upon principles and institutions which claim to transcend culture, and refusing to ground it at all.

NOTES
1. In some of Newman's sermons, his willingness to part with his family sounds uncomfortably eager: "he who has friends or kindred, and acquiesces with an entire heart in their removal while it is yet doubtful, who can say, 'Take them away, if it be Thy will, to Thee I give them up, to Thee I commit them,' who is willing to be taken at his word; he too risks somewhat, and is accepted" (*PS* 4 [20]: 303-04).

2. For the further adventures of Klepper, see Thomas Mozley, 1: 203.

WORKS CITED

Mozley, Dorothea, ed. *Newman Family Letters*. London: S.P.C.K., 1962.

Mozley, Thomas. *Reminiscences: Chiefly of Oriel College and the Oxford Movement.* 2 vols. London: Longmans, Green, 1882.

Newman, John Henry. *Apologia Pro Vita Sua.* Ed. Martin J. Svaglic. Oxford: Clarendon, 1967.

_____. *Letters and Correspondence of John Henry Newman* (Moz.). 2 vols. Ed. Anne Mozley. London: Longmans Green, 1903.

_____. *The Letters and Diaries of John Henry Newman (LD).* Ed. Charles Stephen Dessain *et al.* Vols. 1-6 (Oxford, 1978-84), 11-22 (London, 1961-72), 23-31 (Oxford, 1973-77).

_____. *Parochial and Plain Sermons (PS).* 8 vols. London: Longmans, Green, 1901.

O'Faolain, Sean. *Newman's Way.* London: Longmans, Green, 1952.

Svaglic, Martin J. "Charles Newman and his Brothers." *PMLA* 71 (1956): 370-85.

Tillotson, Kathleen. "Harriett Mozley's Tales for the Young." *The Listener* 48 (31 July 1952): 187-89.

Ward, Maisie. *Young Mr. Newman.* New York: Sheed & Ward, 1948.

Women's Theology and the Novel

Evangelical Theology and Feminist Polemic:

Emma Jane Worboise's *Overdale*

Julie Melnyk
Central Methodist College

Denied the opportunity to preach from the pulpit, many devout Victorian women decided to "preach" in the Circulating Library: they wrote religious novels, novels that I analyze as "women's sermons." These "women's sermons" reflect traditional sermons through stylistic traits and rhetorical methods. Individual episodes and even the novels as a whole participate in the homiletic tradition of the *exemplum*; rhetorical devices such as the "concatenation of passages," or series of allusions, appear in both novel and sermon;[1] and the novelists often do biblical exegesis, sometimes filtering their textual analysis through an admirable character, sometimes speaking in their own person to a "congregation" of readers. Perhaps most significant, however, is the novelists' use of the homiletic "we": rather than writing entirely in the third person or using the first person singular to represent the author or narrator as in most Victorian fiction, these women writers, like preachers, more often use the first person plural. This shared use of the homiletic "we" signals a similarity in the operative conception of the addressee in traditional sermons and "women's sermons": the novels, like the sermons, are addressed to a congregation gathered to receive spiritual, theological, or moral teaching, hoping for entertainment but expecting encouragement and enlightenment.

There are, however, crucial differences between conventional sermons and "women's sermons". A sermon is essentially oral, a speech genre, while these religious novels are written.[2] A sermon is presented publicly to a physically-present congregation; a religious novel speaks silently and privately to an absent audience. A conventional sermon is univocal; a "woman's sermon" is multivocal. This multivocality might seem to work against the traditional aims of the sermon -- teaching, persuasion, enlightenment -- since it undermines the authority accorded to any one voice, even the "preacher's" own. Some female novelists do resist this destabilization, trying to use their narrative voice to retain the authority of univocal discourse. Often, however, this qualification of authority actually enhances the didactic content, since many women's religious novels, such as

Emma Jane Worboise's *Overdale*, dramatize the undermining of univocal, socially-sanctioned religious authorities who nevertheless fail to teach truth. Women authors could exploit the multivocality of their genre to make room for their own (silenced) voices.

In these multivocal novels, Victorian women "preached" many different kinds of sermons: sermons concerned with individual conversion or societal reform,[3] sermons of exhortation and encouragement for the converted, sermons applying moral doctrine to particular moral problems, and, increasingly through the century, theological sermons.

The prevalence of the theological or polemical sermon resulted from the conflicts of nineteenth-century Christianity: within the Anglican church, conflicts between the parties -- High, Low, and Broad; outside, conflicts between Anglicanism and Catholicism, Dissent, and infidelity. In *The Reader's Repentance* Christine Krueger notes that Methodist doctrine originally permitted women preachers as an extraordinary response in a time of crisis; she shows how the nineteenth-century novelists who followed their lead also represented themselves as responding to crises, manufacturing them where necessary. But such manufacture was largely unnecessary, and the chronic state of crisis created opportunities for female apologists: women were allowed, even encouraged to undertake theological polemics in their novels. In these novels, women preachers were not peacemakers, "evangelists of reconciliation" (Krueger 232), expected to "...deliver a predictable, ameliorist message" (231) but front-line troops, expected to fight theological battles -- and there were women writers in almost every major fighting force. Women's theological sermons were supposed to inculcate one set of doctrines and stop the spread of contrary doctrines or systems, although in practice, partly because of the genre's multivocalism, they often did more than that -- and sometimes less.

The seriousness with which these works were regarded is made clear by the phenomenon of "response novels" -- novels written to oppose the errors of previous novels, a kind of rebuttal we associate with solemn genres such as sermons or journal articles. Emma Jane Worboise, for example, wrote several such responses. *Thornycroft Hall*, as Elisabeth Jay demonstrates in *Religion of the Heart*, is a reply to *Jane Eyre*, defending the Evangelical methods of the school attacked by Charlotte Bronte under the name of Lowood and revising some of the ethical judgments of the famous novel.[4] Worboise also replied to a Tractarian novel by Elizabeth Sewell, *Amy Herbert*, which emphasizes the importance of baptism into the Established Church, with her Evangelical *Amy Wilton*, which supports the claims of Dissenters to Christian communion and salvation. She responded to the other major Tractarian novelist, Charlotte M. Yonge, in *Hearts-ease in the Family*, whose title mimics that of her opponent's *Hearts-ease, or the Brother's Wife*. Elisabeth Jay suggests economic motives for these sound-alike titles:

she proposes that Worboise intended her books to be mistaken for those of the Tractarian novelists on book-stalls and in circulating libraries. But though deception may have been part of her intent, Worboise's titles also signal that these books are intellectual and moral responses to other "women's sermons". Some men, too, regarded women's religious fiction as a potentially serious challenge: J.H.Newman's *Loss and Gain*, perhaps the best-known religious novel of the century, was written in response to a woman's novel: Elizabeth Harris's *From Oxford to Rome* (Maison 139-40).

While not a response to another specific work (though see the allusion to Frances Trollope, below), one of Worboise's novels demonstrates clearly the tendency of women's theological "sermons" to concern themselves simultaneously with religious issues and women's issues: *Overdale, or the Story of a Pervert* (1869). "Pervert" lacked its modern sexual connotations in the nineteenth century; its primary meaning was religious: "one who has forsaken a doctrine or system regarded as true for one esteemed false" (*OED*), the opposite of "convert". Obviously, the application of the word depended upon the speaker's own religious convictions, but it was most frequently used to describe Anglicans who, like J.H. Newman, converted to Roman Catholicism. In its very title, this "woman's sermon" reveals its polemical ambitions.

The woman who preached this polemical "sermon", Emma Jane Worboise, was born in Birmingham in 1825, the daughter of an Anglican clergyman; she published her first novel, *Alice Cunningham*, at the age of twenty-one. Although at first her fiction was published by an obscure house in Bath, she soon began her lifelong affiliation with James Clarke & Co., a religious publishing house in London. In addition to the usual range of religious novels, printed sermons, and devotional books, Clarke published a variety of religious newspapers and magazines: *The Christian World and General Intelligencer Containing the News of the Week*, an ambitious penny-journal with a circulation reported at over 100,000 copies a week (Farningham 86); *The Sunday School Times*; *The Literary World*, a Christian review; and *The Christian World Pulpit* (Farningham 105). When in 1866 Clarke needed an editor for a new monthly magazine designed to complement the popular *Christian World*, he turned to Worboise, his most successful contributor. She edited *The Christian World Magazine* from its inception until her death in 1887. In her lifetime, she published at least forty-six novels, a volume of religious poetry, and a biography of Thomas Arnold.

Her religious views do not fit well into traditional categories; although her obituary in *Literary World* calls her "the novelist of Evangelical Dissent" (209), it is not clear that she ever left the Anglican Church. Her laudatory biography of Broad-Church hero Thomas Arnold and her affiliation with *The Christian World*, a "wholly unsectarian, but decidedly evangelical" publication ("A Word") indicate that her Evangelicalism was tempered by a Broad-Church tolerance. Nevertheless, with whatever refinements, Evangelical she was, and it is largely Evangelical doctrine that informs this polemical novel.

Evangelicalism held certain benefits for women that Tractarianism failed to provide.[5] First, while the High Church emphasized the Apostolic Succession and the authority of the clergy, Evangelicalism, whether Anglican or Dissenting, emphasized lay participation in church life and government and insisted on the doctrine of the "priesthood of the believer," the ability of the individual Christian to pray, worship, and interpret Scripture without benefit of clergy. This emphasis was particularly important for women, who were excluded from clerical authority; it provided opportunities to exercise leadership generally denied them by the more priest-ridden High-Church party. Moreover, Evangelicalism was known as "the religion of the heart." While Tractarianism began in Oxford, that exclusively male preserve of higher education, and emphasized the importance of an educated clergy, Evangelicalism inherited the Methodist emphasis on the importance and validity of emotional response and direct inspiration. Since women were assumed superior in their religious feelings, and since direct inspiration could not consistently be confined to men, women were not marginalized to the same extent by their lack of education but took their place nearer the center of the movement. Finally, there is the issue of class. As its designation might indicate, the High Church tended to be a movement of the upper-middle class and the aristocracy, while the Low Church generally attracted members of the lower-middle and even working classes; the class distinction was even stronger between Anglicanism and Dissent. Some lingering class discrimination has probably been a factor in the nearly universal neglect of the Low-Church novel in the twentieth century,[6] but for nineteenth-century women of the Low Church, their inferior status actually held some advantages. In general, High-Church novelists and heroines had to concern themselves with high standards of genteel behavior; Christian service had to remain "lady-like". The Low-Church women, less encumbered by such ideas, were allowed much greater scope for action. These Evangelical advantages make it easier for Worboise to combine an attack on High-Church doctrine with a call for female freedom and self-assertion in *Overdale*.

The novel begins as Agatha Bevan, the orphaned heroine, goes out as governess to the children of Eustace Aylmer, a widowed clergyman just embarking on his first parish in the village of Overdale. Unfortunately, "his theological views were those of the Keble and Pusey school" (17) -- High Anglicanism. His Christian name, however, warned contemporary readers that he would not rest content in the Anglican church: "Eustace" recalls Frances Trollope's religious novel *Father Eustace* (1848), a rabidly anti-

Catholic tale about a dangerous Jesuit let loose in England. Agatha falls under the spell of the fascinating young vicar, gradually giving up the self-determination that Evangelicals value so highly, as Worboise makes clear:

> If, indeed, Mr. Aylmer did say so, it must be true. Agatha did not say so much to herself, but she felt a sort of conviction at her heart that what he taught must indeed be of the very purest and truest. All unconsciously she was setting up an idol for herself; an idol of such excellence, and wisdom, and power of mind that she would humble herself before his shrine with the humility of a little child. (61)

Agatha is rebuked by her author for returning to a state of childishness, for allowing a man -- whatever his "power of mind" -- to determine her beliefs, and the language of the rebuke suggests the theological issues at stake. Agatha is guilty of "idolatry", a charge frequently leveled against Roman Catholics because of their un-English use of saintly images and crucifixes. Moreover, she worships at Eustace's "shrine" -- traditionally a richly decorated repository for the relics of a saint. Such saint worship is as dangerous to female self-determination as it is to Evangelical freedom of conscience; here Evangelicalism and feminism coincide.[7]

But Agatha's willingness to accept Aylmer's opinions as authoritative is not merely an expression of her romantic devotion to him; it is what he, as "the priest of Overdale, the authorised minister of the Church," "one having authority from the Most High" (266) demands from all his parishioners. Using his univocal genre, the traditional sermon, Aylmer claims unique authority, exhorting them to accept traditional church doctrine as he explains it to them:

> "Do not be led away . . .; you have accepted the teaching of your mother, the Church, and if anything is brought before you which militates against that teaching, or in any way clashes with it, reject it. Do not resort to controversy; controversy is not for the laity, and a woman may be easily deceived by the specious arguments of a sophist. A sound rule of faith is provided for you; hold to it, and you will be safe." (91)

Only the Church can interpret for them God's will, and only Eustace Aylmer can interpret for them the teachings of the Church. He tries to represent the Church as a female authority, rather than a patriarchal one; he promises safety in conformity and danger in controversy. He first enjoins all the laity against engaging in controversy, but quickly shifts focus to address his real interest, and, I think, that of the novel: women and religious controversy. Some women novelists used clergyman characters as mouthpieces through which they could preach their own univocal sermons. (See, for instance, Catherine Long's *Sir Roland Ashton*.) But, in what is at once an Evangelical and a feminist move, Worboise refuses to give the man in the pulpit the role of conduit of the author's truth or, indeed, of God's truth; he is in error and must be resisted and corrected by female members of his congregation.

Fortunately, not every woman in the parish is so quick as Agatha to accord Mr. Aylmer the authority he demands: several women, each in her own way and in her own words, resist Aylmer's claims. Roberta Roberts, while otherwise unexceptionable in her behavior, insists on judging for herself.

> And Mr. Aylmer respected her, and knew that of all the lady-workers in the neighborhood she was the most useful, the most thoroughly efficient; but he could not like her: his tastes were fastidious, and her loud tones and manly tread jarred upon his sensibilities. Then she had a terrible habit of speaking her mind, and she hit the right nail upon the head very often with a precision that was both startling and amusing, but not exactly entertaining to the person who happened to have the worst of the argument. (77)

Here Worboise simultaneously satirizes the over-fastidious refinement of the High-Church party and restrictive standards of femininity in general. She gives her female model masculine traits and virtues, and even a masculine name, implying that a good Christian woman is one who usurps the privileges of a man, speaking her mind in "loud tones." Roberta has no illusions about the clergyman's view of her; she good-humoredly complains to a friend:

> "Oh! Lady Jane, Mr. Aylmer has been scolding me terribly; he has been charging me with insubordination, and irreverence, and self-dependence, and obstinacy, and presumption, and several kinds of heresy. And he finishes up by granting all my requests." (78)

Eustace Aylmer's list of Roberta's sins sounds much like Ruskin's accusations against female theologians in "Of Queens' Gardens," but here Worboise lets Roberta herself give voice to the list, undercutting by her tone the negative connotations of the words themselves. Aylmer tries to treat her like a child in his "scolding", but unlike Agatha, she refuses to accept the child's role. And her righteousness is established not merely by her tone, but also by the success that Worboise grants her; Roberta gets what she wants, even from a self-important clergyman.

For her own rather different reasons, young Kate Chennery also suspects Aylmer's claims of authority, and explains her views to her mother:

> "Well, mamma, obedience was never one of my predominant virtues. And as to obeying a man just because he happens to be the clergyman of the parish in which I live, it is altogether out of the question. I tell you fairly that I never will submit myself to Mr. Aylmer. While I was in town I heard a good deal about the set to which he belongs, and I made up my mind to withstand him...all this assumption of authority that Mr. Aylmer has been professing for the last year or so is simply absurd, and I am sure it is to be resisted. You may call it what you will, but I call it *priestcraft*...And it seems to me that all this nonsense about the clergy tends to Romanism." (116)

Kate refuses to accept the authority of societally endorsed and traditional positions, calling them "absurd"; she submits herself only to a truth which transcends these forms, a truth which she can find for herself. These are the words of the New Woman, albeit one who holds to old-time religion, as Worboise's description makes clear: "She had little faith in Mr. Aylmer's pretensions simply because she was a girl of independent, fearless spirit, as frank and outspoken as she was rash and hasty, and because she had more sound sense of her own, when she chose to use it, than many young ladies of her age could command" (119).[8] Kate wins her author's approval for her independence, not only in religious matters, but in her attitude toward life. The novel allows the independent voices of two admirable independent women to harmonize in their opposition to monolithic clerical authority.[9]

Meanwhile, Eustace Aylmer falls in love with his children's governess and wants to marry her, but has scruples about the traditional Anglican practice of married clergy. His scruples exemplify a theme common in women's religious novels which deal with Roman Catholicism: the rejection of women implicit in the celibacy of the all-male clergy becomes explicit in these novels, when converted clerical husbands leave their wives and children in order to become priests in the Roman Catholic church. (Margaret Oliphant in *The Perpetual Curate* presents just such a situation in the hero's family, albeit with less doctrinal commitment than more pious novelists.) Struggling with his doubts, Aylmer writes to an old Oxford friend, Herbert Vallance, who soon arrives in Overdale. Unbeknownst to the reader, and even to Aylmer himself, Vallance is a Jesuit in disguise, who behaves coldly toward the parish women and urges strongly the incompatibility of marriage and priesthood.

Vallance represents Oxford, with its Tractarian traditions, its exclusivity, and its claims of cultural and religious authority. "Women's sermons" regularly pit pious women against the University in a struggle for dominance in religion, usually represented by the competition for the souls of University-trained brothers or lovers. In Anne Howard's *Mary Spencer* Edward Spencer renounces his commitment to his fiancee Emma because of new-found doubts about married clergy, and Emma and his sister Mary unite to bring him back to true Christianity; uncharacteristically, they are still waiting for his return at the end of the novel. A subplot of Felicia Skene's *Hidden Depths* has the heroine's brother falling prey to the later, even more dangerous scourge of Oxford: infidelity, or unbelief. Herbert Vallance represents the University side by his disdain for women, but also by the breadth and depth of his learning, as Aylmer's daughter Gertrude gushes:

> "And then he knows everything...Of course, he speaks French, and Italian, and German, as if they were each one his mother tongue. I know he is a wonderful Spanish scholar and Portuguese comes as a matter of course...he knows every history, every legend, every tale of old romance. He beats papa in the classics, at least papa says so: then as for science and 'ologies, he is well up in them all. He seems to have studied law and physics as much as divinity, and he can tell you all about the councils of the Church; and as for ecclesiastical history, he has Bede, and Mosheim, and Milner at his fingers' ends...Oh, he can do everything, and he knows everything." (271-72)

Of course, much of Gertrude's speech serves to provide clues to Vallance's hidden identity: his easy familiarity with the languages of Catholic countries such as Italy and Spain and his suspicious interest in Church tradition, both legend and history, point to his Jesuitical tendencies. Moreover, his knowing more law and science than he knows divinity alludes to the broad education traditionally received by Jesuit priests, even as it undermines any claim he might make to specifically religious authority. But in the power-struggle between the religion of the University and the religion of the heart, he represents all men who base their claims to religious authority on superior education: in the character of Vallance, Worboise discredits education itself as any guarantor of correct belief or behavior, exalting the less informed but infinitely more practical religion variously practiced by the women of Overdale.

Despite Vallance's best efforts, he loses to his friend's passion for Agatha, and Eustace Aylmer makes up his mind to marry the governess. Aylmer's friend Lady Jane points out to him the obvious religious differences between them, but Eustace dismisses her reservations:

"That is nothing; she can have no settled views, and she is docile and tractable in the extreme...she will recognize in me the Divine authority which as a duly-ordained priest I hold, and she will learn readily. I fear nothing on that head, Jane." (236-7)

In a moment of weakness, as she recovers from a serious illness, Agatha Bevan accepts his proposal, and they are married.

Here a lapse of many years in the narrative allows Worboise to demonstrate the long-term consequences of Aylmer's doctrines for his wife and children. His eldest daughter Rosamund is now morbidly pious; she dresses in a black veil like a Roman Catholic "Sister of Mercy", and she argues for the extreme obedience of the convent: "We are not to judge the actions of our spiritual guides: we have only implicitly to obey. To argue cases of this sort is dangerous presumption" (405).[10] But while she accepts the asceticism of her father, and the additional obedience enjoined on her as a woman, her younger siblings Claude and Gertrude rebel against silly restrictions and rituals "and in their anxiety to steer clear of superstition, they were in real danger of falling into a practical infidelity" (252). Eustace Aylmer remains an Anglican minister, but he is clearly edging "Romewards", and his ritualistic tendencies have begun to foment open rebellion among the women of the parish. This rebellion, of course, reflects Evangelical doctrine of individual conscience, but, in accordance with the narrativization that Carol Gilligan has identified in female moral thinking, it is thoroughly contextualized; the rebellion is justified by the whole set of circumstances and personalities, not merely by abstract principles.

The most radical voice of rebellion is that of the sixty-year-old spinster Miss Grierson. The author carefully distances herself from this unlikely rebel -- "I am afraid she was rather an unreasoning champion of the truth" -- but she does not silence her voice. Miss Grierson says and does things too radical to be openly acknowledged, but Worboise clearly values her extreme contribution. This elderly woman actually takes over as her own minister, and she justifies her action to the group of women debating at the circulating library:

"So I thought I had better say my prayers at home, and I bought a volume of sermons -- good, sound Church sermons, with no nonsense in them -- and I rang the bell about half-past ten, and called in my Jenny and the boy Dan, and I began with, 'When the wicked man,' and went straight through to the prayer of St. -- what's his name? -- that comes just before the end; and then I read a sermon, and said the Benediction, and Dan and Jenny went back to the kitchen." (246)

She does not go so far as to write her own sermons, but she does perform service and read a sermon of her own selection. High-Church Miss Harrison is disturbed -- "I hope you did not read the Absolution!" -- and her sister Laura agrees: "it would have been terrible!" But feisty Miss Grierson is not to be intimidated:

> "Stuff and nonsense, my dear! I've as much right to read the Absolution as the Archbishop of Canterbury has, if it's in accordance with God's Word. If it is not, nobody ought to read it." (246)

Miss Grierson refuses to acknowledge any Church authority, and her radical vision of woman-as-priest shines forth in the novel, although Worboise never has to commit herself to such a radical position.

Mrs. Bellamy is more temperate in her views, but no less adamant:

> "The change in our Church service has grieved both Mr. Bellamy and myself greatly, and we have come to the resolution respectfully but urgently to bring the matter before our pastor...If he will not listen,...we have but one course open to us -- we must leave our parish church....my husband will be the priest of his own household. We are a large family, ourselves, eight children, a governess, and including outdoor labourers, seven servants...we shall make no rules for our servants; no man, woman, or boy or girl, being of an age to judge for himself or herself, ought to be controlled in matters of conscience." (247-48)

While she more traditionally cedes priestly authority to her husband, she also generalizes the freedom to judge for "himself or herself", pointedly including women. She comes to this generalization, however, only after carefully describing the context of her moral dilemma -- the doctrine arises from the narrative.

Despite these multiple acts of individual self-assertion, only Roberta Roberts moves into open, public defiance of Aylmer, in the only fully dramatized scene of conflict between the clergyman and a female parishioner. He goes to her to forbid her further teaching, her public work:

> "I am not going to dispute with you any more, as you say it is all in vain; I am going, as your pastor, as one having authority from the Most High, to issue a command -- I cannot permit you any longer to continue to make those visits of which you speak."
>
> "You cannot permit me!" said Roberta, turning round with flashing eyes.

Her spirit rose at the haughty tone in which she was addressed; she was not one tamely to submit to unwarrantable coercion.

"I cannot permit you to spread error in the fold of the Holy Church. It is not I, Eustace Aylmer, who command you -- it is as the priest of Overdale, the authorised minister of the Church, who yet claims you as her child, that I desire you to render to me obedience in this particular." (266)

But Roberta Roberts remains unmoved by his commands and by his invocation of the feminine symbol of the Holy Mother Church:

"Dear Mr. Aylmer, you know how I have honoured you, how I have loved you as my pastor and my friend, but when my Bible teaches me one thing and you another, it is you whom I must perforce disbelieve and disobey." (267)

She can justify disobedience to patriarchal authority by calling on the higher obedience to the patriarchal God of the Bible; she continues her public work and her public speaking in defiance of Mr. Aylmer and the authority that wishes to silence her.

The vicar's wife Agatha, who allows herself to be silenced, does not fare so well. When he finally decides to become a Roman Catholic, Aylmer sends her and the children to France, where she begins to understand and to reproach herself for her silence and submission:

"for whenever Eustace and I began to converse on religious subjects, -- when even our discourse led that way, as it continually did, of course, I was either constrained to silence or to protest; and, Jane, I kept silence. I was unfaithful to my God who had enabled me to see clearly His own simple and eternal truth..." (465)

If Roberta Roberts's defiance teaches the success that attends self-assertion in religious matters, Agatha Aylmer's silence teaches the complementary lesson about the dire consequences of self-abnegation. The truth was "clear" and "simple", easily available to the young woman, somehow unavailable to the hyper-educated Vallance and his friend Aylmer. She who can see the truth is responsible for defying any authority that would silence her.

As the very title of the novel indicates, the story of Overdale, the conflict between clergyman and lay-women, between monolithic clerical authority and the individualist rebels, is the center of interest for the novel. But the romance plot remains important, because it is here that the Evangelical polemic and the feminist polemic most closely coincide. For Agatha, Eustace is both clergyman, claiming the Divine authority of the

Church, and husband, claiming traditional authority over his wife. As Roberta Roberts notes: "Her position is a very critical and a very sad one, for she is a devoted wife; and now for the first time she is feeling that it is her duty in many cases to testify against the teaching of her husband" (360). Agatha's failure to rebel not only against a dangerous Tractarian doctrine, but also against her husband's authority, leads them both to disaster. The Christian's responsibility to stand firm for the truth as she understands it becomes, through the narrative, a woman's, even a wife's, right of moral and theological independence.

Worboise's method of simultaneous polemics appears clearly in a debate near the end of the novel, between Aylmer's Tractarian daughter Rosamund and his rejected, but enlightened, Evangelical wife Agatha, on the subject of Apostolic succession:

> "You, Rosamund, hold that only those are 'authorised' who receive their commission directly from those whom you believe to be the successors of the apostles themselves. I believe that they whom Christ calls to preach His gospel, they whom He teaches and gifts with His Holy Spirit, are as worthily the ambassadors of God as any who can show the credentials on which so much stress is laid."
>
> "Mamma!" said Rosamund, gravely, "if you cannot believe in the one true Church, you surely hold that some kind of consecration is required before a person should pretend to take upon himself the office of the ministry?"
>
> "I hold in the setting apart of certain persons for the work of the ministry and all such persons should be duly examined by those whose age and experience give them weight in the churches; but the true call -- the only call that should be obeyed and recognised -- must be from God Himself. Unless He send them forth as heralds and ambassadors, they are certainly 'unauthorised,' and they may well tremble at the responsibilities they have dared to assume...all they who love the Master, and are willing to devote themselves to His work, need not fear. He will own and bless their work, under whatever name they enrol themselves as His true captains." (454)

Worboise, through Agatha, is combatting a heresy, but this heresy is, in particular, one that would deny women positions of authority. By arguing against the need for continuity with tradition represented by Apostolic succession, by refusing this patriarchal authority in favor of God's immediate authority, by denying the power of the past and asserting the power of the present, Worboise, through Agatha, frees women to assume positions of power. Her careful manipulation of pronouns supports her scarcely-hidden agenda: while Rosamund refers to her hypothetical preacher using a masculine pronoun ("take upon himself"), Agatha uses "persons" where she might have used "men" and keeps her pronouns deliberately in the plural, where gender is unspecified. Women are implicitly included in the ministry and in other positions of authority. Note that would-be preachers are not to be examined by the University, by those who have mastered some abstract body of knowledge, but "by those whose age and experience give them weight in the churches." Experience is the knowledge of narrative: it is the knowledge of narrative that here justifies the exercise of authority in woman or man. Gone are all the restrictions that exclude women from public, religious authority: the religious and the feminist polemics have succeeded together.

But this hard-won authority is not necessarily confined to theological topics. When women wrest from masculine control the theologies by which men claim to justify their power, the act has consequences beyond the narrowly religious realm; during the Victorian period in particular, biblical interpretation and theological doctrine could influence and justify many different forms of public and private behavior. Moreover, while female self-assertion, based on claims of spiritual equality or superiority, may begin in the religious realm, it does not always remain there: both Roberta Roberts and Kate Chennery move from religious independence to a personal independence more broadly conceived. These women gain not merely religious authority, but a strong sense of self-determination and societal power.

Nevertheless, Agatha has come to her freeing revelation of women's authority too late. She dies at Rouen, surrounded by her "unperverted" children, the victim of her husband's Roman Catholicism and her own silence. The novel ends seven years later, when Eustace, now rescued from the Catholic Church as a result of a letter written by his late wife, recognizes Agatha's fundamental rightness and righteousness.[11] Worboise closes her "sermon" with a vision of unity, and a traditional benediction:

> In all three churches the Word of truth is preached in simplicity and power; all unite as brethren and Christians, and great is the blessedness and peace of Overdale, now that the dark tempestuous clouds of error have rolled away, and the Sun of righteousness shines upon its people, even as the earthly sun shines upon its woods, and its breezy downs, and upon its glittering sea!
>
> May God grant us all "the knowledge of His Truth, and in the world to come the life everlasting. Amen!" (463-4)

These final paragraphs seem to return to religious ideas and rhetoric that the novel attempts to combat, but the context of the narrative has worked a change on the traditional words and phrases. The "Word of truth" sounds like the monolithic ecclesiastical authority that the female parishioners rejected, but this Word is preached not by the Church but by three churches of different denominations. The truth for a Christian author is, perhaps inevitably, one Word, but its incarnations here on earth are multiple: the multiple voices of the novel, each expressing a different facet or style of Truth, are reflected in the three different churches of Overdale, each preaching in its own manner some part of the Truth. The three churches can be identified with the three natural features -- woods, downs and sea -- on which the "earthly sun" shines, celebrated for their differences, without any question of unique authority. The phrase "brethren and Christians" similarly seems to recant the novel's assertion of women's religious significance by excluding them from fellowship, but Roberta Roberts and Kate Chennery and the rebellious women of the parish have made the term inclusive -- unless, that is, one wanted to argue that by the end of the novel, the word "Christian" tended to exclude men. The narrative context changes and redeems traditional Christian language.

Between invocation and benediction, Worboise's congregation heard a message of women's intellectual independence, their right and their ability to make their own decisions concerning religion and personal behavior, in the teeth of patriarchal opposition, whether it come from the clergy or from a husband. Overdale has been saved by the efforts of strong-minded women who refused to submit to external authorities; Eustace has been saved by his wife's devotion to truth; and the principle of female assertion in matters theological and religious has been vindicated, both by the plot, and by the sheer existence of the "woman's sermon."

NOTES

1. The term "concatenation of passages" was coined by G. Campbell Morgan. I use it to describe any long list of Biblical passages or allusions that together make some point or establish the pedigree of an idea. I take the following example from Alexander McCaul's sermon "Advice and Consolation":

> If we go forth to seek a supply for the necessities of nature, we are not safe: Abraham was tempted to deceit, when he went down into Egypt to escape the famine. If we retire to the loneliness of our chamber, we are not secure, for in such retirement David was led into the sin of adultery. Even the solitude of the wilderness can afford no protection; for there Satan tempted our Lord. (341)

2. Of course, since sermons are both oral and written, spoken and then printed, and Victorian novels were liable to be read aloud, the distinction is not sharp, but it is nevertheless important.

3. In *The Reader's Repentance*, Christine Krueger shows how fruitful regarding religious novels as women's sermons can be, but she focusses on sermons which call for individual and societal reform, thus limiting her homiletic model to only one kind

of (largely Evangelical) sermonizing and excluding many other kinds of "women's sermons."

4. Charlotte M. Yonge's *The Daisy Chain* also responds to Bronte's novel.

5. For more on the doctrinal advantages of evangelicalism for women, Christine Krueger, *The Reader's Repentance* (*passim*).

6. Valentine Cunningham similarly identifies class prejudice as a significant factor in the treatment of Dissenters at the hands of novelists and critics alike: "The novelists' imperception is often undergirded by common snobbery toward Dissent" (*Everywhere Spoken Against* 13).

7. Despite her High-Church views, Charlotte M. Yonge in *The Heir of Redclyffe* also portrays a heroine, Laura, who cedes her "heart and soul" -- and her moral sense -- to her beloved Philip, and suffers when he leads her into deception. Philip does not represent clerical authority, only traditional masculine authority, but Yonge and Worboise make similar points about the need for women to judge for themselves in matters of morality and theology.

8. Although feminist criticism generally focusses on the secular or sexual aspect of the New Woman, she also had her theological side. In *Red Pottage* Mary Cholmondeley unfavorably describes typical guests at Sybell Loftus's dinner parties: "the 'new woman' with stupendous lopsided opinions on difficult Old Testament subjects; the 'lady authoress' with a mission to show up the vices of a society which she knew only by hearsay" (20). The New Woman is here defined by her theology.

9. Of course, even as both women express their independence from traditional doctrines and allegiances within the novel, both remain dependent in that they serve Worboise's larger ideological aims. Still, the voices of the sensible, middle-aged Roberta Roberts and the headstrong, young Kate Chennery sing in harmony, but hardly in unison; while both voices express some of Worboise's own ideas, they remain interestingly different, even slightly dissonant. Neither is merely an authorial ideal: like Miss Grierson, both enjoy general authorial approval tinged with authorial distance and irony.

10. In other "women's sermons," the empowering aspects of Roman Catholic and Anglo-Catholic sisterhoods are emphasized: the escape from middle-class marriage and domesticity, the solidarity of a community of women. Here, however, the emphasis is placed upon vows of obedience taken, obedience ultimately to a male-dominated Church hierarchy. See Colleen Hobbs, "'Vestal Priestesses': The Devout Woman, Anglican Sisterhoods, and the Politics of Female Spirituality," *The Library Chronicle of the University of Texas at Austin* 23.1: 11-31.

11. The power of deceased women's private religious writing is a recurring theme in women's (public) religious novels. In Charlotte M. Yonge's *The Daisy Chain*, Mrs. May's last letter becomes a sacred moral guide for her family; in *The Heir of Redclyffe*, a journal takes on this quasi-Biblical status.

WORKS CITED

Bronte, Charlotte. *Jane Eyre*. 1847. New York: New American Library, 1960.

Cholmondeley, Mary. *Red Pottage*. 1899. London: Virago, 1985.

Christian World Magazine. Ed. Emma Jane Worboise (Guyton). 1866-1887.

Cunningham, Valentine. *Everywhere Spoken Against: Dissent in the Victorian Novel*. Oxford: Oxford University Press, 1975.

"Emma Jane Worboise." Obituary. *Literary World* 2 Sept. 1887: 209-10.

Farningham, Marianne. *A Working Woman's Life: An Autobiography*. London: James Clarke, 1907.

Gilligan, Carol. *In A Different Voice: Psychological Theory and Women's Development*. Cambridge, Mass.: Harvard University Press, 1982.

Harris, Elizabeth. *From Oxford to Rome, and How it Fared with Some Who Lately Made the Journey*. 1847. New York: Garland, 1975.

Hobbs, Colleen. "'Vestal Priestesses': The Devout Woman, Anglican Sisterhoods, and the Politics of Female Spirituality." *The Library Chronicle of the University of Texas at Austin* 23.1:11-31.

Howard, Anne. *Mary Spencer*. 1844. New York: Garland, 1975.

Jay, Elisabeth. *The Religion of the Heart: Anglican Evangelicalism and the Nineteenth Century*. Oxford: Oxford University Press, 1979.

Krueger, Christine L. *The Reader's Repentance: Women Preachers, Women Writers, and Nineteenth-Century Social Discourse*. Chicago: University of Chicago Press, 1992.

Long, Catherine. *Sir Roland Ashton*. 1844. New York: Garland, 1975.

Maison, Margaret M. *The Victorian Vision: Studies in the Religious Novel*. New York: Sheed & Ward, 1961.

McCaul, Alexander. "Advice and Consolation." *Plain Sermons on Subjects Practical and Prophetic*. London: Wertheim, 1840. 337-54.

Newman, John Henry. *Loss and Gain*. 1848. Ed. Alan G. Hill. Oxford: Oxford University Press, 1986.

Oliphant, Margaret. *The Perpetual Curate*. 1864. London: Virago, 1987.

Ruskin, John. "Of Queens' Gardens." *Sesame and Lilies*. 1865. Philadephia: Henry Altemus, 1899.

Sewell, Elizabeth. *Amy Herbert*. London: Longmans, 1844.

Skene, Felicia. *Hidden Depths*. 1866. New York: Garland, 1975.

Trollope, Frances. *Father Eustace*. London, 1847.

Worboise, Emma Jane (Guyton). *Alice Cunningham*. London, 1846.

---. *Amy Wilton*. Bath: Binns & Goodwin, 1852.

---. *Heart's-ease in the Family*. London: James Clarke, 1874.

---. *Overdale, or The Story of a Pervert*. London: James Clarke, 1869.

---. *Thornycroft Hall: Its Owners and Its Heirs*. London: James Clarke, 1866.

---. "A Word To Our Readers." *The Christian World* 9 Apr. 1857:4.

Yonge, Charlotte M. *The Daisy Chain, or Aspirations. A Family Chronicle*. 1856. 2 Vols. New York: D. Appleton, 1871.

---. *Heartsease: or, The Brother's Wife*. 1854. New York: Appleton, 1855.

---. *The Heir of Redclyffe*. 1853. London: J.M. Dent "Everyman Library", 1909.

Reverent and Reserved:
The Sacramental Theology of Charlotte M. Yonge

Virginia Bemis
Ashland University

Can one who would have disclaimed the title be considered a theologian? Charlotte Mary Yonge would never have called herself a theologian, nor would she have allowed anyone else to do so. She was, after all, a woman, and neither a priest nor a university professor, hence lacking in qualifications. Yet no one did more to communicate the ideals of the Tractarians in an instructive and entertaining manner, both in best-selling novels like *The Heir of Redclyffe* and in the *Monthly Packet*, which she edited and wrote for. If to communicate ideas about God, to engage in God-talk and to teach and explicate doctrine is to be a theologian, than Yonge can properly be given the title she would never have claimed for herself.

"A theology mediates between a cultural matrix and the significance and role of a religion in that matrix." This, says Bernard Lonergan in his great reflection, *Method in Theology*, is the basis of theological scholarship. Yonge's cultural matrix was the Victorian era, her religion the Church of England, her theology Tractarian. As a writer, she used the high church teachings of Keble, whose disciple she was, to mediate between an increasingly fragmented and unsure society and the role of the Church and its sacraments in producing personal and collective certainty, stability and peace.

There are several ways, which Lonergan denotes as functional specialties, by which such mediation may be accomplished. The first is *research*, assembling data thought to be relevant; *interpretation*, ascertaining their meaning; *history*, finding incarnate meaning; *dialectic*, investigating the conflicting conclusions of the previous specialties; *foundations*, locating and measuring the horizon effected by a conversion; *doctrines*, which uses foundations as a guide in selecting from the alternatives presented by dialectic; and *systematics*, which seeks an ultimate clarification of the meaning of doctrine; followed by his eighth functional specialty, *communication* (355).

In her role as theologian, Yonge is engaging in the eighth of Lonergan's functional specialties. While following as loyally as Keble could have wished the doctrine of reserve, she is using both her fiction and her didactic work in the *Monthly Packet* as means of communicating religious knowledge and experience. The readers, as they share lives of the characters, develop or further a common knowledge and a body of common meaning, that which Lonergan names as a prerequisite for community (317). For Yonge, that community is the Church, its common meaning to be located in the Sacraments.

These then serve as the basis for society, a society that for Yonge replicates the ideal English home and ideal parish community. As Lonergan has said, a community may start in moral, religious or Christian principles. "The Christian principle conjoins the inner gift of God's love with its outer manifestation in Christ Jesus and in those that follow him" (360).

In her novels, and most of all in articles (later collected in book form) for the *Monthly Packet*, Yonge set forth and developed the views she had inherited from her mentor, John Keble, on the sacraments, on grace, on baptismal regeneration, and developed the beginnings of a Christology. These she presented to a wide range of readers, who might never have attempted reading a theological treatise.

In the world of Yonge's novels, religion was the central fact of life and the Church was the key social structure. Tractarianism as interpreted by Keble was the philosophical basis for every part of life, and Yonge remained faithful to that creed throughout her writing career.

Yonge had a partly didactic purpose in writing, and acknowledged her wish to share with her readers the benefits of Mr. Keble's spiritual insights. However, she managed to spare those readers the large sections of undiluted preaching common in the religious novel of the 1850's and 1860's. She felt that it was improper for a lady to devote much time to strictly theological discussion. It was also, in her view, uninteresting to the reader, who needed something more subtle in order to accept and profit by instruction. Her favored mode of teaching was the parable rather than the sermon. Through a story, one could see how doctrine was lived out, in a way that would allow readers to apply such lessons to their own lives. Far better than a discussion of substitutionary atonement is to look at the edifying life and death of a Guy Morville or Felix Underwood, whose death teaches the survivors about repentance and forgiveness. Rather than an explicit talk about baptismal regeneration, show a person, such as Fernan Travis, whose life is transformed by baptism.

Yonge describes the daily lives of families in the middle, professional and upper classes, in an atmosphere of comfortable Tractarian piety. She breaks from the mainstream of the domestic novel in showing the Church of England as an active and vital force in the lives of her characters. The moral questions, worldly triumphs, sufferings, deathbeds and happy endings that form the stock scenes in so many novels of the period are not part of an atmosphere of vague general goodness. In Yonge's hands, they become part of a living Anglican framework. The Church provides her characters with the strength they need to face their trials, and the humility needed in success.

The Church is the principal consistent factor in Yonge's work, and the Church, as shown through the lives of its members, is her constant subject. Rather than preach its doctrines directly, she prefers to illustrate them in life. She considers it more effective not to engage in direct debate on the merits of confirmation, the Holy Communion, auricular confession or Baptismal Regeneration. She prefers to illustrate such a principle in operation, and show its benefit to a character in whom the reader has taken an interest. The reader who sees the comfort or joy given to a character through participation in the sacraments of the Church of England is likely to be moved, even if not convinced.

Yonge's work is narrowed by her refusal to question the doctrines she had learned as a child. She enjoys the confidence that comes from knowing what is right, and doing what follows from that knowledge.

A contemporary review of Yonge's *Musings Over the Christian Year* shows clearly one source from which she gained this tendency. In discussing Keble's few "defects of character," the author remarks on Keble's own narrowing:

> He scarcely ever ventured on exercising his own character and judgment on doctrines or on disputed ecclesiastical questions. It was his bliss to receive and to rest in what he had received. He felt that his safety lay in the shadow of reverent example...No caution was more frequently given to young people by him than that against arguing on doctrines or Church matters. When some one was inclined to question the ground of something connected with the Church of England, he pointed to his sister, and asked whether anything could be substantially wanting to a Church which had nourished a saintly life like hers, that had been all untroubled by hint of dissatisfaction. He turned hastily away from whatever even seemed to cast an irreverent glance at what he held sacred. (*Sunday Magazine*)

Following this example, Yonge's preferred mode is to create a character to whom she can point as Keble did to his sister, and for the same effect. Doubt and discussion are irreverent and dangerous and therefore to be avoided, particularly for the audience of "young maidens" to whom she addressed herself. Her novels provide a comforting refuge from doubt and rational inquiry for any reader feeling threatened or simply fatigued by too much exercise of the mind on such matters.

Her articles in the *Monthly Packet* are quite different, and are directed toward those who ought to work at understanding, particularly candidates for confirmation. Here, Yonge becomes a teacher/theologian, and shows that she had thought (though not "for herself", which would have been wrong) and based her opinion on scripture study, early Church Fathers and most especially the Book of Common Prayer.

One primary reason for this reticence in preaching was the doctrine of Reserve in Communicating Religious knowledge. This had been a key point of Keble's theological method, and one of the primary ways in which the Oxford Movement differentiated itself from other renewal movements then and later. Adherents of this doctrine refrained from excessive discussion and were careful to temper their discourses according to the relative level of sophistication of their hearers. This removed much from Yonge's potential subject matter, for many among her intended audience were children and young people. By contrast, it allowed her focus on the topics she chose and gaze at them with intensity, free from the demand to construct a systematic theology.

Reserve appealed strongly to a naturally reticent writer, and Yonge welcomed its series of admonitions to guard and conceal one's intellectual understanding of the Church. Making a parade of such things would be prideful, so she replaced that with description of the delight her characters took in missionary meetings and decorating the church building on holy days. Where a teacher's duty prompted, examination of doctrine and what amounts to a theological pattern, if not a system, could take a proper place.

Loyalty to the doctrine of Reserve created a largely indirect and implied theology, hinted at in parables rather than spoken in sermons. Much of Yonge's theology must be discerned from events and conversations in her novels, from the importance of confirmation in *The Castle Builders* or Guy's many personal struggles in *The Heir of Redclyffe* to Felix's deathbed teaching on the sacraments and Angela's reconversion in *The Pillars of the House*.

Yonge does find it entirely appropriate to speak of doctrines in a teaching setting, as one might when teaching Sunday School. Her years of experience doing so in Keble's parish at Hursley had taught her that it was often one's duty to lead catechumens toward fuller understanding, as long as this teaching was done under the supervision and direction of a priest. This in itself is a theological statement on the priesthood, an ecclesiology that endows priests with the sacramental representation of divine authority. In numbers of the *Monthly Packet* extending over years, Yonge discusses theology as teacher to pupil, especially in the "Conversations on the Catechism," but also in a series of articles on the Book of Common Prayer, and occasionally in the "Cameos from English History." Here she is performing one of Bernard Lonergan's functional specialties of theology, that of communication. This is the stage, in Lonergan's schema, where theological reflection bears fruit.

In Yonge's view, the relation of the individual to the Church should be that of child to parent. As each individual was a child of God, the Church, to which all were jointed in Baptism, was the family of God. Within the family the ordained priests and deacons fill the paternal role, interpreting scripture and guiding the behavior of the laity. The teachings of the Church as interpreted by the clergy were to be obeyed as implicitly as a child would obey his parents and with as little question. As the lawful, divinely established authority, the clergy were the primary guiding force against secularism, fragmentation, doubt and false doctrine. Only a priest, properly trained in theology and Church history, and drawing all his conclusions from Scripture and tradition, was qualified to act as final arbiter.

In her direct discussion of religion, Yonge tends to concentrate on the Sacraments as a supremely important part of Christian life. This emphasis on the Sacraments was particularly Tractarian, part of an attempt to restore their vitality in a society that neglected them. Most Anglicans had become used to thinking of Sacraments as rites of passage rather than as channels for divine grace. The Holy Communion, which Yonge stresses particularly, was all but ignored, and the Tractarians were thought of as dangerous ritualists for encouraging weekly celebrating and frequent reception where four times a year (the canonical minimum) had been thought sufficient.

Yonge pays particular attention, in both fiction and nonfiction, to Baptism and Confirmation, which latter admits one to full Christian privileges, including the Holy Communion. These were the only sacraments really common to all Anglicans and necessary, in Yonge's eyes, for renewing one's submission to God and obedience to the Church. She realized that only a few chosen men could receive Holy Orders, and that many people might not marry, but to her mind Baptism and Confirmation were absolutely imperative.

Baptism as admission into the church, and its concomitant theme of baptismal regeneration, feature prominently in *The Pillars of the House*. The baptism of the newborn twins, Stella and Theodore, by their dying father, a priest, highlights the necessity of baptism, as does the shock and horror felt by all when Fernan Travis, nearing his teens, is found never to have been baptized. His careful preparation for baptism and confirmation follows, doctrinally, the pattern of "Conversations on the Catechism."

A fuller examination of Yonge's sacramental theology in *Pillars* comes during the long decline and death of Felix Underwood. Angela, one of his twelve younger siblings, is finding the high-church ways she was raised in unsatisfying, uncomforting in her grief for Felix and little brother Theodore, killed in an accident she caused. In her mingled guilt and grief, she abandons what she saw as formalism for the low-church ways of some pious neighbors.

Felix understands that "excitability can pass for devotion" (411), and that Angela has been exposed to excessive party spirit. "She thinks because the Cross has been decked with flowers it has been no cross at all" (412). Yonge's Christology, while usually focused on Christ the Redeemer, here reminds the reader that the Suffering Servant is also present.

What Angela needs most is a sense of repentance, and of individual spiritual contact, a "personal relationship with Christ," though Yonge would never use such terminology. This is properly to be received through the sacraments. "Individual pardon through faith" (501) is the center of it all, but the sacraments are what nourish and grow that faith, far more than forms. Felix tells Angela "I can no more doubt of the grace, comfort, and strength imparted through them than I do of the refreshment of food or of air" (462).

The sacraments are as necessary to Christian existence as food or air, in Yonge's cosmos. They function also as "lamps of faith" (*Pillars* 461) to guide the believer through the world. In the *Monthly Packet* series, "Preparation of Prayer Book Lessons," which ran from 1884-1887, Yonge took the various parts of the Book of Common Prayer, examining them in a way suitable for those preparing to teach Sunday school classes, especially for young people preparing for Confirmation. While many of the lessons deal with liturgy, scripture and prayer, the overall thrust of those that do focus on sacraments and underlying doctrine is remarkably consistent.

To a Yonge character, Baptism is the most important event in life. It is absolutely necessary for salvation and must be administered as soon as possible after birth. People like Guy Morville, hero of *The Heir of Redclyffe* and Yonge's pattern of fictional holiness, speak of Baptism as the greatest gift they ever received. In like terms in the "Prayer Book Lessons" series, Yonge herself speaks of Baptism and Communion are the essentials, the "great bond of the Universal Church" (Jan.1884:49). Baptismal Regeneration is an absolute truth, and every baptism bears witness to the Resurrection of the Dead, or else it is a mere vain ceremony" (Oct.1887:351).

Confirmation assumes nearly equal theological importance, particularly as it admits one to communion, though less absolute necessity. As being voluntary, it was far more useful to an author. Yonge could safely assume that her readers' experience of confirmation would be varied. Many of them were still preparing for confirmation, which customarily took pace in the mid-teens; assuming the same importance that "coming out" did in more worldly families. Still other readers had only recently been confirmed. The devout remembered their Confirmation with as much joy and awe as Yonge herself, and for her it had been the high-point of her conscious life. Even the parents in her audience could be expected to read with an eye towards guiding their children. They, and those children, were particularly influenced by the *Packet* series of "Conversations on the Catechism."

All of these groups could be expected to take an intense interest in stories of solemn preparation for confirmation, and an equal interest in theologically sound materials. The doubts, strivings, fears and triumphs attending the process would be their own. The questions answered by Yonge as teacher would be those they needed answers for. They would sympathize with the many plots Yonge evolved in which the confirmation of one or more characters is an important element.

In Yonge's interpretation, the person confirmed gains strength against the temptations of the world through taking on voluntarily the submission made at Baptism. As well, there is the direct contact with God made possible through Communion. Unless undertaken with false scruples or failures in absolute obedience, the commitment changes life. Selfishness and careless living grow directly from refusing to be confirmed or from neglecting the duties that come with the status of confirmand. Arthur Martindale's bad character, dissipated life and failure as husband and father all stem directly from such an attitude.

> It had been grace missed and neglected, rather than wilfully abused...his confirmation had taken place as a matter of form, and he had never been a communicant; withheld at once by ignorance and dread of strictness, as well as by a species of awe. Even his better and more conscientious feelings had been aroused merely by his affections instead of the higher sense of duty; and now it was through these that the true voice had at length reached him. (*Heartsease* 433)

Only through proper obedience and regular attention to the sacraments can Arthur become a reformed soul and obtain the help he needs. Grace now operating through the sacraments nourishes Arthur's struggling conscience.

Confirmation is the center of *The Castle Builders*, in which two sisters defer their confirmation, first through feelings of unworthiness, later through more worldly motives. Unconfirmed, they cannot receive Communion, and so are separated from God. This causes them to sink into self-will, disrespect to their elders, flouting of clerical authority and mixing with Dissenters. Nothing in their lives goes right while they remain unconfirmed.

> ...though they acknowledged the duty of attending to Church ordinances, these were to them duties in themselves, which stood

alone, unconnected with practical life, and without influence over it. So as confirmation was to come but once in their lives, why not at one time as well as another? And the thought of the Holy Communion made them still more inclined to defer it, since they would be afraid to stay away and yet dreaded to go without due preparation. They did not feel in their hearts, though in some degree they knew with their understandings, that prayers, Church services, confirmation, Communion, were all steps to lead them on in the track of daily life, the waymarks set about their faith; nay, further, the wings which might bear onwards their steps." (*Castle Builders* 49)

This feeling in the heart, this process of development of Christian life through the sacraments indeed is Lonergan's development of community through common meaning. "The genesis of common meaning is an ongoing process of communication, of people coming to share the same cognitive, constitutive and effective meanings" (357).

In greater detail, Yonge covers this process in the "Preparation of Prayer-Book Lessons" series. Through 1884-1887, she examines each segment of the Book of Common Prayer, discussing explicitly doctrines she discusses with more reserve in her fiction. Baptismal Regeneration, the Real Presence of Christ in the Eucharist, the Substitutionary Atonement, all find a place, each in its turn, as each service, each sacrament, follows in order. Included as well we find her rejection of Predestination, disavowing of the necessity of a conversion experience or the requirement that a person found a Christian life on the realization of a sense of sin.

The sacraments are "the great bond of the Universal Church" ("Prayer Book Lessons", *Monthly Packet*, Jan. 1884). Baptism "bears witness to the Resurrection of the Dead, or else it is a mere vain ceremony" (July 1887). Christ is our Advocate, Elder Brother and Redeemer (Oct. 1887).

The Eucharist, the central sacramental act in the life of the Church, is indeed marked by the presence of Christ. "How we cannot tell, but by eating of the Bread and drinking of the Wine, we are made to partake of the Body and Blood which were offered for us....Christ's Body and Blood spiritually, and therefore really and absolutely present, so that we actually partake of them" (March 1886). Here we find Atonement, the Real Presence, and the sustaining power of the sacrament for the recipients, all together in one place.

For Yonge, the sacraments are not symbols, but real and absolute means of grace, always to be shared, always to be experienced, always to be continued. It is in her feeling for the sacraments that we find the center of her theology, and it is this she is working to communicate in fiction, reproducing daily life as it should be experienced, by Christians who struggle and yet persevere, who weep and yet hope.

In her sacrament-focused theological system, dogma is a presence, but she would not agree with Dorothy L. Sayers that the dogma is the drama. The worship, the life of prayer, the experience of the sacraments and their assistance in the growth of conscience and faith, these make a living religion, an active faith that can be lived. The sacraments, instituted by Christ and taught by the Church, make of the Church a living being, not a re-enactment of the Incarnation, but a community that does in very truth incarnate Christ on earth. It has sometimes been said that the Church of England is the Church of Christmas because of its emphasis on the Incarnation as the center of its teaching. While Yonge would not say so directly, following, as always, the doctrine of reserve, she illustrates the centrality of the Incarnation through her sacramental emphasis, and through the lives of her characters.

Yonge was convinced that women ought not to preach, yet sure that they might tell stories and, properly supervised, might teach. No feminist theologian, she nonetheless develops a hermeneutic of experience that, paradoxically, uses women's experience as often as men's. The use of experience is not, as Rosemary Radford Ruether reminds us, unique to feminist theology, though the use of women's experience is such a criterion. In using women's experience, Yonge is not opening up classical theology to critical view. She is instead affirming it, through her presentation of women's experience as typified by her own, of the faithful and silent disciple, subduing her will to that of the properly trained and divinely ordained male leaders. Yet she is perhaps the most successful at showing the world what the Tractarians taught, in a way that can be both understood and felt. The *Tracts for the Times* and Keble's sermons were breakthroughs, relevatory experiences of an unusual order. But "relevatory experiences become socially meaningful only when translated into communal consciousness" (Ruether 13).

Without such translation there is no theology in its full sense. Ruether's concept of translation and Lonergan's specialty of communication meet, and are in fact the same. Here is Yonge's place in the theological continuum; her calling is to act as a communicator, a maker of community. Those who do theology, in whatever specialty, are theologians, whether or not they would claim the title for themselves. It is interesting to look at Yonge through the lens of feminist theology, or simply with the knowledge that feminist theology is part of the continuum. But space prevents a detailed analysis of the tension between her use of women's experience and her belief in women's subordinate status.

Reserve hedged in Yonge's theology as it did her novel-writing. Still, something speaks to the contemporary reader, as Yonge gives us both a window into the Victorian domestic world and into the theology that informed and energized her sector of it. While she would never call herself a theologian, she acts as one, and hence is one. Without her contribution, the Catholic wing of Anglicanism, and indeed Anglicanism as a whole, would not be what they are today.

WORKS CITED

Lonergan, Bernard. *Method in Theology.* New York: Seabury Press, 1979.

Ruether, Rosemary Radford. *Sexism and God-Talk: Toward a Feminist Theology.* Boston: Beacon Press, 1983.

Sayers, Dorothy L. "The Dogma is the Drama." *Strong Meat.* London: Hodder and Stoughton, 1939. Rpt. in *Creed or Chaos?* London: Methuen, 1947. 14-24.

Yonge, Charlotte M. *The Castle Builders, or the Deferred Confirmation.* London: J. and C. Mozley, 1854. (*Monthly Packet* Apr.1851-May 1853).

---. *Conversations on the Catechism.* (*MP* 1851-1857).

---. *Hearts-ease, or the Brother's Wife.* London: Macmillan, 1864.

---. *The Heir of Redclyffe.* 1853.

---. *Musings Over the Christian Year and Lyra Innocentium.* (*MP* Nov.1868-Nov.1870).

---. *Preparation of Prayer Book Lessons.* (*MP* Jan.1884-Oct.1888).

---. *The Pillars of the House, or Under Wode, Under Rode.* London: Macmillan, 1873. (*MP* Jan.1870-Dec.1873).

The Moral Irrelevance of Dogma:
Mary Ward and Critical Theology in England

Mark M. Freed
Central Michigan University

I

German biblical scholarship and its influence in England have for a very long time been foundational for understanding Victorian culture. Benjamin Jowett and Matthew Arnold are perhaps the most famous English voices of German biblical criticism in the period. George Eliot's translations of Strauss's *Leben Jesu* and Feuerbach's *Wesen des Christenthums* are two of a very few commonly cited examples of a woman's participation in the predominately masculine arena of Victorian Anglican theology. There is a strong case to be made, however, that the single most culturally resonating advocacy of German critical theology in England was made by a woman hardly read at all today.

Mary Augusta Ward's *Robert Elsmere* was one of the very best-selling novels of the nineteenth-century. It was published February 1888 and by the first week in June 3,500 copies of the triple-decker edition had been sold to lending libraries. It is estimated that by November 100,000 copies had sold in America alone; that by March 1889 between 30,000 and 40,000 copies of various editions had been sold in Britain, with sales continuing at the rate of 700 copies a week. In 1909, eleven years after its publication, Ward estimated that nearly one million copies of *Robert Elsmere* had been circulated in English-speaking countries.[1] This kind of success can only be taken as an indication that Ward's novel touched a tender Victorian nerve.

Robert Elsmere deals with the fairly common Victorian crisis of faith occasioned by the failing belief in the historical veracity of the Bible. The novel's supreme celebrity attests not only to the ubiquity of that problem but also to the dexterity of Ward's treatment of it. The importance of *Robert Elsmere* in Victorian religious culture goes beyond the mere popularity of a late-century summing up of the liberal argument against the Oxford Movement. Ward's novel elicited remarkable response from a range of reviewers. One count lists fifty reviews in the first two years alone, including one from then ex-Prime Minister William Gladstone.[2] It is clear that Gladstone received the novel as theology, judging that it would make a deep impression "not, however, among mere novel-readers, but among those who share, in whatever sense, the deeper thought of the period" (Gladstone 767). Although notable reviews by Walter Pater, Henry James, and Mark Twain[3] treated the novel as literary art, Gladstone's theological reception was the norm (Peterson 161).

Randall T. Davidson, then Dean of Windsor, acknowledges that Ward had set forth "a new faith, of necessarily tremendous import, in a popular and attractive form," but, he adds, "when the argument is couched, as here, in the form of a romance, it is possible to skip each inconvenient stage and lead the unwary reader to suppose he has had the full case fairly argued out before him" (681-682). Another reviewer, Henry Wace, also recognizes that Ward had "invested with the attraction of a personal tragedy some of the most characteristic questions of the critical and theological debate of the past generation" (274). Nevertheless, the self-stated goal of his very long piece for *The Quarterly Review* is to supply "some slight representation of the arguments on the other side" (276). These reviews are remarkable (though not unique) for the fact that one does not usually feel the need to rebut a novel.

That most reviewers did feel such a need in the case of *Robert Elsmere* can be taken as an indication of their fear of the novel's religious consequences. R. H. Hutton's anxiety about *Robert Elsmere*'s probable cultural effect is typical: "we do not agree with Mrs. Ward that there is any likelihood of such a faith as Elsmere's holding its ground against the scientific agnosticism of the age" (480). Hutton's slippery slope implication is that when Elsmere's new brand of faith eventually fails (and it will), Christianity fails altogether, so it is better not to go along with Elsmere at all. William Peterson has duly noted the "professed great alarm" in the *London Quarterly Review*'s statement that "there is a latent skepticism in many a young mind which this book will call to the surface and confirm" (Peterson 172).

In addition to a theological reception in the periodicals, there were at least twenty sermons delivered specifically on *Robert Elsmere* between 1888 and 1890. Far beyond treating it simply as dangerous popular literature, what these sermons register is a full theological reception of the novel. What *Robert Elsmere* had so forcefully to say to Victorian religious sensibilities made it all the way into the pulpits, if only to be denounced there. Through her novel, Mary Ward became a high-profile player in Anglican theological debate.

What positioned *Robert Elsmere* (and Ward) so centrally was its combination of imaginative literature, German theology, and the subject position of its author. Reading Ward back into public Anglican theological debate adds to our understanding of the ways in which marginalized women's voices managed to speak from high religious places. Beyond this, it expands our sense of how imaginative literature participated in the theological and ethical reconstruction of post-Anglican moral understanding in Victorian England.

II

While other Protestant sects offered women opportunities to participate fully in essential Church business, those opportunities were severely restricted in the highly patriarchal Church of England where women were denied the pulpit as well as formal, advanced university training. Even so, Mary Ward was uniquely positioned in the landscape of Victorian religious controversy to make important contributions to the popular reception of theological argument. For one thing her family was involved at the highest levels of public religious and theological debate for several generations. Ward's grandfather, Dr. Thomas Arnold, stood as the primary antagonist to Newman, Pusey, and the other Tractarians throughout the notorious Oxford Movement. Ward's even more famous uncle, Matthew Arnold, was equally public in his religious opinions. Arnold's *Literature and Dogma* and *God and the Bible* are perhaps the most famous English treatments of German critical theology in England.

Theological and religious debate penetrated so deeply into the Arnold-Ward family that it occasionally defined family composition and determined family well-being. Ward's father, Thomas Arnold the younger, vacillated several times between Anglicanism and Catholicism. William Peterson reports that upon hearing of her husband's conversion, Julia Ward, Mary's mother, "threatened to leave him,...begged him not to take the fateful step...and on the day in January 1856 when he was finally received into the Catholic Church in Hobart Town [New Zealand], she hurled a brick through the church window" (37). After teaching for a couple of years at Newman's Catholic University in Dublin and at his Oratory school in Edgbaston, in 1865 Thomas reverted to Anglicanism and moved to Oxford to take up private tutoring. Then, in 1876, on the eve of his probable election to the Chair of Anglo-Saxon at Oxford, he once again announced his conversion to Catholicism. This time when Tom retreated to London, Julia and Mary remained in Oxford where they continued to experience money problems until *Robert Elsmere* became a financial success.

As an Arnold, Ward was highly accustomed to regard public theological debate as a matter of private family business. A long tradition of interweaving the two was not the only thing Ward had going for her. For those who seek it, power can frequently be found on the margins of an institution. Armed with the example of her famous relatives, and as a woman on the perimeter of Oxford society, Mary Ward was able to find and develop that power. She was, for example, able to benefit from

Oxford's most famous scholars in ways their own students could not. As a woman Ward was prevented from matriculating. Paradoxically, however, she was therefore not subject to the constraints of Oxford's theological establishment -- an advantage Ward herself was aware of:

> But I should like to ask you what possibility is there in this country of a scientific, that is to say an unprejudiced, an unbiassed study of theology, under present conditions? All our theological faculties are subordinate to the Church; the professors are clergymen, the examiners in the theological schools must be in priest's orders. ("The New Reformation" 467)

Mark Pattison, Oxford's most famous "pure" scholar of the period was also aware of the hopeless conservatism of Oxford as a theological institution. He, too, saw that Oxford had become a bastion of the Anglican Church rather than a place for scholarship that recognized developments outside England. Ward recalls in her memoir that Pattison regretted along with Dean Arthur Stanley that "the whole course of English religious history might have been different if Newman had known German" (1: 143). Pattison's challenges to Oxford's theological ethos facilitated Ward's pursuit of equally independent lines of thought.

Ward was a close personal friend of Pattison, and he strongly encouraged her to pursue her own historical scholarship on Spanish history: "Get to the bottom of something," "choose a subject and know *everything* about it!" he advised her (Pattison quoted in Trevelyan 21). If from Pattison Ward learned the discipline of historical scholarship, then it was very likely from another famous don, T. H. Green, that she learned the cultural potential of applying historical scholarship to theology.

Ward was also a close friend T. H. Green and his wife, Charlotte. It was to their parlor that she immediately went for consolation and advice upon hearing that her father had for a second time converted to Catholicism (Trevelyan 27). Green was Whyte's Professor of Moral Philosophy at Oxford from 1878 until his death in 1882. By the last quarter of the nineteenth century, Green's name was firmly associated with the foundation of a British school of German idealism. His German example provided both the spiritual and intellectual model for much of Ward's own theological articulations.

Robert Elsmere is dedicated to T. H. Green, and, in addition to containing a thinly disguised portrait of him, makes use of quotations from his lay sermons.[4,5] Clearly, what Ward found most compelling in Green's German example were the cultural implications he drew from the historical hermeneutics of critical theology. Ward's daughter and biographer, Janet Trevelyan, reports that Ward was most interested in the question of "*historical testimony*" on which the fabric of Christianity rested (Trevelyan 32). Historical criticism of the Bible led to different conclusions in the hands of German scholars than it did for most English receivers of German ideas. The most important things Ward had to contribute to Anglican theological debate are grounded in just this difference.

III

In an essay on the relationship between nineteenth-century biblical criticism and Victorian fiction, Stephen Prickett leads us to Hans Frei's observation of the difference between English and German biblical scholarship:

> In [eighteenth-century] England, where a serious body of realistic narrative literature and a certain amount of criticism of the literature was building up, there arose no corresponding cumulative tradition of criticism of the biblical writings, and that included no narrative interpretation of them. In Germany, on the other hand, where a body of critical analysis as well as general hermeneutics of the biblical writings built up rapidly in the latter half of the eighteenth century, there was no simultaneous development of realistic prose narrative and its critical appraisal. (Frei quoted in Prickett 1)

According to Frei, the relative lack of narrative prose criticism in Germany created a tendency to recognize the narrative realism in the Bible as a species of history, not literature. Conversely, the relative underdevelopment of an historical hermeneutical tradition in eighteenth-century England led to the nineteenth-century treatment of biblical narrative in more metaphorical than historical terms.[6]

Frei's observation is corroborated in one very important Victorian instance by Matthew Arnold's *Literature and Dogma* (1873). Arnold's effort there is to redirect attention away from the (faulty) historical nature of biblical miracles to the emotional experiences they are supposed to represent. In short, Arnold urges replacing the historical understanding of the New Testament with a metaphorical one. With this shift in perspective Arnold hoped to *preserve* the Bible as a locus of moral and cultural authority. In this way, his biblical criticism is essentially conservative: an attempt to provide new reasons for retaining old Christian beliefs and habits. In a way analogous to his famous touchstones, Arnold viewed the Bible stories *themselves* as the final remaining anchors of Christian spiritual value in England.

As much as she relished being an Arnold and revered her famous uncle, Mary Ward did not follow his example. Ward's treatment of biblical narrative in *Robert Elsmere* and the implications of that treatment are fundamentally different from his. It is for one thing German and historical as opposed to English and literary. Glossing Frei's observation, Prickett agrees that it is not difficult to see how German historical critics "judged the prose narratives of the Bible by their own standards of history and found them of such dubious value" (Prickett 7). The implications of this "dubious value" is what separates Ward from Arnold's strong attachment to the stories themselves. In her hands, critical theology leads not to a reassertion of Biblical authority but to a radical abandonment of Anglican orthodoxy. The combination of imaginative literature and theology in *Robert Elsmere* domesticated German critical theology in England in a way strictly theological argument could not easily have done.

The great crisis of *Robert Elsmere* is the title character's loss of orthodox faith. Robert takes holy orders at Oxford and accepts a clerical living in Surrey where, through contact with a local landowner and scholar, Squire Wendover, he begins to question the historical veracity of New Testament miracles.

Wendover's thirty years of inquiry into the nature of testimony have convinced him that testimony has "developed" in the sense that "man's power of apprehending and recording what he sees and hears has grown from less to more, from weaker to stronger, like any other of his faculties" (317). His sense of the developmental character of testimony is coupled with an urgent advocacy of "what is meant in history and literature by 'the critical method,' which in history may be defined as the 'science of what is credible,' and in literature as 'the science of what is rational'" (317).

Robert finds the logic of Wendover's "scientific" approach so compelling that it dramatically changes his conception of Christ and Christianity:

> In the stillness of the night there rose up weirdly before him a whole new mental picture -- effacing, pushing out, innumerable older images of thought. It was the image of a purely human Christ -- a purely human, explicable, yet always wonderful Christianity. It broke his heart, but the spell of it was like some dream-country wherein we see all the familiar objects of life in new relations and perspectives. (321)

Wendover's introduction of a *scientific* point of view brought about an *imaginative* change in Robert's conception of Christ. This, in turn, precipitates what Robert describes as a "failure of *feeling*" for the habits of Anglican worship (341).

The final break with Anglican orthodoxy comes when Robert begins to consider the implications of critical scholarship *a propos* of St. Paul's witness to the Resurrection.

Between the Paul of Anglican theology and the fiery fallible man of genius -- so weak logically, so strong in poetry, in rhetoric, in moral passion, whose portrait has been drawn for us by a free and temperate criticism -- [Robert] knew, in a sort of dull way, that his choice was made. The one picture carried reason and imagination with it; the other contented neither. (330-331)

Robert arrives at the conclusion that "miracles do not happen" (342) through a modified understanding of Christian documents characterized by the combined faculties of science and imagination. Science (reason in the form of historical scholarship) establishes new perspectives toward sacred texts, which, in turn, precipitate a reconception -- a reimagination -- of Jesus and other central biblical figures.

The heterodoxy to which critical theology led Ward is represented in *Robert Elsmere* by the protagonist's resignation of his clerical living in order to take up social work in London's East End. In a speech to the Workmen's Institute Robert articulates his reformed religious position:

My friends...the man who is addressing you to-night believes in *God*; and in *Conscience*, which is God's witness in the soul; and in *Experience*, which is at once the record and the instrument of man's education at God's hands. He places his whole trust, for life and death, "*in God the Father Almighty*," -- in that force at the root of things which is revealed to us whenever a man helps his neighbor, or when a mother denies herself for her child; whenever a soldier dies without a murmur for his country, or a sailor puts in the darkness to rescue the perishing; whenever a workman throws mind and conscience into his work, or a statesman labours not for his own gain but for that of the State! He believes in an Eternal Goodness - - and an Eternal Mind -- of which Nature and Man are the continuous and only revelation.... (494)

Robert's "religious" beliefs are couched in the unmistakable language of philosophical idealism. He explains that he now believes in a depersonalized "Eternal Goodness -- an Eternal Mind -- of which Nature and Man are the continuous and only revelation." The translation of Christian stories into the language of idealism registers Ward's abandonment of Anglican orthodoxy -- including even the metaphorical or exemplary value of biblical stories themselves. Whatever spiritual and moral truths those stories once represented to past generations can now be found in the fabric of ordinary human interaction.

The theological thesis of one of the nineteenth-century's best-selling novels might well be "the moral irrelevance of dogma" -- the idea that moral agency can and does exist apart from Anglican orthodoxy. This thesis unifies the novel's narrative of doubt with its major sub-plot: the chasm created between Robert and his devoutly Anglican wife, Catherine, who is described as "the Thirty-Nine Articles in the flesh." When Catherine discovers that Robert has been pursuing exactly the same social projects in London's East End that he did while in holy orders in Surrey, she re-evaluates the implications of his heterodoxy. She initially interpreted his resignation of clerical duties as a relaxation of moral fiber occasioned by heretical ideas. What she learns, however, is that his work in the East End is characterized by the same energy and moral commitment that impelled his work as an Anglican minister.

Forced to reconsider her own reluctance to acknowledge Robert's newly formulated religious position, Catherine makes the following explanation:

> 'You were right -- I *would* not understand. And, in a sense, I shall never understand, I cannot change...My Lord is my Lord always; but He is yours too. Oh, I know it, say what you will! *That* is what has been hidden from me; that is what my trouble has taught me; the powerlessness, the worthlessness, of words. *It is the spirit that quickeneth*.' (530)

Finally Catherine says "I am past thinking. Let us bury it all, and begin again. Words are nothing" (530).

By devaluing the linguistic -- in essence doctrinal -- differences between Robert and Catherine, and by re-grounding their new beginning on a shared moral commitment, *Robert Elsmere* transfers the locus of spiritual significance from biblical narratives to moral and social practice. In a quasi-allegorical way, Anglicanism is eventually brought to acknowledge alternative articulations of spiritual and moral truth.

IV

The thesis that spiritual truth can be articulated in language other than Christian dogma elicited excited response from a variety of sources. One especially long and critical review entitled "*Robert Elsmere* and the Battle of Belief" was written by William Gladstone. Gladstone objected to the inadequate representation of Anglican apologetics in the novel. It is generally true as he charges that in *Robert Elsmere* "there is a great inequity in the distribution of arms. Reasoning is the weapon of the new scheme; emotion is the sole resource of the old" (Gladstone 778). But if Gladstone's criticism of Ward's elision is accurate, he misjudges its cause. He falsely attributes the lack of Christian apologetics to a lack of knowledge on Ward's part:

[T]here is nowhere a sign that the authoress has made herself acquainted with the Christian apologists, old or recent; or has weighed the evidence derivable from the Christian history.... (778)

Gladstone's objection that Ward did not know enough should certainly be seen as a play to exclude her from theological debate altogether. Other important reviewers made this same attempt as well.[7] Beyond pronouncing Ward unfit for public theological discussion, Gladstone's criticism reveals his expectation that her novel give the same even-handed treatment one would expect from a theological or philosophical treatise. It is clear he received the novel as much as a piece of theology as a piece of fiction.

The body of his review bears this out. It is divided between answering specific tenets of critical theology and refuting Ward's conclusion that dogma is morally irrelevant. Regarding the first category, Gladstone argues that there can be no strictly philosophical or scientific *a priori* objection to miracles "until philosophy or science shall have determined a limit, beyond which [an] extraneous force of will, so familiar to our experience, cannot act upon or deflect the natural order" (774). Similarly, Gladstone rejects on historical grounds the argument that early Christians were inordinately disposed to believe in miracles and therefore especially susceptible to metaphorical extravagance in reporting their experiences. In rejecting this argument, Gladstone attacks critical theology's assertion that biblical testimony is historically contingent and must therefore be historically understood -- and that it is only therefore historically relevant.

The part of Gladstone's review that reveals the most about Ward's reception as a theological writer, however, is his alarm at the cultural implications of her heterodoxy. Gladstone understands the rhetorical purpose of *Robert Elsmere* to be

to expel the preternatural element from Christianity, to destroy its dogmatic structure, yet to keep in tact the moral and spiritual results. (773)

He objects that it is morally and culturally disastrous to try to separate "Christian character" from the history and culture that produced it.

What right have we to detach, or to suppose we can detach, this type of personal character from the causes out of which as matter of history it has grown, and to assume that without its roots it will thrive as well as with them? (784)

His fears of the consequences of such a separation are clearly for the well-being of the Church of England itself:

It abolishes of course the whole authority of Scripture. It abolishes also Church, priesthood or ministry, sacraments, and the whole established machinery which trains the Christian as a member of a religious society. (777)

From his 1837 *The State and its Relation with the Church* to his participation in the disestablishment of the Church of England in Ireland (1868), much of Gladstone's political life was concerned in one way or another with the function of the Anglican church in Victorian culture. At the time he wrote the review, Gladstone had lost the government over the issue of Home Rule in Ireland. There can be little doubt that some of his antipathy for *Robert Elsmere* is traceable to this concern for the cultural importance of the Anglican Church. By choosing to discuss points of theology in his review, Gladstone drew Ward's novel into a theological debate that was being carried out at the level of national politics.

In response to Gladstone, Ward wrote a long fictional piece for *The Nineteenth Century* entitled "The New Reformation: a Dialogue." In this piece two old college friends take sides and debate the relative merits of Anglican and German theology. Ward's ostensible first purpose is to defend herself against Gladstone's charge that she did not know enough about Christian apologetics or about critical theology to have treated them satisfactorily in her novel. Much of the dialogue is given to recounting the basic tenets and developmental stages of historical criticism of sacred texts in Germany. The piece is a veritable *tour de force*. The command of the history and development of German and French critical theology she evidences in "The New Reformation" is impressive. Ward thoroughly reviews the history of biblical scholarship in Germany and France, and the reception of these ideas in England, including the cultural and institutional conditions of that reception. She also evidences detailed familiarity with Christian apologetics in both Europe and England. In so doing, Ward defends her fitness to participate in public theological debate.

In addition to reasserting herself as a capable theological writer, Ward uses the occasion of "The New Reformation" to respond to Gladstone's objection that *Robert Elsmere* advocates "a vague and arbitrary severance of Christian morals from the roots which have produced them" (Gladstone 781). Ward counters Gladstone by arguing that the cultural "roots" of Christian morality are really only an epiphenomenal accretion -- that critical theology has already made this plain, but that the Anglican theological establishment has been incapable of acknowledging it.

The theological basis for the view of dogma as epiphenomenal is present in critical theology from the beginning. Ward points out in "The New Reformation" that critical theology really began in 1835 with Strauss's *Leben*

Jesu, which reasserted the Hegelian distinction between *Begriff* and *Vorstellung*:

> The particular system of dogmas put forward by any religion is the *Vorstellung* or presentation, the *Begriff* or idea is the underlying spiritual reality common to it and presumably other systems besides. Why in Christianity have you gone so far towards identifying the two?...Examine [Christian evidence] carefully and you will see that the particular statements which it makes are really only *Vorstellung* as in other religions, the imaginative mythical elements which hide from us the Idea or *Begriff*. ("The New Reformation" 470)

We find grounds for Ward's decision to dedicate *Robert Elsmere* to Green not only in their personal friendship, but also in the context of this passage. Ward's intellectual debt to Green is evident in the use she made of his explication of the *Begriff-Vorstellung* distinction.[8]

Green undertook a translation of F. C. Baur's *Geschichte der Christlichen Kirche*, the essential argument of which is distilled in Green's "Essay on Christian Dogma." There he explains that "'Faith' is a certain condition of the spiritual consciousness. Dogma is the expression of this consciousness in terms of the understanding" (181):

> Christianity, on its first entrance into the world, whatever else it may have been, was not, in the natural sense of the word, a theology. By theology we understand a connected system of ideas, each qualified by every other, each serving as a middle term by which the rest are held together. The theological consciousness...is a consciousness which approaches its object, God, through the medium of such a system of ideas. Christianity, in its simplest primary form, is involved in the divine consciousness of Jesus and in that of St. Paul...Now this consciousness of the divine...was an essentially immediate consciousness...It was, therefore according to the definition we have given, no theological consciousness, nor could its utterances constitute a theology. (164)

The cultural implications Green found in this distinction are clear enough in his own decision to abandon Anglican orthodoxy for philosophical idealism as the language of spiritual and moral truth. Green was in fact the first don allowed to remain at Oxford without taking orders.

Ward not only followed Green's theological lead, but she followed him all the way to the ends of orthodoxy, as is clear in her decision to couch Robert's reformed "religion" in the language of philosophical idealism. Both Ward's novel and her response to Gladstone end with the assertion that moral agency is *the* spiritually significant fact, and that this fact is bound up with the *Idea* (*Begriff*), not with its *representation* (*Vorstellung*). She concludes "The New Reformation" this way:

> We must submit to the education of God...but we must keep firm hold all the while of that vast heritage of feeling which goes back, after all, through all the overgrowths of dream and speculation to that strongest of all the forces of human life -- the love of man for man, the trust of the lower soul to the higher, the hope and the faith which the leader and the hero kindles amid the masses! (480)

"The New Reformation" makes explicit the theological background of Ward's effort to reassure Victorian readers that they can be good moral agents even if they no longer can accept Anglican dogma at face value. The popularity of *Robert Elsmere* represents the popularity of the secular moral redemption offered by Ward's theological-fictional utterances.

V

One year after she published *Robert Elsmere*, Ward has one of the characters in "The New Reformation" voice what must have been her own hope and expectation:

> For my own part, I believe that we in England, with regard to this German study of Christianity, are now at the beginning of an epoch of *popularization*. The books which record it have been studied in England, Scotland, and America with increasing eagerness during the last fifteen years by a small class; in the next fifteen years we shall probably see their contents reproduced in English form and penetrating public opinion in a new and surprising way. (468)

Although it is impossible to tell if Ward was specifically referring to her own work in this passage, the immediate and stunning success of *Robert Elsmere* might lead us to believe she was. In any event, the truth is that *Robert Elsmere* and "The New Reformation" were an important part of the penetration and popularization of German critical theology in England.

What Ward found characteristic of critical theology -- its improved translation, a faculty "half scientific, half imaginative" -- is equally true of her own work. Both her novel and her dialogue present highly rational theological argument through the voices of imaginative characters in fictional situations. The importance of this fact goes beyond being merely another example of how women used literary genres to participate in discourses from which they were institutionally excluded. By fully integrating imaginative literature and theology, Ward adapted her thesis to the conditions under which theological ideas lived and breathed in Victorian England. The theological mode of her fiction addressed the Anglican habit -- following Matthew Arnold's example -- of always taking one's theology with literature. In the last analysis, Ward's importance as a theological writer is given not only by the popularity of *Robert Elsmere*, but also by the efficacy of her fiction as a mechanism of theological, ethical, and cultural change.

NOTES

1. Later there were 1,000 copies of a two-volume library edition, and 20,000 copies of a half-crown edition had sold before the end of 1890. That adds up to about 128,000 copies in three years. Two decades later, still another cheap edition sold 50,000 copies in two weeks, and 100,000 copies within a year. For a fuller account of sales see Peterson 221. The edition I cite is the authorized one-volume American edition (Macmillan and Co: London and New York, 1888), reprinted from the seventh London edition.

2. See Peterson 248.

3. For Twain's remarks see Kipling, xvi, 278-279.

4. The sermons Ward cited on the dedication page are from Green's *The Witness of God, and Faith, Two Lay Sermons*. Ed. A. Toynbee, London, 1883. See *Works* iii, 230-276.

5. I am not the first to comment on Green's presence in *Robert Elsmere*. Among the most significant are Lionel Trilling, Melvin Richter, William Peterson, Rosemary Ashton, Bernard Lightman, Robert Lee Wolff, and John Sutherland. While Richter gives the most detailed attention to Green's philosophy, he says very little about the novel itself. Conversely, the others, mentioning Green in passing, give no serious attention to Green's ethics and religious philosophy and their implications as they are represented in the novel. Moreover, none gives any treatment of the way(s) in which Robert's critique of dogmatic theology prefigures the alternatives he pursues after he abandons orthodox Christianity.

6. Frei argues that in neither Germany nor England did a purely narrative reading of the Bible develop -- i.e. apart from both questions of its historical accuracy and the religious significance of its stories if "true." In this restricted sense there was no purely "literary" understanding of the Bible. The distinction between Green and Arnold I am drawing here depends not on the presence or absence of a purely narrative reading, but rather on an attitude toward the relative importance of the stories themselves. While both Green and Arnold are primarily interested in what the stories represent, Arnold is much more concerned than Green to maintain the religious significance and moral authority of the Bible's stories themselves.

7. See especially Randall Davidson, "The Religious Novel."

8. Ward herself gestures toward this debt by having her advocate in "The New Reformation" attribute his own progress in theological understanding to a reading of Baur's *Geschichte der Christlichen Kirche*: "I can only describe what I felt in the words lately attributed by his biographer to Professor Green: 'He thought the *Church*

History the most *illuminating* book he had ever read'" (*NR* 460). Green's biographer, R. L. Nettleship, reports Green as having said in regard to Baur: "'I have found him . . . nearly the most instructive writer I have ever met with'" (see Nettleship, "Memoir" xxxvii).

WORKS CITED

Arnold, Matthew. *God and the Bible*. Ann Arbor: U of Michigan P, 1970. Vol. 7 of *Complete Prose Works of Matthew Arnold*. Ed. R. H. Super. 11 vols. 1960-77.

---. *Literature and Dogma: An Essay Towards a Better Apprehension of the Bible*. Ann Arbor: U of Michigan P, 1968. Vol 6 of *Complete Prose Works of Matthew Arnold*. Ed. R. H. Super. 11 vols. 1960-77.

Ashton, Rosemary. "Doubting Clerics: From James Anthony Froude to *Robert Elsmere* via George Eliot." *The Critical Spirit and the Will to Believe*. Ed. David Jasper. London: Macmillan, 1989, 69-87.

Baur, Ferdinand Christian. *Geschichte der christlichen Kirche*. Tübigen: L.F. Fues, 1863.

Davidson, Randall T. "The Religious Novel." *Contemporary Review* 54 (1888): 674-682.

Frei, Hans. *The Eclipse of Biblical Narrative: A Study of Eighteenth- and Nineteenth-Century Hermeneutics*. New Haven: Yale U P, 1974.

Gladstone, William E. "*Robert Elsmere* and the Battle of Belief." *The Nineteenth Century* 23 (1888): 766-789.

Green, Thomas Hill. *Works of Thomas Hill Green*. Ed. R. L. Nettleship. 3 vols. 1908. New York: Kraus Reprint Co., 1969.

---. "Essay On Christian Dogma." *Works of Thomas Hill Green*. Ed. R. L. Nettleship. Vol. 3. New York: Kraus Reprint Co., 1969. 3 vols.

---. "Faith." *Works of Thomas Hill Green*. Ed. R. L. Nettleship. Vol. 3. New York: Kraus Reprint Co., 1969. 3 vols.

---. "The Witness of God." *Works of Thomas Hill Green*. Ed. R. L. Nettleship. Vol.3. New York: Kraus Reprint Co., 1969. 3 vols.

Hutton, R. H. "Robert Elsmere." *The Spectator* 61 (1888): 479-480.

James, Henry. "Mrs. Humphry Ward." *English Illustrated Magazine* 9 (1892): 399-401.

Kipling, Rudyard. *From Sea to Sea*. New York: Charles Scribner's Sons, 1899. Vol.16 of *The Writings in Prose and Verse of Rudyard Kipling*. 36 vols. 1897-1899.

Lightman, Bernard. "*Robert Elsmere* and the Agnostic Crisis of Faith." *Victorian Faith in Crisis: Essays on Continuity and Change in Nineteenth-Century Religious Belief*. Ed. Richard J. Helmstadter. Stanford: Stanford U P, 1990.

Nettleship, R. L. "Memoir." *Works of Thomas Hill Green*. Ed R. L. Nettleship. 3 vols. London: Longmans, Green, and Co., 1906.

Pater, Walter. "Robert Elsmere." *Guardian* 63 (1888): 468-469.

Peterson, William S. *Victorian Heretic: Mrs. Humphrey Ward's Robert Elsmere*. Leicester: Leicester Press, 1976.

Prickett, Stephen. "Poetics and Narrative: Biblical Criticism and the Nineteenth-Century Novel." *The Critical Spirit and the Will to Believe*. Ed. David Jasper. London: Macmillan P, 1989.

Richter, Melvin. *The Politics of Conscience: T. H. Green and His Age*. Cambridge, MA: Harvard U P, 1964.

Sutherland, John. *Mrs. Humphry Ward: Eminent Victorian, Pre-Eminent Edwardian*. Oxford: Clarendon P, 1990.

Trevelyan, Janet Penrose. *The Life of Mrs. Humphrey Ward*. London: Constable and Co., 1923.

Trilling, Lionel. *Matthew Arnold*. New York: Meridian Books, 1955.

Wace, Henry. "Robert Elsmere." *The Quarterly Review* 167 (1888): 273-302.

Ward, Mary Arnold (Mrs. Humphrey Ward). "The New Reformation: A Dialogue." *The Nineteenth Century* 25 (1889): 454-480.

---. *Robert Elsmere*. London and New York: Macmillan and Co., 1888.

---. *A Writer's Recollections*. 2 vols. New York: Harper Brothers, 1918.

Wolff, Robert Lee. *Gains and Losses: Novels of Faith and Doubt in Victorian England*. New York: Garland Publishing, 1977.

Reformers Write

"And Your Sons and Daughters Will Prophesy":
The Voice and Vision of Josephine Butler

Lucretia A. Flammang
U. S. Coast Guard Academy

"She reads Scripture like a child and interprets it like an angel"--John Henry Newman of Josephine Butler[1]

Josephine Elizabeth Grey Butler (1828-1906) has been variously described as a moral reformer, a Christian feminist, a visionary prophet and a mystic.[2] She has also been recognized as a brilliant political strategist. According to Judith R. Walkowitz, Edwardian suffragists hailed Butler as the "great founding mother of modern feminism" (*Prostitution* 255). From 1868 until nearly three years before her death, Butler spoke and published in defense of numerous social causes, particularly women's rights to higher education and viable employment and the rights of the Irish and native South Africans. She is mostly remembered, however, in connection with the sixteen–year crusade to repeal Britain's Contagious Diseases Acts (1870-1886), a series of laws that sought to arrest the spread of venereal diseases by regulating prostitutes through registration, examination, and incarceration.

Butler argued that the source of women's oppression is their vulnerability to sexual servitude, which results from the sexual double standard inherent in patriarchal culture. She found this double standard most evident in the prevailing attitudes toward the legal regulation of prostitution, whereby only women were punished for an act in which men also engaged. Yet Butler's concern exceeded the immediate goal of repeal of the Acts; ultimately, she hoped to bring about a world in which women and men would live in freedom and harmony -- a world that in her view would fulfill God's covenant with humanity.

Butler's polemics are largely hortatory, for to achieve her vision she had to educate her audiences. She based most of her teaching on traditional Christian theology, being very much influenced by the prophetic understanding of God's nature and his relationship to humanity and history. Yet, because she wrote on behalf of the rights of prostitutes, a wholly traditional theology could not support her: while the Biblical prophets championed the rights of "innocent" widows, children, and the poor, they never championed the rights of "sinful" prostitutes. Moreover, her opponents could easily invoke the Pauline prohibition against women's sermonizing to silence her exhortations.

Thus, where traditional theology failed Butler, she employed an alternative theology, drawn from her own feminist interpretations of the Bible. As Gerda Lerner has observed, such interpretations have the power to "[subvert] and [transform] patriarchal doctrine" (138). Butler's exegesis challenged patriarchal doctrine by positing three feminist principles: that God created women and men in perfect equality; that this inherent equality demands liberty for all; and that God has authorized women's prophecy, as foretold by the prophet Joel. In this essay, I will show how Butler developed these principles and combined them with the traditional theology of the prophetic tradition to produce an idiosyncratic and heterodox explanation of the nature of God, the nature of woman, and their relationship with each other. Indeed, Butler believed that when she acted on behalf of prostitutes, she was obeying the will of God: her theological convictions made her public actions possible.

I: EQUALITY AND LIBERTY

Before examining Butler's theology, I must place the topic within the proper framework. In a lengthy study of the role religion played in Butler's social actions, Nancy Boyd observes that Butler cannot properly be considered a theologian. Boyd bases her argument on the fact that Butler never addressed the existence of evil in a systematic way, a requisite consideration in theological thought (82). Indeed, Butler neither considered herself a theologian nor produced a comprehensive theological treatise (Boyd xv). My goal here, however, is not to present a fully developed theology for Butler but to focus on a set of principles that underpin her feminist thought and action -- principles that without doubt are theologically based.

One of the most obvious features of Butler's theology is its traditional view of the role of the prophet, who, in the Christian tradition of understanding the Hebraic prophets, provides the people knowledge of God's role and presence in human history. According to this tradition, God will ultimately create a new history when he establishes the New Jerusalem through Christ's second coming, but for now the prophet must interpret and reveal God's purpose, his nature, and his will for humanity. A second traditional feature of Butler's theology is its origins in a very literal interpretation of the acts and philosophy of Christ. In him, Butler found the perfect model of just and moral living. From daily study of the Gospels, she developed her theological understanding of the nature of humanity, an understanding reflected in her three principles.

Butler's first theological principle established the foundation for all of her feminist Biblical exegesis: God created women and men in absolute equality. In the introduction to her edition of essays by noted women's rights activists, *Woman's Work and Woman's Culture* (1869), Butler clearly elucidates this principle: "...it seems to me impossible for any one candidly to study Christ's whole life and words without seeing that the principle of the perfect equality of all human beings was announced by Him as the basis of social philosophy" (lix). Earlier in the essay, she explains that the equality to which she refers is not exclusively intellectual or physical or moral but is "on a wider and deeper basis..." (lv). In a speech she delivered to the Ladies' National Association in 1885, "The Principles of the Abolitionists," Butler defines equality more fully: "The equality that I desire is equality of judgment towards all alike, men and women; an absolute equality in all human laws...which bear upon personal liberty and legal rights, and that all this should be based upon the highest law..." (3). That women had been denied this equality for centuries was all too apparent to Butler, as she observes in the polemic *Hour Before the Dawn* (1876): "Christ's teaching in this matter has been practically frustrated and denied century after century, and upon its denial have been founded legislation, customs, and public institutions, criminally and cruelly immoral and unjust" (64).

Butler recognized that very few Christians understood the Gospels as she did. It was apparent to her that the principle of equality between women and men was missing from contemporary Victorian political and social attitudes. This lack was manifest most clearly for Butler in the conventional wisdom about prostitution. Although many Victorians were concerned about the numbers of prostitutes in urban areas -- referring to prostitution as the "Great Social Evil" -- most agreed with William Lecky, who declared in the *History of European Morals* (1869) that it was "ultimately the most efficient guardian of virtue" (qtd. in Bullough 197).[3] Butler challenged this prevailing wisdom that prostitution was necessary: consistent with her principle of the absolute equality between women and men, from which the principle of liberation obviously follows, she conceived of prostitution as slavery.

As Jenny Uglow has argued, Butler's analysis of prostitution advanced the nineteenth-century women's movement by redirecting the focus of the "Woman Question" from legal and educational inequalities to "a more radical and comprehensive view of women's oppression within a total economic, political, and sexual power relationship" (146). The broader focus involved revisioning prostitution as an egregious departure from God's will that women and men be equal, that women as well as men are created for freedom from the oppression of others. The abolition work of Butler's father, John Grey, had taught her as a girl to be sensitive to how people developed relationships of power over others. She recognized then that enslaved women had a unique set of horrors visited upon them.[4] Beginning in 1865, her own work with prostitutes in Liverpool confirmed her perception that tyranny and despotism characterized the relationship between powerful men and vulnerable women. Working to aid the women who inhabited the bridewells of the Liverpool workhouses, she discovered not hardened sinners but mostly poor, uneducated women whose circumstances prevented them from aspiring to less miserable conditions.

In various polemics and biographies, Butler narrates the stories of these women's lives, emphasizing that many were unable to support themselves or their sick parents on the wages they earned as laborers. In an 1868 pamphlet, *The Education and Employment of Women*, Butler underscores this economic foundation of prostitution:

> Many a woman rejected from the shop-till or housekeeper's room for ignorance and inefficiency, is compelled to offer herself among the lowest class of nursery governesses, or, failing all, to embrace the career, the avenues to which stand ever wide open, yawning like the gates of hell, when all other doors are closed. (16)

Others had been seduced and abandoned, and, as Butler understood, social conventions often prohibited these women from re-entering what Victorians considered acceptable society:

> ...the lapse of a woman of the humbler classes, though that lapse has been induced by the pressure of poverty or the allurements of love, is made the portal for her of a life of misery and shame. Society drives such an one out of bounds, sets its hell-hounds on her track, and makes recovery all but impossible. (*Hour* 64)

Butler recognized that the sexual double standard informally created two classes of women. Indeed, because of the widespread tolerance of men who indulged "irregular" sexual tastes, a group of women had to be available to service those desires. Butler reiterates the point in numerous polemics, and in *Social Purity* (1882), addressed to students at Cambridge University, she expresses it most lucidly:

> Worldly and impure men have thought, and still think, they can separate women, as I have said, into two classes, -- the protected and refined ladies who are not only to *be good*, but who are, if possible, to *know* nothing except what is good; and those poor outcast daughters of the people whom they purchase with money, and with whom they think they may consort in evil whenever it pleases them to do so, before returning to their own separated and protected homes. (9-10, emphasis in original)

According to Butler, the Contagious Diseases Acts institutionalized the sexual double standard by legally regulating a slave-class of women to keep them free of disease. Under the Acts, women suspected by the police of being prostitutes could be arrested and forced to undergo a vaginal examination to detect venereal disease. If the woman was infected, she could be incarcerated in a Lock Hospital for up to nine months.[5] Women were subjected to these actions solely on the authority of the police -- and virtually any woman could be arrested if the police considered her suspect. In a long constitutional argument against the Acts, *The Constitution Violated* (1871), Butler defines the regulated women as slaves:

> I have already said that these Acts virtually introduce a species of villeinage or slavery. I use the word not sentimentally, but in the strictest legal sense. Slavery means that condition in which an individual is not master of his own person, and the condition of slavery is defined in the Magna Charta by the omission of all slaves from the rights which that charter grants to every one else. There could be no more complete, galling, and oppressive deprivation of freedom than this which takes place under these Acts. (28-29)

Underlying Butler's constitutional argument was her belief that men were as guilty as women and should not be protected by unjust laws.

As Butler legitimized her campaign against the Contagious Diseases Acts and the sexual double standard with her principle of the equality of women and men, she cast the campaign as a revolution for liberty. Indeed, she and her followers described themselves as the new abolitionists, for which she could apply the quotation from Isaiah that was central to her father's abolitionist crusade: "Is not this the fast that I have chosen: to loose the bonds of wickedness, to undo the heavy burdens, and to let the oppressed go free, and that ye break every yoke?" (58:6).[6] Moreover, Butler used Christ's life as the divine model for the treatment of prostitutes. She interpreted his behavior toward them as completely compassionate rather than judgmental; he always emancipated them: "His dismissal of each case [of prostitution] was accompanied by a distinct act of *Liberation*" (*Woman's Work* lviii, emphasis in original).

Equality is an obvious axiom for liberty; those who are equal under God have no authority to prevent others from experiencing their full humanity, as ordained by God. To Butler, liberty was an imperative commandment, for without it, one could not exercise free will. According to traditional theology, God imbues humanity with the free will to choose to accept him and his love or to reject him and be damned. Those who are oppressed cannot choose freely, thus they are prevented from receiving God's grace. Butler believed the treatment of prostitutes forcibly prevented them from seeking forgiveness for their sins and achieving ultimate union with God. In her "Letter to the Members of the Ladies' National Association" (1875), Butler explains her point: "This system [of enslaving women] necessitates the greatest crime of which earth can be witness, the crime of blotting out the soul by depriving God's creatures of free-will, of choice and responsibility, and by reducing the human being to the condition of a passive, suffering minister to the basest passions" (19).

Since Butler believed that men were largely responsible for perpetuating women's sexual oppression, she argued that women's liberation depended upon profligate men adopting the moral standards the law sought to impose upon women:

> That portion of the mighty task appointed to us at this day, which is in danger of being again and again lost sight of, is the elevation of the moral standard of our sons and our brethren. If this is neglected, the work of rescuing women will continue to resemble the attempt to dry the bed of a river by turning away its waters, while the fountain-head continues actively to pour forth its ever-renewed floods. (*Hour* 92)

In passages such as this, Butler attempts to teach her audience that the source of prostitution was not the depraved nature of the prostitute but the depraved nature of the profligate. In *Hour Before the Dawn*, she suggests that women were seduced not because of their greater capacity for sin but because of their greater capacity for self-sacrifice: "...and who shall say that that self-abandonment in woman, which will make her fling herself away for another, is altogether devoid of some trace of unselfishness, which men would do well to mark and shield in her, and to imitate for themselves in a pure and good cause?" (35).

In depicting the prostitute as a victim or, as she suggests in the quotation above, as an ideally self-sacrificing woman, Butler sought to liberate prostitutes and thereby restore to them the essential equality of humanity with which God had endowed them. But this important principle of Butler's theology seems to have been misunderstood by most of her contemporaries. What many audiences heard when she spoke was a condemnation of the sexual double standard that was intended not to liberate women but to seek punishment for both men and women. Philippa Levine has argued that Butler's Christianity ultimately worked against her: "what had begun, in the heady days of the L[adies'] N[ational] A[ssociation] and at the start of the social purity movement as a direct questioning of male-imposed inequity was recaptured and co-opted back into male-dominated conservatism" (99). Conservatives seeking to eradicate vice blanched Butler's arguments of their theology, focusing solely on a superficial moralism. Her theology of equality was simply too radical to gain acceptance. Although she warned people about the potential repressiveness of anti-vice movements, she was unable to reclaim the discourse. Sadly, like the prophets she sought to emulate, Butler demanded an equality that remained an unattainable human standard.

II: WOMEN'S PROPHECY

The first public act of the Ladies' National Association, the woman's arm of the campaign against the Acts, was the publication of its manifesto in the *Daily News* on 31 December 1869. Signing it were 124 concerned citizens, including two of the leading women's voices of the era, Harriet Martineau and Florence Nightingale. Despite the venerable reputation of such women, however, the initial reaction to the manifesto was shock and outrage. One member of Parliament wrote to Butler, "Your Manifesto has shaken us very badly in the House of Commons; a leading man in the House remarked to me: 'We know how to manage any other opposition in the House or in the country, but this is very awkward for us -- this revolt of the women" (qtd. in Bell 80). The awkwardness issued from the general response to women's participation in public affairs; on the eve of 1870, Victorian Britain had not fully accepted women who expressed their sentiments and opinions publicly. Women discussing prostitution, sex, and venereal diseases, moreover, transgressed social taboos. Accordingly, the legitimacy of women's public voice became a dominant theme throughout Butler's polemics.

Butler's understanding of the authority of women's voice was informed by the third principle of her theology. Founded on the first two principles of equality and liberty, Butler's third principle asserted that God authorizes women's prophecy. If men could be suitable prophets, then by the logic of equality, so could women. Furthermore, if God authorizes women to prophesy his will, then no social or political prohibitions should prevent their public orations and writing. Butler cited the prophet Joel to defend her position: "I do not think that women are excluded from [Joel 2:28-29], for it goes on to say that 'your daughters shall prophesy'" (Letter to Fanny Forsaith). From this principle that God authorizes women's prophecy issued Butler's greatest contribution to the early feminist movement.

The tradition of Old Testament prophecy influenced Butler's own understanding that prophets were sages divinely inspired to express God's will for humanity. Those chosen as prophets shared with God a special relationship, most likely developed through hours of silent communion and prayer. In his classic study *The Prophets*, rabbinical scholar Abraham Heschel explains this relationship as one requiring a unique consciousness. Heschel posits that the source of God's consciousness is his pathos: "This notion that God can be intimately affected, that He possesses not merely intelligence and will, but also pathos, basically defines the prophetic consciousness of God" (2:4). Enabled by what Heschel labels the "prophetic consciousness," prophets are capable of responding to God's pathos with sympathy, "the central feature of the [prophet's] life" (2: 87). Through sympathy, then, the prophet experiences the divine pathos, interprets it, and then communicates it to others.

Although Butler never explicitly claimed that she was a prophet, she implied as much in numerous polemics and in the biographies *Catherine of Siena* (1878) and *Recollections of George Butler* (1892). In *Hour Before the Dawn* (1876), she describes most extensively her prophetic consciousness. Like the Old Testament prophets, she sought to understand the heart of God; through hours of silent supplication, Butler experienced what she believed was a divine revelation. Claiming to have seen into God's heart, she proclaims a knowledge of his love:

> This is the only passion, the true, the all-absorbing passion, the Love which is my Lord and King; not a tyrannical Lord to-day and forsaking me to-morrow, but a Lord who has bound me His captive for ever. The utmost heights and depths of human passion, in all its beauty, its power, its sweetness, its self-abandonment, are to this love as the feeble flicker of a rushlight compared with the mid-day sun. (99)

Having witnessed the enormity of God's love, in prophetic fashion, Butler knows she then must share it with others:

> Christ reveals to us the secrets of his heart, and then it is, and not till then, that he sends us, with his own seal and commission, back to the world for which he died, that we also may die for it. It is from the heart of Christ alone that I venture to speak these words to you. I know nothing except what I have learned upon my knees before him, and I will speak nothing except that which I have so learned. (103)

In enacting the role of a prophet as she did in *Hour Before the Dawn*, Butler worked to authorize her criticism of the sexual double standard and the Contagious Diseases Acts and assumed the authority to attack publicly the practices of profligate men. She revealed God's love for prostitutes, teaching her audiences that a prostitute's sins do not preclude her from ultimate salvation (*Hour* passim). Moreover, in various polemics Butler pointedly tells her audiences that, of profligate men, only those who seek forgiveness for their sins will receive God's grace. Of course, she did not encounter universal acclaim for her prophecy or her position; she was even accused of being "no better" than the women she defended (Fawcett and

Turner 69). Indeed, Christian audiences throughout history have regarded women's prophecy with suspicion, a phenomenon for which scholars have advanced various explanations. For instance, Amy Lang has argued that the antinomian Anne Hutchinson threatened the Puritan community because her status as a prophet placed her outside the communal law: by wholly giving herself up to Christ, she subverted the hierarchy of the church (42). The implication is that women prophets evoke suspicion because they transcend the patriarchal order: they answer to no man, but to God.

Butler's work not only distanced her from men, but also from most other women in her society. Her efforts to help prostitutes conflicted with the expectation that she be a "good" woman, who should maintain ignorance about the entire topic of prostitution. More importantly, in prophesying God's love for only those profligate men who seek forgiveness, Butler not so subtly censured other men's behavior. Rather than acknowledging the depraved nature of prostitutes, Butler implicitly criticized expressions of male sexuality that most people tacitly tolerated. Moreover, because she enacted the role of a prophet sent to reveal God's will to humanity, men who submitted to Butler's expression of that will were seen to do so because of the demands of a woman. In short, Butler's prophecy disrupted and inverted centuries of patriarchal discourses aimed at controlling the sexuality of women.

To Butler, prophesying against the sexual double standard seemed women's special province. She did not believe that men could fully understand the injustices arising from women's subjection to the double standard. As she wrote in her introductory essay to *Woman's Work*,

> There are few men who can thoroughly know the minds of women in a state of society in which the reality of woman's nature is repressed, and it is especially difficult for those who are in a position of life which confines their intercourse to women of their own class... (lvi).

Only Christ was capable of fully comprehending women's lives, for "[he] is the Person in whom all virtues which are considered essentially womanly, as well as those which are considered essentially manly, found their perfect development" (*Education* 19). Because women shared the qualities that Christ manifested in his treatment of prostitutes, women were therefore more sympathetic to a divine call to liberate prostitutes from the slavery imposed by the sexual double standard and the Acts.

Yet Butler realized that her cause repelled many women. In the first two years of the campaign, she had to appeal openly to women to end their silence and join her. In 1872, however, when the Ladies' National Association had a larger membership than the men's arm of the movement, the National Association, Butler began to see the fulfillment of Joel's prophecy that an age would come in which numerous women would prophesy. The phenomenon seemed to be occurring for the first time in history, as she explains in her polemic *The New Era* (1872):

> The voice of God has, for the first time so far as we know in the world's history, summoned to deal with this question [of the Contagious Diseases Acts] not an individual heroic woman here and there, but an entire class, who, like a nation born in a day, have, by the force of peculiar circumstances to which I shall refer, identified themselves with the down-trodden and degraded of their own sex; have been aroused by a great shock; and, by the leading of a hand controlling these events, have been carried to the heart and true stronghold of the causes of this misery. (41-42)

Butler believed that women's mass participation in her campaign was a sign that the apocalyptic predictions in Joel were emerging in her lifetime. In *Hour Before the Dawn*, she narrates the events of this apocalypse most completely in a sermonic appeal for profligate men to forsake their sinful lives:

> The holy rebellion proclaimed aloud in our day, the revolted cry of womanhood against her enslavement to the licentiousness of man, and against the falsehoods by which the greatest of social evils is maintained, has more than anything in our memory, more perhaps than any event in the history of Christendom, awakened echoes from all parts of the earth, shaken the ancient strongholds of privileged licentiousness, and called out of its guilty slumber the conscience of the Churches. That revolted cry is the herald of a sifting season. (106-7)

Using temporal metaphors such as "sifting" or changing season, Butler describes the imminence of the Lord. Where night was the period of darkest sin, the dawn marks the new era of righteous life in a sinless world. The great battle between good and evil would therefore take place in the hour before the dawn:

> We see the beginning only, not the end, or nearly the end, of the horrors which are yet to be revealed. It would appear as if the powers of evil were about to combine, at the hour before the dawn, for one last gigantic effort to turn God's dear earth into hell... (109)

Butler's vision of the battle itself departs from traditional Biblical narratives of the final battle; instead of imagining universal destruction, Butler constructs a battle in which the enemy abandons his position to join the forces of good: "Shall we not see the hostile cohorts melting away like mist before the full light of the glad morning, and recognise our foemen of the night to be our 'brothers at break of day'?" (110).

Butler's transformation of the traditional apocalyptic narrative provides the basis for her final vision, a New Jerusalem that emerges from the existent world, rather than one that replaces the world. In the new era, harmony reigns:

> Fetters shall no longer be wrought out of the intelligence and civilisation of one zone to entrap the unwary simplicity and enslave the generations of another. The light of day will fall upon all the dark places of the earth, now full of the habitations of cruelty, and there shall come forth, at the call of the Deliverer, the thousands and tens of thousands of the daughters of men now enslaved in all lands to cruelty and lust. (*Hour* 111)

The source of the harmony is the liberation of slaves, and Butler imagines the freeing of all slaves, men and women, European, African, and Asian. She also reveals a hope often absent in traditional views of history, a hope that the present world can be transformed without destruction. This hope arises from her belief in the unlimited transformative power of women's love itself. Like God's love, women's love is healing, and it can save the world:

> We [women] are all mothers or foster-mothers....It would be wise of the State to avail itself of this abundance of generous womanliness, of tender and wise motherliness which lives in the hearts of thousands of women who are free to bring their capacities to bear where they are most needed. (*Education* 20)

Clearly, Butler incorporated in her vision assumptions central to the domestic ideology, particularly that women were morally superior to men (Banks 91). Helsinger, Sheets, and Veeder suggest that the concept of women's moral superiority led to a form of feminism they have designated "apocalyptic": "there is a radical version of the angelic ideal which combines a belief in woman's distinctive nature with claims for a leadership role in the world -- a female savior leading the way to a fuller humanity and ushering in a new era of community and love" (xv). Butler's theology of women's prophecy, which she associated with the second coming, clearly was a form of apocalyptic feminism (160). And although her vision was not to be realized, her polemics breached an important social barrier that had prevented women from addressing one source of their oppression, their vulnerability to sexual servitude. After Butler had begun to write openly about the sexual double standard, other women followed, in particular Ellice Hopkins, Francis Swiney, Annie Besant, and Christabel Pankhurst.

While Butler's theology was unique in content, she was not the first reformer to establish a political movement upon the foundation of Christian tenets, and given her goals, her gains were rather modest. But it is improbable that any visionary leader will force politics to conform with theological principles. What is perhaps most striking about Butler's theology is the courage it provided her. Indeed, it was this courage that inspired other women to continue the fight for women's emancipation, a courage that earned her the reputation of "great founding mother" of modern feminism. Millicent Garrett Fawcett acknowledged as much when she wrote, "Mrs. Butler's victory [in repealing the Contagious Diseases Acts] was an immense encouragement to us; for her task had been immeasurably more difficult than ours, and her triumph helped us to believe that all things were possible" (128).

In the later years of her life, Butler herself suspected that she had genuinely and significantly advanced women's rights. In 1893, Butler speculates about her legacy in an editorial in the newsletter *The Dawn*:

> Who shall say how much of the present awakening of women to an equality with men, and of men to the justice of that equality, is the outcome of the educational process of our old agitation and crusade against state-aided immorality? We English women began that crusade when a female figure on a public platform was rare, and a woman's voice there almost unknown. But two decades have passed away since then, and to-day women possess all franchises except the vote for Parliament... (7)

Butler's achievement clearly emanated from her theology, as her theological thinking provided her the conviction upon which to base her political activity. Thus by virtue of her political actions, her theology ultimately had a profound impact on the political and social achievements of the early women's movement. Indeed, her inspiration to others was a fulfillment of her own prophesying: "Women have found a voice; women now preach (or prophesy); and God has set His seal upon their word and work" ("Catherine Booth" 650).

NOTES

1. Quoted in Bell 209.

2. For excellent biographies see E. Moberly Bell and A.S.G. Butler. For studies of the impact of Butler's participation in the campaign against the Contagious Diseases Acts and of her influence on early feminism, see Judith R. Walkowitz, Barbara Caine, and Jenny Uglow.

3. Bullough and Bullough quote from William Edward Hartpole Lecky, *History of European Morals* (1869; New York: George Braziller, 1955) 283.

4. In a 1905 letter to colleagues in Switzerland, Butler described her childhood reaction to the accounts that her father read about the abuses slaves were forced to endure: "I say women, for I think their lot was particularly horrible, for they were almost invariably forced to minister to the worst passions of their masters, or be persecuted and die (qtd. in Johnson 14).

5. For comprehensive studies of the Contagious Diseases Acts, see Walkowitz and Paul McHugh.

6. This translation from the King James Bible is the one Butler quotes in the biography of her father, *Memoir of John Grey of Dilston* (49).

WORKS CITED

Banks, Olive. *Faces of Feminism: A Study of Feminism as a Social Movement.* New York: St. Martin's, 1981.

Bell, E. Moberly. *Josephine Butler: Flame of Fire.* 1962. London: Constable, 1963.

Boyd, Nancy. *Three Victorian Women Who Changed Their World: Josephine Butler, Octavia Hill, Florence Nightingale.* New York: Oxford UP, 1982.

Bullough, Vern and Bonnie Bullough. *Women and Prostitution: A Social History.* Buffalo, NY: Prometheus Books, 1987.

Butler, A.S.G. *Portrait of Josephine Butler.* London: Faber, 1953.

Butler, Josephine. "Catherine Booth." *Contemporary Review* Nov. 1890: 639-653.

---. *Catherine of Siena: A Biography.* London: Dyer Brothers, 1878.

---. *The Constitution Violated.* Edinburgh: Edmonston and Douglas, 1871.

---. Editorial. *The Dawn* 1 Mar. 1893: 7.

---. *The Education and Employment of Women.* London: MacMillan, 1868.

---. *Hour Before the Dawn: An Appeal to Men.* London: Trubner, 1876.

---. Introduction. *Woman's Work and Woman's Culture.* Ed. Butler. London: MacMillan, 1869.

---. Letter to Fanny Forsaith. 20 Jan. 1905. Butler Collection. Fawcett Library, City of London Polytechnic, London.

---. "A Letter to the Members of the Ladies' National Association." Liverpool: T. Brackell, 1875.

---. *Memoir of John Grey of Dilston.* Edinburgh: Edmonston and Douglas, 1869.

---. *The New Era.* Liverpool: T. Brackley, 1872.

---. "Principles of the Abolitionists." Ladies' National Association. London, 20 February 1885.

---. *Recollections of George Butler.* 2nd ed. Bristol: J. W. Arrowsmith, 1892.

---. *Social Purity.* 3rd ed. London: Dyer Brothers, 1882.

Caine, Barbara. *Victorian Feminists.* New York: Oxford UP, 1992.

Fawcett, Millicent Garrett. *What I Remember.* London: T. Fisher Unwin, 1925. Westport, CT: Hyperion, 1976.

--- and E. M. Turner. *Josephine Butler: Her Work and Principles, and Their Meaning for the Twentieth Century.* London: Association for Moral and Social Hygiene, 1927.

Helsinger, Elizabeth K., Robin Lauterbach Sheets, and William Veeder. *Social Issues.* Vol 2 of *The Woman Question: Society and Literature in Britain and America 1837-1883.* 3 vols. Chicago: U of Chicago P, 1983.

Heschel, Abraham J. *The Prophets.* 2 vols. New York: Harper Torchbooks, 1962.

Johnson, George W. and Lucy A. Johnson, eds. *Josephine Butler: An Autobiographical Memoir.* Bristol: J. W. Arrowsmith, 1911.

Lang, Amy Schrager. *Prophetic Woman: Anne Hutchinson and the Problem of Dissent in the Literature of New England.* Berkeley: U of California P, 1987.

Lerner, Gerda. *The Creation of Feminist Consciousness: From the Middle Ages to Eighteen-Seventy.* New York: Oxford UP, 1993.

Levine, Philippa. *Feminist Lives in Victorian England: Private Roles and Public Commitment.* Oxford: Blackwell, 1990.

McHugh, Paul. *Prostitution and Victorian Social Reform.* New York: St. Martin's, 1980.

Uglow, Jenny. "Josephine Butler: From Sympathy to Theory." *Feminist Theorists: Three Centuries of Key Women Thinkers.* Ed. Dale Spender. New York: Pantheon, 1983. 146-164.

Walkowitz, Judith R. *Prostitution and Victorian Society: Women, Class and the State.* 1980. Cambridge: Cambridge UP, 1991.

Ellice Hopkins and the Defaced Image of Christ

Susan Mumm
The Open University, Milton Keynes

In her own time Jane Ellice Hopkins was as famous as Josephine Butler, more famous than Dr. Elizabeth Blackwell, and certainly more notorious than either. Today she is the forgotten member of the trinity of Victorian purity activists. Hopkins was an important religious thinker and popularizer, and the founder of the White Cross Army, an international non-denominational movement devoted to overthrowing the sexual double standard. She is central to the tradition of Christian feminism, and her work linked advocates of women's social equality with religiously inspired purity activists. Her 'theology of altruism' combines reformist elements of the evangelical tradition, some heterodox ideas about the purpose of suffering, and a militant sexual politics.

Born in 1836, Jane Ellice was the younger daughter of William Hopkins, who began life as a farmer, but abandoned it to enter Cambridge at the age of thirty. He became a celebrated lecturer in mathematics at Cambridge, and gave his daughter a rigorous education in the sciences and classics. Her public work began shortly before his death in 1866, when she began addressing large meetings of bricklayers and fossil diggers in a working-class suburb of Cambridge. It was here that she discovered her remarkable oratorical powers. Her preaching combined the emotional appeal of the tent evangelist with rhetorical skill and a strong ability to create vivid images. Her ability to control and contain the most difficult and unruly audiences was remarkable. During her public career, her oratory held miners, medical students, and factory operatives spellbound, despite her childlike size, weak health, and lack of conventional attractiveness. An American auditor described a talk she gave when she was about twenty-five, at the very beginning of her work in Cambridge:

> I have listened to the most eminent revivalist preachers in America, and to many of the most impressive ministers in England; but I

never heard an address more calculated to melt an audience of common men than hers; and I never saw an audience more deeply moved. In diction and argument it was beautiful and powerful; but in fervour and pathos it was indescribable. (Burritt 15-16)

Hopkins found herself attacked by the clergy of several denominations who criticised her presumption in preaching to hundreds of working men, a task they considered improper for a woman. She was fully aware of the underlying sexism driving their condemnation of her activities, writing, "It was hard that the power which would have been a glory to me if I were a man, should be held a shame and disgrace to me because I was a woman" (*English* 43).

It was her own experience of the clergy's bitter opposition to her preaching that forced her to reassess her initial belief in the literal inerrancy and ahistorical truth of scripture. She came to reject all such claims, and instead argued that the Bible must be reinterpreted for each age, especially where it deals with the position of women. She came into repeated conflict with the Anglican clergy over her position on this, and never neglected to rebuke them for falling prey to:

the old foolish tendency to stick to the letter of Scripture, and [to] sin against its divine, progressive spirit, to bind women, after nineteen centuries of freedom, with precisely the same worn-out bandages and restrictions which were necessary to preserve social order when first the great truth of the equality of the sexes was proclaimed (*English* 42).

She wrote to a friend on the same topic, making clear her distrust of the text-based exegesis so dear to the evangelicals of the time:

Are you going to be guided by the maxims of Christianity? For if so I give it up in despair. You can get into any amount of muddle and contradictory and mischievous conduct by sticking hard and fast to the maxims of Christianity....[It] is a religion of spirit and life which cannot be bound down to maxims, to rules, which the changing conditions of life must constantly falsify....So we are not going to judge this question by texts, are we? (Barrett 140)

During this period Hopkins underwent a crisis of faith which forced her back to what she described as the elements of belief; she found herself compelled to abandon many of the traditional elements of Christian theology in favour of a single-minded focus on the Incarnation; the Atonement was meaningful only in so far as it helped to explain human suffering. The core of Hopkins' theology was her conviction that the fact of the Incarnation, that God became a man, meant that life on earth mattered profoundly. The fact of the Atonement, that God had to suffer to redeem humanity, meant that reformers would have to suffer to bring about the changes required of Victorian society before it could be truly termed 'Christian'.

As a result of her crisis of faith, she retained a solid respect for honest doubt for the rest of her life, strongly preferring it to complacent religiosity. Her religious opinions were considered dangerous by her contemporaries, not so much because of their nature (many secretly shared her rejection of Biblical inerrancy) but because she declared them openly and sought to promulgate them. Her refusal to interpret the Bible literally was most troubling since, as a woman, she should have left such issues unexamined. Ruskin had convinced many that theology was the only dangerous science for women, and consequently the only acceptable feminine approach to Scripture was to venerate it as the infallible rule of conduct, without challenging the historical or cultural attitudes embedded in it. The general public, untouched by the higher criticism, was scandalised by her insistence that the message of the gospels must be reinterpreted for every generation and society. Also troubling was her suggestion that Christ's redemptive sacrifice may need to be repeated (sometimes she suggests, completed) by the suffering of the innocent and guiltless in later generations.

At the age of 30, Hopkins moved to Brighton where she worked at the Albion Hill Home, a reformatory for prostitutes, from 1866 to 1870. These years of experience with fallen women led her to conclude that penitentiary work (homes for the voluntary rehabilitation of prostitutes were usually called penitentiaries in this period), while necessary, failed to address the root cause of the vice (Mumm 527). She argued that it was senseless for women reformers to provide "tender and merciful ambulances at the bottom of the precipice, while men are pushing them over at the top faster than we can save them at the bottom" (*Black* 8). Hopkins decided that the real problem was men's belief that chastity was only for women; if men could be taught self control and respect for women, much (but not all) prostitution would disappear, as would many of the social and moral problems accompanying it. She also rejected the commonly held idea that sexual sins were somehow uniquely contaminating for women in a way that other offences against the moral law were not. Prostitution, she claimed, was no more sinful than intemperance, and indeed was often less so, in that it was driven largely by economic necessity: part of her mission in seeking the sexual single standard was to "break down the artificial distinction between this and all other sins" (*Work* 40). Moral cures for prostitution attacked the wrong problem; Hopkins declared that low female wages, overcrowding, and a general absence of alternatives for women combined tragically with male lack of self-control. She saw prostitution as a rational, although deplorable, economic choice for women, but felt that the moral and social damage caused by the trade made it intolerable. While women were without economic self-determination, men lacked a willingness to take responsibility for their sexuality. She also suggested that men were responsible, not only for the existence of prostitution, but for the low wages that drove women into it; writing of a prostitute: "She was once dragged down, not necessarily by any individual man, but rather by the trade in the bodies and souls of women which the money of men sets up -- the standing bribe formed by its miserable gains when compared to the starvation woman's wage" (*Lost* 7). It followed that Hopkins campaigned for the opening of more trades to women. Unlike many reformers, she approved of factory work for women, since it was a relatively better paid occupation than traditional women's work, and she felt that it encouraged a sense of independence and self-sufficiency. She also made an early and interesting case for linking wages to need rather than to the fluctuations of trade, arguing that demand should not be permitted to determine women's wages; these should be keyed to self-sufficiency, in defiance of "our accursed English laissez faire" (*What Can* 15). The real and final cure for prostitution would be raising the wages of women to a decent level.

After four years of active work in Brighton, Hopkins spent seven years confined to bed as the result of a botched medical procedure (she is silent about the nature of this illness). She suffered greatly from depression during this time; eventually she recovered a moderate level of health and re-entered public life, becoming a full-time lecturer and writer after her mother's death in 1881. Hopkins began her crusades of the 1880s with a nagging sense of wasted time and lost opportunities, which seems to have never completely left her. By the time she resumed her active work, she was a woman with a mission from God, and the seven years spent in forced retirement were a constant spur to her ceaseless work for the next decade. Her health remained a problem for the rest of her life, and her drive to compensate for this probably contributed to the complaints about her overwhelming and "too powerful" personality.

During her years of invalidism she wrote her only novel, *Rose Turquand*, which was highly sensational but introduced many of the ideas that were to dominate her later work. Her second book of poetry, *Autumn Swallows*, deals very explicitly with the issues that Hopkins was to concentrate on in her theological writing, especially the mystic relationship between the crucified Saviour and the fallen woman; many of the poems suggest that the redemptive work of the Cross is at least paralleled, and perhaps completed, by the sexual exploitation of Victorian women and children. Women held a privileged place in Hopkins' view of the Christian story, especially fallen women. Hopkins began relatively early her recasting of the Atonement: in it the two sacrifices of two outcasts (Christ and the emblematic prostitute) are equal, but Christ's suffering is completed in that of women. *Swallows* too was favourably reviewed, and both it and *Turquand* indicate Hopkins' utter absorption in the problems of suffering, especially suffering caused by social or sexual inequality. In her eyes, her society's refusal to admit the equality of the genders meant that Britain was turning its back on the work of God in the nineteenth century. She claimed that the inequality of women, typified most vividly for her in the depersonalisation of the public image of the prostitute, was thus a violation of the very heart of the Gospel -- a second rejection of Christ.

She saw working-class women as the most vulnerable and the most exploited group in British society. It followed naturally that this was the group which produced the bulk of prostitutes and abused children. Hopkins argued that sexually exploited working-class women and children represented the suffering of Christ to the nineteenth century, and were, actually as well as symbolically, "the crucified body of your Redeemer" (*Touching* 10). They were the "defaced image" of Christ witnessing to the modern world, who could only be restored and healed by reclaiming their equality. "For some strange reason the whole weight of this evil in its last resort comes crushing down on the shoulders of a little child -- infant Christs of the cross without the crown, 'martyrs of the pang, without the palm'" (*Power* 23).

At some point during the 1870s Hopkins had been trained in medicine and reproductive physiology by a noted surgeon, James Hinton, who wanted to be remembered as "the man who went mad over the wrongs of women." As well as pioneering aural surgery, Hinton was the founder of the altruistic school of philosophy in Britain, who later lost much of his influence (although not Hopkins' loyalty) through his guarded defence of free love and passionate advocacy of prostitutes. At his deathbed Hopkins promised to finish his work by devoting herself to the cause of redressing women's wrongs. She was to spend the next twelve years fulfilling this pledge, and additionally, kept alive and popularised Hinton's "theology of altruism" (*Life* 187-8).

In 1876 Hopkins founded the Ladies' Association for the Care of Friendless Girls, which grew to have countless branches and which established more than two hundred refuges and training homes for young women throughout Great Britain. The goal of this organisation was to provide better job training for girls and women, in the hope that increased wages would remove the principle motivation of many who entered prostitution. She felt that ordinary middle-class women, by being actively involved with such projects, could signal their refusal to any longer sanction the setting aside of "a class of our own sisters" for moral and physical destruction (*Ladies'* 6-7).

In the short term, Hopkins' greatest achievement was undoubtedly the organisation that she and Bishop Lightfoot of Durham founded in 1882: the White Cross Army. This organisation's structure was based on that of the temperance movement: men, mostly of the working class, attended large mass meetings where they were urged by Hopkins and other speakers to "take the pledge" of chastity until marriage. An important secondary goal of the movement was the raising of the social standing of women, which Hopkins believed had been injured by their sexual commodification. Other groups were formed with a similar intent but appealed to sectionalised audiences. The Church of England Purity Society (which also claims Hopkins as its founder although it was technically all-male) aimed to influence the moral climate through persuading Anglican men of the upper classes to embrace the cause of purity: this group was noteworthy for its lack of success. Unlike the CEPS and many other denominationally structured groups, the White Cross Army attracted a following from all churches, and from those who were outside organised religion altogether. No declaration of religious belief was imposed. All that was required was that the members pledge to carry out the five aims of the society, which included, centrally, "To treat all women with respect, and endeavour to protect them from wrong and degradation," and "To maintain the law of purity as equally binding upon men and women." This was deliberate policy on Hopkins' part. She insisted that the White Cross Army had to be non-denominational. Some branches were Anglican; others non-conformist; others contained a mixture of all denominations, Jews, and those of no religion. The mixture of religiously motivated men with atheists and secularists in the organisation was extremely unusual for a purity movement.

Hopkins always envisaged an organisation whose most important work would be carried out by permeation of other associations, especially the temperance movement and the YMCA. In general, it attracted the same constituency who also became involved in temperance, the anti-Contagious Diseases Act programme, and self-improvement organisations of many kinds. The White Cross Movement had considerable success, particularly in the industrial north and midlands. In its first year alone, over 2000 men (mostly coal miners and industrial workers) signed the pledge. There were also active branches in the universities. Overall, 102 formally affiliated branches of the White Cross Army were formed in Great Britain in its first year of operation, as well as in India, Canada, Australia, the United States, and Germany.

Hopkins used the White Cross Army as a venue to spread her demand for purity, equality, and the theology of altruism; especially important to her reformist agenda was the White Cross Series, published by Hatchards in the mid 1880s, which spread her ideas widely in a popular form. Her best selling title, *True Manliness*, sold more than three hundred thousand copies within a year of publication. By her death in 1904, over two million copies of her works had been distributed. Hopkins's books and pamphlets were widely read; twenty to seventy-five editions of a single title were common, with some remaining in print until the 1940s. She did not profit financially from these enormous sales, as she gave the proceeds to further the work of the White Cross Army.

In preparation for her public work as lecturer and writer she studied Puritan theologians, the writings of Bunyan, and the sermons of contemporary Evangelicals such as Charles Spurgeon. She scoured ancient and modern authors for racy anecdotes, telling examples, and memorable stories to attractively convey the message of social purity to a late-Victorian audience. Unsurprisingly given her scientific education, many of her most telling examples were drawn from geology and zoology. Like many of her contemporaries, she was convinced that advances in science would reveal more of the nature of God: "So thin has the material veil grown under the touch of modern science that everywhere the spiritual breaks through" (*Power* 162).

Hopkins loathed latinate and what she called Pulpit English ("the most vicious English in existence"). She claimed that women made the best preachers and writers, for "women never wrong their thoughts with pulpit English, but preserve the strength and sweetness of their mother tongue....they speak not from theological systems but from the heart and the life" (*Work* [1879] 79). Her writing contained little of the "water-gruel and brown sugar" which she felt constituted most religious writing. Over time Hopkins' rhetoric became more radical, and she abandoned the stereotypes and religious cant that deface some of her earlier writing. She herself rejected most devotional literature, finding it unreal, escapist, and incapable of grappling with the real problems of the Christian life: "only in the Divine Book do I find the deep, human cry, only in the Psalms of David, and in the Word made flesh, do I find what suits my struggling humanity" (Barrett 32-3).

Even though her writing style was generally vigorous and earthy, she felt constrained by the decorums of publishing; much of what she wanted to convey could not be put in print without offending Victorian decency. Consequently, Hopkins preferred lectures to writing: "In everything one publishes, one is tormented by the sense that one has to stop just short of the useful" (*Grave* 39). Even her audiences sometimes found her speeches too shocking to be acceptable; after a long debate, the Norwich branch of the Ladies' Association for the Care of Friendless Girls rejected her as a potential speaker, because "many people considered her to be far too plain spoken to be generally acceptable": this from a branch of the organisation she had herself founded (Norwich 1886). Her radical rhetoric barely remained within the constraints of her society, as she savaged the double standard and demanded a re-examination of the central truths of Christianity.

Despite the all-male composition of the Army, Hopkins placed increasing stress on the role of women in reforming society as time passed. While women could not join the Army, they were urged to take steps toward ensuring purity. Initially, most were individual rather than collective: educating their children about sexuality, demanding purity from men of their own class, developing a higher standard of female courage, and devoting themselves to the reversal of the nation's moral decay through loving and compassionate responses to their fallen sisters. Work for women by women would "prove a most powerful protest to men, that we simply will not have a class of our own sisters set apart to moral and physical destruction" (*Grave* 27).

She demanded that women learn to identify with one another on the basis of gender; class differences were much less significant than shared female experience. Women betray other women if they socialise with men who degrade working class women. Men who are known to practice the sexual double standard should be ostracised as much as a prostitute might be, and with greater reason: she has an economic motive, while he has no defence. To marry one's daughter to a 'gallant' man is to "sell her pure and innocent girl to a man who has done his best to make her womanhood a vile and desecrated thing" (*Work* 101). Society will become pure

> only when no mother worthy the name will, for the sake of wealth or position, -- what is called 'a good match,' -- give her pure girl to a man on the very common conditions...that some other ten or twenty young girls -- some poor mothers' daughters -- have been degraded and cast aside into the gutter, that she, the twenty-first in this honourable harem, may be held in apparent honour as a wife. (*Power* 37)

In Hopkins's worldview, ignorance is no defence; she argues that the purity of ignorance is positively evil, because it leaves others to perish. Christ without his wounds was no saviour; similarly, women who refused to suffer social damage and psychic pain in the cause of reform were not Christian (*Visitation* 27-8).

> "It is this divine motherhood, which all evolution, the whole 'process of the suns,' has gone to strengthen, and which Christianity has enshrined at the very heart -- it is this that makes her for ever the

Christ factor in the world, the supreme expression of the redeeming Love -- that care of the strong for the weak. " (*Power* 162)

Hopkins' thinking placed great emphasis on the shared sisterhood of all women. Women's worth came from their place in God's redemptive plan, rather than from their social or sexual value. She argued that for women to permit themselves to be separated by class barriers resulted in a state of society that was both unnatural and false. Shared gender transcended class difference. This sisterhood should not be expressed simply through intellectual or emotional assent; it demanded social integration of all women. Class snobbery, distance and prejudice were responsible for much of the degradation of their sex. Women should learn to respect themselves and to love themselves, instead of being mirrors of men's opinions and desires. There could be no dignity for any woman without the single sexual standard.

> For the misery as things are is this: -- that men divide us into two classes -- we pure women for whom nothing is too good; and those others, whom they never associate with us, for whom nothing is too bad. And what we have to teach them is this -- that our womanhood is ONE, that a sin against them is a sin against us, and so to link the thought of us to them that for the sake of their own mothers, for the sake of their own sisters, above all, for the sake of the future wife, they cannot wrong or degrade a woman or keep up a degraded class of women. (*Power* 147)

She saw one of the great crimes of Victorian society as being its deification of social class. The incarnate Christ's message, Hopkins always insisted, was the absolute equality of all human beings. She claimed that where class differences in morality existed, the advantage was with the working class, even claiming that a House of Commons composed entirely of the sons of working women would be an improvement in moral terms over the current upper class Parliament. Hopkins also believed that increased working class democracy would be in the long term the best means of procuring justice for women, as working class men (she never discusses the possibility of working class women having the vote) would insist on purity legislation, in order to protect the women of their own class. She felt artisans would lead the movement for sexual protection, just as they had been leading demands for the franchise: democracy would result in the "moralising of our laws, and getting some recognition of the sacredness of individual life and moral personality which emphatically does not consist in the abundance of things which are possessed" (*England's* 5,

Damaged 6). In a pamphlet aimed at a working-class audience, Hopkins wrote:

> I find educated men talking of degraded women as a necessary class
> -- a necessary thing that your daughters should be sacrificed, body
> and soul, and that our Christian and civilised life should be based on
> ruined girls -- your girls, remember! the girls of the working class
> -- fast men talking of it as a jolly life for them, though God knows
> it would break their heart for their own daughter or sister. (*On the
> Early* 15-6)

The sometimes inflammatory class argument employed again and again by Hopkins is admirably summarised in this passage from *What Can We Do?*, where she speaks of the

> almost total want of protection it [the law] affords the young and
> helpless, unless they have property and belong to the protected
> classes. And these protected classes seem deliberately to prefer that
> hosts of the young and the helpless should perish rather than laws
> should be passed for their protection, which would entail the risk to
> their own well-protected persons of a false accusation. (14-15)

Hopkins was especially outraged, as were many social reformers, by the reluctance of Parliament to raise the age of consent. Voices in favour of increasing the age of sexual self-determination were overruled by those who preferred the status quo. Some MPs (named and criticised by Hopkins in her writings) even advocated lowering the age of female consent to ten or under, in order to protect men from charges of assault. Speaking more generally of class legislation, she noted angrily that legislation for the good of the people was crowded out session after session, while acts such as the Explosives Bill were passed in twenty-four hours, because it provided extra security for the wealthy and powerful.

Alongside her attack on the social attitudes of the property owning classes ran a deep hostility to the class prejudices ingrained in the Church of England. By its reluctance to democratize its structure and its clergy, the Establishment only reinforced the belief that religion was for the affluent. Her explanation for the disinterest of the masses in Anglicanism was that the Church had, knowingly or not, chosen to exclude them:

> If the Church of England will insist on making herself an exclusively
> aristocratic institution, where only broadcloth is allowed a voice and
> a work, she must expect to lose the democracy. Yet, surely such a

Church is in a most anomalous position; recognising a Working-man as her Lord and Head, yet tacitly excluding working-men. (*English* 92)

She felt that attempts to convert the masses were doomed to failure unless the Church became fully committed to social reform and social justice; only then would preaching begin to have any effect.

While critical of the Established Church, she shared with many Christian feminists of her time the belief not only that Christianity had raised the status of women wherever it had been accepted, but that moral progress was as inevitable as evolutionary advance. Like Josephine Butler, she saw Christ's mission as primarily as one of liberation: of women, of slaves, of all outcast and downtrodden groups. Because the purpose of the Incarnation was to liberate groups unjustly oppressed by their societies' religious traditions and cultures, true Christian theology would also insist on the eradication of inequality in Victorian Britain. Throughout her life she was an ardent advocate of all aspects of female emancipation, and repeatedly urged purity organisations to keep in touch with what she called the "Women's Movement among women". Hopkins thus aligned herself with a number of progressive causes: unionisation of women; the female franchise; the raising of the age of consent; and the punishment of male users of prostitutes on the same basis as solicitation (*Power* 284). It was largely through her work that social purity became a popular issue in radical circles; trade union leaders, socialists, Irish nationalists, all were drawn into sympathy through their espousal of the single sexual standard as advocated by Hopkins (Bristow 111-13). She never overlooked the radical potential of the purity movement, and indirectly influenced some very unlikely people. The best known of these is probably Oscar Wilde, who portrayed her movement sympathetically in several of his plays.

Hopkins was convinced that the tendency of Christianity had been to raise the position of women in society. Where Christianity had failed was in teaching men to respect and endorse that raising. Thus progress could not take place until the sexual double standard was replaced by a single standard of purity before marriage and fidelity afterwards. She pointed to earlier advances in moral feeling such as the abolition of the slave trade, the revolution in the treatment of the insane, and the temperance movement, as examples of how ethical progress can only take place once the public expresses moral revulsion against the status quo. She hoped that the White Cross would join these other successful campaigns as part of "the march of a victorious movement", purifying late Victorian society.

Hopkins insisted that Victorian definitions of purity were a derisory parody of the Christian view. Purity was not merely the absence of contamination; it required social and economic confrontation. Purity of life without social commitment was not purity at all. Educated women were urged to confront local landlords who permitted overcrowding, or whose cottages did not allow for decent sleeping arrangements. Women who were unable to attack the sexual double standard directly were encouraged to devote themselves to a related issue, such as improved work or educational opportunities for working-class women. A woman, however chaste, who turned an indifferent shoulder to the suffering of other women, was not pure, in Hopkins' eyes. Pure women will quietly struggle to transform their society from within.

> We must institute a new and higher order. To do so we women must unite in a great silent movement, a temple slowly rising up beneath our hands without sound of axe or hammer. It will not make itself heard on platforms; its cry will not be heard in our streets. It will go on beneath the surface of our life, probably unheeded and unnoticed of men. Women must educate women; those who know must teach those who are in ignorance. (*Power* 222-3)

Women's mystical role in the redemption of the nation was also important. England's moral decay was certain if women did not begin to respond to "the depths of human pain." Hopkins preferred to see women's role as one of immense spiritual power, rather than of conventional influence. Women needed to be convinced of the importance of demanding moral purity of men; if they would, they could effect more and greater change than any institution or organised body could do. But to make the changes necessary would require "sacrifices amounting to a silent revolution in our life" (*Power* 226). The true remedy was two-fold: the inner involved the development of mental, moral, and spiritual strength among women; the outer nothing less than the transformation of society. But the inner change would bring about the outer: "The remedy, like the evil, must be from within, and must to a great degree revolutionise our life....the first step we have to take, the step which must precede all others, if anything is to be of the least avail, must be to restore the moral law and get rid of the double standard" (*Power* 27).

Hopkins always insisted that theological insights were valueless unless they could be worked out on a very practical level. The gospel imperative to purity of life applied not only on Sunday mornings but should transform the lives of Christians at every level, including their sexuality. Since women are expected to be virgins at marriage, the same demand should be made of men; in another publication she sardonically describes non-virgin bachelors as "fallen men" (*Moral* 7-8, 11).

It is simply a moral Q.E.D., that if chastity is a law for women --
and no man would deny that -- it is a law for every woman without
exception...and if it is a law for every woman, it follows necessarily
that it must be for every man, unless we are going to indulge in the
moral turpitude of accepting a pariah class of women made up of
other women's daughters and other women's sisters -- not our own,
God forbid that they should be our own! -- set apart for the vices of
men. (*Power* 30-1)

Her writings combine a demand for the sexual single standard with two
strands of thought regarding the ideal relationship of men to women. The
true man, moral inheritor of Christ, will use his sexuality responsibly as a
form of atonement to women: she was quick to appreciate "the infinite
possibilities of self-sacrifice and self-control that lie hidden in the common
natures and in the deep heart of man " (*Greeley* 7). At the same time she
demands a sexual single standard as a simple matter of justice for women,
as well as claiming divine origin for it.

It is God who has made us -- not we ourselves, with our false codes,
false notions, and false necessities; and God has made the man to
love the woman and give himself for her, not to degrade her and
destroy the very function for which she was made the blessed
'mother of all living.' Only be sure of this: that men will rise to the
level of any standard that we set them. (*Power* 36)

Hopkins was angered by the familiar argument that prostitution
provided a necessary safety valve for men: if prostitution was needed to
ensure the purity of Victorian homes, she argued, then it should receive the
sanction of both the state and the church: the parsonage should be built on
one side of the parish church and the brothel on the other. As it was, the
argument was incompatible with real Christianity, as Hopkins defined it.

I have even met with Christian women who have serenely averred
to my face that they have been told, on authority that they could
not question, that, were it not for the existence of an outcast class,
no respectable woman would be safe and we could not insure the
purity of the home! So low had the moral consciousness fallen,
through ignorance and thoughtless acceptance of the masculine code,
that women calling themselves Christians could be found who
seemed wholly unconscious of the deep inner debasement of
accepting the degradation of other women as a safeguard to our own
virtue and of basing the purity of the Christian home on the ruined

bodies and souls of the children of the poor. Truly the dark places of the world within, as well as of the world without, are full of cruelty! (*Power* 35)

Hopkins blamed three primary causes for the incredible willingness of middle class Christian women to accept the double standard: they shrank from facing the unpleasant facts; they were morally blighted by the "desolating individualism" which caused them to see personal salvation as the central tenet of Christianity; and they participated in a debased family spirit, which cared little for the injustices done to others as long as their own family life remained serene (*Grave* 3). Hopkins pointed out that merely to articulate this "monstrous theory" of the necessity of prostitution tended to its refutation. "Something divine within us, something higher than mere logic, rises up in wrath, and cries 'It is not so. I refuse to accept life on such conditions; I would die rather'" (*Work Among* 30). Women had been imposed upon by self-serving men in believing such arguments; it was time for women to think and act for themselves, and work out their own line of belief on such issues. Salvation of the individual soul without regard for social transformation was, in her theology, pointless if not impossible. What might save the soul, regardless of the state of faith, was commitment to a cause and sacrifice to that cause.

It is the amount of flabby half-conviction in the world, the number of men and women who are content to be jelly-fish with only a mouth to swallow and a stomach to fill, flapping about hither and thither with every wave that ebbs and flows, and when death comes leaving only a gelatinous smear behind them; it is this that keeps back the world. (*Conquering I* 6)

Her principles were that sexuality should be held in check in both sexes until the reasoning ability was mature; that chastity does not cause infertility or other medical problems, and that sexuality involves another person, with the possibility of creating a third, so it cannot be viewed as merely harmless self-indulgence (*True* 120-3). It was unnatural for a man to bring a child into the world and then to fail to take care of it; more unnatural than abstinence before marriage. Not a garden-variety ascetic, she rejected the belief that the body itself is evil, using the metaphor of horse and rider instead; the horse is in subjection to the will of the rider but has rights and needs by virtue of its animal existence. "And the teaching of Christ is: Neither hate nor fear this part of your nature with the ascetic, nor pamper and stimulate it with the Hedonist, but let it alone to act on its own plane" (*Power* 43). She pointed out wryly that male desire and male lack of self control were often overlooked as factors affecting prostitution. At a conference held in the

1870s on the subject, Hopkins noted that of the 30 or 40 causes of the degradation of women listed, "the masculine pronoun did not once occur" (*Conquering II* 27).

Just as she despised the elitism and snobbery of the Church, Hopkins attacked the class assumptions inherent in the medicalized defenses of the double standard. In response to the many Victorian doctors who claimed that regular intercourse was medically necessary for men, she suggested that such physicians should be asked if "his own daughter or sister was available for the carrying out of the prescription, since he so freely prescribed the degradation of other men's daughters and sisters" (*Conquering II* 25). On the scientific merits of this claim, she concluded that if this was so (which she denied) then men should pay the price of less-than-optimal health in order to crush the trade in female flesh. She denounced "...the talk about this evil being a necessity, as if men were made jackals that must have their carrion, or they cannot live" (*Rolling* 10). Since doctors had previously advocated the practices of bleeding, alcohol abuse, and the flogging of the insane as sound medical practice, she argued that their insistence on the necessity of intercourse for male health was also suspect (*Work* 48-9).

Hopkins saw the so-called purity of sexual ignorance, encouraged in Victorian women in so many ways, as one of the worst evils of her time. She encouraged women to inform themselves about sexual matters so that they could teach their sons and daughters accurately about sexual function, and to view sexuality as a wholesome natural appetite which required responsible control. Women should "insist on knowing -- refuse to acquiesce any longer in the babyish ignorance that unfits them for the care of their own sons " (*Work* 42). Sex education was especially important for girls. Hopkins was disgusted by the attitude of women who boasted that their adolescent daughters believed babies were purchased from the doctor. She advised mothers to

> aim for our girls not so much at Innocence, with her fading wreath of flowers -- fading, as, alas! they must ever fade in a world like this -- but to aim at Virtue, with her victor's crown of gold, tried in the fire. May it not be that His divine providence is constraining us to take as our ideal for our womanhood, not the old sheltered garden, but a strong city of God ... a city of refuge for all who are oppressed with wrong, and from which all foul forms of evil are banned by the one word '*Without*'? (*Power* 172-3)

This passage powerfully re-interprets Biblical images of women, rejecting the passivity of the secluded garden, an image of female sexual innocence since at least the time of Solomon, for that of the militant city of sanctuary, armed against evil with knowledge.

Hopkins saw purity as a positive spiritual force, not a simple abstaining from certain activities. The key to its power was its sacrifice of self-interest. For men, her "new commandment of love" was chastity in the service of women, not for the protection of his own virtue (*Work* 54-5). For both sexes,

> Surely the great central fact of Christianity is not personal salvation, not saving our own soul, not just getting to heaven, but a life poured out for the good of the world. (*Touching* 4)

This pouring out could take many forms, but she insisted the goal must always be the care of the weaker and the helpless. The means mattered less: the 'poured-out life' could be spent advocating improved working class housing, factory reform, unionisation, or as with her own life, the promulgation of a sexual single standard which would bring justice to women. "That passion for the weak, the wronged, and the defenceless" was a passion for purity in the world, regardless of the form it might take in the life of the individual activists, but she insisted that only passion could cast out passion (*Standard* 23, *Wild* 15).

Unlike most purity literature, the emphasis in Hopkins' writings was not on protecting one's own virtue; men and women were expected to remain virtuous while devoting their energies to the care of the weak and defenceless in their society. Those who risked contamination through knowledge of evil, and through caring for the sinful and tempted become the Christs of the nineteenth century; just as prostitutes and abused children became Christs through their unmerited suffering.

Hopkins poured out her contempt on what she termed, "mere passive purity, the purity of which the noblest utterance is, 'I know how to take care of myself', and which is intent on saving its own alabaster skin " (*Work Among* 99). Selfishness is probably the unforgivable sin in her theology; even the woman who gives in to the demands of her lover is praised, in contrast to the selfishness which makes those demands. The purpose of Christianity is not the salvation of one's own soul, but the response to the need to "*love*, have a response to every claim upon you....live a life poured out for the good of the world" (*Girls'* 8; emphasis Hopkins'). The focus of the White Cross was always a robust emphasis on purity rather than a sneaking fascination with impurity; this helped them to largely avoid the prurient interest in vice which dogged some groups. Hopkins confessed to an abiding unease at the motivation of some purity activists who seemed to find their crusade titillating: "some subtle odour of the sewer will still cling about the heart of the shrine, a nameless sense of something impure in the whole subject; an undefinable something in his way of looking at it, which has often made the purity of men -- blameless in their outer life -- sadden and perplex me almost as much as the actions and words of confessedly impure men" (*Power* 103).

She assured women that learning about evil in order to save others would never be morally contaminating; the true defiling evil for women was the embracing of wilful ignorance; however, even a tainted woman was preferable to a selfish one, unwilling to risk danger in the service of others: "That hand may be white, but in God's eyes it is white with the whiteness of leprosy" (*Power* 10-11). Of course, the Army was not immune to sexual scandal. Hopkins mused, "there is some mysterious connection between the religious emotions and the lower animal nature; and the religious forcing-house, of whatever school of theology, will always be liable to prove a hot-bed of impurity" (*Power* 81).

At times she seemed to be going beyond a demand that men take responsibility for their sexuality, towards the declaration of a sex war. She complained that penitentiaries for the rehabilitation of fallen women left the real culprit, the man, untouched and unpunished, and she demanded that public opinion, "break down the artificial distinction between this and all other sins. " (*Plea* 9, *English* 53). Women should petition for changes to the laws regarding solicitation, and demand, "a righteous law that will deal with men and women with the same even-handed justice, and not put the prostitute woman in the lock-up and leave the prostitute man in the dining room" (*Rolling* 11). At times too Hopkins suggested that women were morally superior: men should rise, "to the level of the Christ in us, instead of our sinking to the level of the animal in them" (*Work* 44).

Hopkins's premise that the purpose of Christian belief is not personal salvation, but the service and protection of the weak and helpless was derived from Hinton's 'theology of others'. The following passage from her novel, *Rose Turquand*, is absolutely central to an understanding of Hopkins' theological vision, combining as it does her characteristic amalgam of suffering and altruism as the fuel for spiritual power.

> And if the one Cross which was to reveal the unseen to us, the one Cross whose end we therefore see, if the end of the pain, the failure, the shame, the mockery, the forsakenness of God and man that went to make up that Cross, all those things which we think most dreadful and most useless, was to work out an infinite gain for the whole world, may there not be, nay, must there not be...an unseen end working out an infinite good for man, as well as for the sufferer himself?...it is good to be shapely and clever and useful, and successful, and loved; but one thing is better, it is better to be like Christ, to drink of His cup and be baptised with His baptism, and render back the world's pain into the expression of a perfect Love. (vol.2, 262)

One of Hopkins' central themes is the theology of failure. This is based in part upon Hinton's theology of altruism, but at times Hopkins seems to suggest that failure itself is a form of grace. One of the recurrent phrases in her religious writing is 'Wreck yourself on God'; the metaphor is that of shipwreck. What made failure powerful was the element of sacrifice: "in this work God stretches His hand across any number of mistakes, any amount of unwise actions, and blesses SACRIFICE" (Barrett 146-7; emphasis Hopkins'). The Messiah could emancipate only through suffering and apparent failure; she perceived the pain experienced by women and children in her own time as a reprise, or even completion, of that redemptive mission.

Hopkins accused contemporary Protestantism of being overly Pauline in its focus on the Atonement; she preferred to emphasise the Johannian theme of the Incarnation, where the body as well as the soul is capable of experiencing grace. Thus, all her social reform was morally driven. "If the Incarnation means anything, it means not the salvation and sanctification of a ghost, but the salvation and consecration of the whole man, of his body as well as his soul" (*Power* 116). Christ was the prototype of a new kind of man, one who would treat women as his sexual, social, and moral equal, while at the same time reverencing them for their differences from himself; Hopkins saw, "Christ as the revelation of the true man, *the man that is to be*; the Incarnation which enshrines the sanctity of womanhood at the very heart of our Christian faith. " (*Standard* 20; emphasis added).

Implicit in this last quotation is another important theme of Hopkins's writings, premised upon a Victorian version of the ideals of chivalry. Women were not only physically weaker than men, but more importantly, society's inculcation of proper ladylike behaviour turned them into moral cowards. She argued that until men and women were able to become true equals in social and political life, men -- as the stronger and more privileged sex -- would have a chivalric responsibility for the protection of women. Women did require protection from some men until all men learned to take responsibility for their own sexuality. So chivalric protection of women was represented as necessary during a transitional state of society, but was to be abandoned when women came to enjoy full equality with men. Until equality was achieved, men should protect women, rather than degrade them; she attacked the 'pitiful meanness', as well as the unfairness of the double standard. Again, Christ was the prototype of how life on earth should be lived: her focus was on his life always, rather than on the resurrection or the prospect of salvation. Christ was the exemplar who

Came on earth that He might show mankind
What 'tis to be a Man: to give, not take;

To serve, not rule; to nourish, not devour;
To help, not crush; if needs, to die, not live. (*Power* v)

Late in her life, she became troubled by the numbers of young women who denied any positive faith in religion. She was convinced that unbelief could be countered by an emphasis on service mediated by faith:

...if they [young women] were taught that Christianity is only human life rightly seen and divinely ordered, that the Cross is only the uncovering of what is going on all round us, though hidden to a careless gaze, -- the sin, the pain, the misery, which are forever crucifying and forever calling forth that great passion of redeeming Love to which, through the motherhood that is in us, 'one touch of nature makes us kin'; and that the central truth of Christianity is not, as we have too often taught, saving our own souls, but a life poured out for the good of others, and personal salvation as a means for having a life to pour forth -- I cannot but think that much fashionable girlish agnosticism would disappear, and the true woman would reach forth to that divine humanity to which she belongs. (*Power* 169)

She argued that this Christianity, which placed the redemptive role of altruism at its heart, was the only form of Christianity that educated young women of the late nineteenth century could be brought to believe in at all; conventional belief collapses "in the face of the great inequalities of life" (*Girls'* 8).

As a consequence of her campaigns, Hopkins found herself a social outcast, depicted in some circles as "a monster of folly and depravity" (*Conquering II* 3). A number of respectable moral reform organisations, (including several that she had helped to found) expelled or distanced her, fearing that her name might prejudice their reputations. A contemporary wrote, "the very name of Ellice Hopkins, if anyone dared mention it in a drawing room, was spoken in a whisper and heard with a shudder" (Bristow 5). The mental stress of leading an unpopular cause must have been great; she certainly felt the pain of a lack of support, writing rather sadly in 1882 that if she "were fighting against intemperance, heathenism, cruelty to animals, &c., I should find myself backed by five or six of the most powerful Societies in the country. But because I am only fighting for the honour of us women, and the manhood of our sons, I am backed by nothing" (*Grave* 63).

During the ten years of her active work, she came into contact with kinds of evil that she had not before imagined: incest, child abuse, rape, child prostitution, the traffic in white slavery, among other horrors, often in the most respectable of families. It took a psychological toll, as well as destroying her faith in all of the 'respectable' institutions of Victorian society: she wrote

> ...my fellow-creatures used me as a bottomless well into which they could empty their household skeletons; and I used often to reflect with sardonic satisfaction that I should never run dry like other old wells, but that death would come and fill me up with a good wholesome shovelful of earth, and I and my skeletons would lie quiet together. But in this way I gained a knowledge of what is going on under the surface of our life, whether we choose to ignore it or not, which possibly can only come to those who are set apart to be confessors of their kind; and the conclusion was forced upon me that this evil...is more or less everywhere -- in our nurseries, in our public schools...decorously seated on magisterial benches, fouling our places of business, and even sanctimoniously seated in our places of worship. (*Power* 7-8)

In 1888 her health finally broke down, leaving her an invalid until her death in 1904. Although she continued to publish until the very end, she never again wrote so prolifically or so powerfully as she had done in the 1880s. Towards the end of her life she looked back at her crusade and felt convinced that real progress had been made, claiming now that the tone of society had changed with regard to questions of sexual morality. She expressed great satisfaction that women were uniting in common causes in the late nineteenth century, and rejoiced that a sense of 'common womanhood' was being established among woman activists of all kinds. By 1904, the year of her death, the inheritors of Hopkins' thought were able to work through government and municipal bodies in a way that had been impossible for her twenty years earlier (*Power* 3, *National* 6-7). However, she never abandoned her suspicion of public progress without personal sacrifice. In one of her final writings she insisted:

> Now, I contend that the only ground of despair, the only thing that might shut us up to pessimism and to 'a philosophy only just above suicide mark,' would be not the presence but the absence of these great world evils. If this world presented a dead-level of comfortable selfishness that on the whole answered fairly well all round, an economy of petty self-interests in stable equilibrium....then indeed we might despair....Who that gazes on this world, with its infinite depths of pain, its heavy weight of evil, its abysmal falls, its stupendous pressures of wrong and misery, but feels that here, if anywhere, we are in the presence of kinetic energies, of immense moral and

spiritual forces, capable of raising the whole of fallen humanity to the heights of the Divine. For let us remember that in the moral and spiritual world, as well as in the physical, no fall but carries with it the force that can be converted into a rise; no dread resistance of wrong to the right but creates an accumulated force which once let loose can transform an empire; no weight of evil but, in pulling it down, can be made to raise the whole bent of our life.... I ask how else can [humanity] be educated, in the true sense of the word, and raised from death unto life except by being made to deduce his own results and work out his evil premise to the bitter end, till he is forced to go back upon himself, and recognise the right principle which he has violated? The very law of his being, of every being who is being raised from death unto life, is, that he can only know life through death, only grasp good by grappling with evil, only gain knowledge by knowing ignorance; his highest must be sown in weakness before it can be raised in power, must be sown in dishonour before it can be raised in glory. (*Power* 209-11)

Jane Ellice Hopkins was notorious in her time as a result of her refusal to quietly accept the sexual double standard. Her protest, expressed in more than 75 books and pamphlets, demanded equality for women: morally, economically, socially, and politically: an equality which stemmed from her conception of the founder of the Christian faith, "the revelation of the true man, *the man that is to be*." She devoted her considerable literary ability to tabooed issues, especially the double standard of morality and the sexual abuse of children, saying: "Nature made me a singing bird; man has made me a sewer rat". Her unique theology, rejecting Biblical literalism and the centrality of personal salvation in favour of social activism, personal altruism, and the absolute equality of all humanity, was promoted through a torrent of publications distributed in phenomenal numbers in the 1880s. She investigated and publicised subjects which her contemporaries preferred to ignore; her impact was enormous and lasting, even if she has herself been ignored by historians of social and religious reform movements.

WORKS CITED

Barrett, Rosa M. *Ellice Hopkins: a Memoir.* London: Wells Gardner, Darton, [1905].
Bristow, Edward J. *Vice and Vigilance: Social Purity Movements in Britain Since 1700.* Dublin: Gill & Macmillan, 1977.
Burritt, Elihu. 'Preface', *An English Woman's Work Among Workingmen*, by Jane Ellice Hopkins.
Hopkins, Jane Ellice. *Autumn Swallows: a Book of Lyrics.* London: Macmillan, 1883.
---. *The Black Anchor.* London: Hatchards, 1883, 1885.
---. *Conquering and to Conquer I.* London: Hatchards, 1886.
---. *Conquering and to Conquer II.* London: Hatchards, 1886.
---. *Damaged Pearls: an Appeal to Workingmen.* London: Hatchards, 1984; London: D.Gardner, 1895, 95th thousand, reprinted by White Cross League in 1910.

---. *The Defaced Image Restored.* London: Hatchards, 1885.

---. *England's Law for Women and Children.* London: [Hatchards, 1883].

---. *An English Woman's Work Among Workingmen.* New Britain, CT: John A. Williams, 1875. Expanded version titled *Work Among Working Men.* London: Strahan, [1879]; 4th ed. London: Kegan Paul, 1882; 5th ed. New York: Whittaker, 1884; 6th ed. New York: Whittaker, 1886.

---. *Girls' Clubs and Recreative Evening Homes.* London: Hatchards, 1887.

---. *Grave Moral Questions Addressed to the Men and Women of England.* 100th thousand. London: Hatchards, 1882.

---. *The Greeley Expedition.* London: Hatchards, 1886.

---. *Ladies' Associations for the Care of Friendless Girls, being an account of the work in Brighton.* 13th thousand. Reprinted from *Day of Rest,* London, 1878.

---. *Life and Letters of James Hinton.* Edited by Ellice Hopkins; with an introduction by Sir W.W. Gull. 4th ed. London: 1878; London: Kegan Paul, Trench and Co., 1882.

---. *Lost in Quicksand.* London: Hatchards, [1885].

---. *Moral Money-clippers.* London: Hatchards, [1885].

---. *The National Purity Crusade* [1904].

---. *On the Early Training of Girls and Boys: an Appeal to Working Women, especially intended for Mothers' Unions.* New York: Hammett, 1883; London: Hatchards, 1882, 1884, 1886; London: 20th thousand, P.S. King & Sons, 1902.

---. *A Plea for the Wider Action of the Church of England in the Prevention of the Degradation of Women as submitted to a Committee of Convocation.* London: Hatchards, 1879.

---. *The Power of Womanhood; or, Mothers and Sons. A Book for Parents and those in loco parentis.* London: Wells Gardner, 1899, 1900; 11th edition, London: Gardner, Darton, [1904]; New York: Dutton, 1899, 1904.

---. *Rolling Away the Stone.* London: Hatchards, [1885].

---. *Rose Turquand.* London: Macmillan, 2 vols, 1876, New York: Harper & Bros., 1876, New York: G. Munro, 1880; third and cheaper edition published, date unknown.

---. *The Standard of the White Cross: Do We Need It? An Appeal to Clergy and Laity.* London: Hatchards, 1885, 1886.

---. *Touching Pitch.* London: Hatchards, [1885].

---. *True Manliness.* Reprinted in *The Blanco Book: a collection of papers for men.* London: White Cross League, 3rd ed. 1904). First published London: Hatchards, 1886.

---. *The Visitation of Dens. An Appeal to the Women of England.* [1874].

---. *What Can We Do?* London: Hatchards, 1883, 1886; Chicago: Miss R.Gilbert, n.d..

---. *Wild Oats, or Acorns?* London: Gardner, 1890.

---. *Work Among Working Men.* [1879]. See *An English Woman's Work Among Workingmen.*

---. *Work in Brighton, or, Woman's Mission to Women.* London: 9th thousand, with additions and a preface by Florence Nightingale, Hatchards, 1877, 1879.

Mumm, Susan. "'Not Worse than Other Girls': the Convent-based Rehabilitation of Fallen Women in Victorian England." *Journal of Social History* 29 (1996): 527-46.

Norwich Record Office. SO 27/3, Minutes of the Norfolk and Norwich Ladies Association for the Care of Girls, vol.III, May 1886.

Beyond Victorian Christianity

Victorian Women Theologians of the Mystical Fringe:
Translation and Domesticity

Sarah Willburn
Duke University

> *Now let me write down my creed that you may see it with your two eyes clearly...Only, granting that a door is open to evil and uninstructed spirits, I hold that by the same door must necessarily come the good and instructed. I don't believe in your theology about troops of devils coming in by miracle. My theology is simply physical, and has to do with ordinary nature. I understand by a medium a peculiar physical adaptitude...*

Elizabeth Barrett Browning, letter to Mary Hunter, 28, Via Del Fritone, Rome, December 31, 1859 (Browning 8).

The mid-to-late Victorian era seemed to be a conducive environment for mediums to receive instructive communications from beyond the vale. Some Victorian women theologians used seances and mesmerism to gain insight into how to achieve progress, friendships, and wellness, as well as to reconceptualize history. For some theologians of the mystical fringe, such communications from the after-life supplanted the power of religious tradition and displaced time -- eliding the concept of an eventual or apocalyptic Christian *telos*. By this I mean that a Victorian woman's immediate mystical experience might reduce the imperative importance, in her mind, of over eighteen-hundred years of organized Christianity. The point here is that Victorian women who engaged in mystical practices do not fit into the identificatory model of separate spheres.[1] These women are not in a private domestic female space, or a public, male, professional space, they are, instead, in an extra space.

To displace tradition and history, as certain mystical women's practices seemed to do, results in a radical theological enterprise. In the midst of a century marked by its professionalism, writing theology became surprisingly de-professionalized. It was more often the act of the lay man or woman than the religious scholar. As religious practice changed, with even the spirits of the dead ostensibly appearing in living rooms, theology became for some a popular, domestic act not reserved for the clerically-trained professional.

The mid-Victorian age was marked by a growing amount of "popular" theology. Eighteen forty-eight not only marks a year of political revolution in the Western world,[2] but also one of religious domestication with the famous spirit rappings of the Fox sisters in Rochester, New York. In the subsequent decades more serious, pious, conventionally-religious citizens started to communicate with spirits in their own homes, some reports even claiming these guests as the emissaries of God. Often the visited were women. These women not only recorded their ectoplasmic experiences, but also discussed the theological import of such sightings. Many women presented new systematic theologies to incorporate their interactions with the spirit world. These theologies were not based on Biblical or religious history, but on private events in their private lives. This new theology was not a redundant if strange marker of bourgeois hegemonic respectability, but was, instead, often a new, revolutionary world view that, in turn, changed the boundaries of some Victorian women's domestic lives.

The overarching similarity between the women's theologies that we will examine is an expanded present tense and a sense that neither a millennium of linear Christian history in England nor a doctrine of ur-perfectibility define their spiritual lives. These women used a mystical extra sphere to expand and redefine the professional and domestic spheres of which they were also a part. This essay, though, seeks only to illuminate the ways in which their theological writings utilize the concept of this mystical extra sphere. These women present this extra sphere as a liberating space that gives them room to develop their own autonomous extra-Victorian identities.

This essay presents three case studies in Victorian women's mystical practices: Camilla Crosland's seance with her medium's spirit-control, "Vastness"; Harriet Martineau's mesmeric trance-state; and professional novelist Florence Marryat's seances with her friend the professional medium, Miss Showers. Not only do these narrative accounts depict complicated subject/object relations, but they also show the pro-social power and authority a medium can take on. What these instances of mediumship have in common is that they all create an instant community of at least three -- the medium, the witness/recorder of the phenomenon, and the invisible spirit control that ostensibly speaks through the medium. They operate, then, by a sort of multiple personal identity. Intimacy becomes a spectator sport. The situations of all of the mediums and seances we will examine, with their erotic detail and potential for cure, for entertainment, for mediation is never without a witness and secretary/recorder: the history of this new state is instantly written down -- made true -- and also made presentable. In living rooms we find newly constituted sanctuaries fulfilling complicated ritual passing between the natural and the spiritual world. We find alternative theologies. The terms, medium, mesmerist, and spirit-control, are all a part of the epistemology of this *nouveau* theology. These alternative theologies are volatile and lead to cure, community, Christ, with otherwise demure women reinscribed as militant and triumphant. The medium is a part of a new, if ephemeral, political space several decades before suffrage.

The Reverend and Mrs. Crosland: Theology at Home

The Croslands were one prominent mid-Victorian theologically inclined couple. Newton Crosland was a minister, and his wife, Camilla, a literary woman of note, for her children's books, biographies, and for her personal acquaintance with such famous activists as Harriet Beecher Stowe and Margaret Fuller. The Croslands are both notable for their complicated (and antagonistic) theologically intoned interpretations of spirit manifestations. The Rev. Newton Crosland's *Apparitions; a New Theory* (1856) blends the budding technology of photography with the epistemologically -- and theologically -- established ethic of learning by example. Crosland elucidates his photographic spirit-theory as follows:

> The candid ghost-seer, in relating his experiences, is baffled by the scoffing logician, who exclaims -- "I have no objection to believe in the apparition of the soul of your grandmother, but don't tell me that you really and literally saw the ghost of her night-cap and apron!".... To meet the difficulty, I venture to offer as a solution the following hypothesis: that every significant action of our lives -- in the garments we wear, and in the attitudes and gestures of our humanity -- is vitally photographed or depicted in the spirit-world; and that the angels, under God's direction, have the power of exhibiting, as a living picture, any specific circumstances or features to those who have the gift of spiritual sight, and who are intended to be influenced by the manifestations.... What an idea of infinity and divine government does it give us, to suppose that after death we shall move through a grand picture-gallery of our own deeds self-delineated! What a subject of contemplation and awe to those who are debating in their own minds the character of their actions! What a check to those who have not yet quite decided to perpetrate something unworthy of future exhibition! And what a consolation to believe that true repentance for any vicious deeds may secure the removal of the portraits of such deeds from this gallery of celestial art! (N. Crosland 28-30).

Rev. Crosland's bold theory is simultaneously technologically progressive and religiously conservative. Newton is ready to incorporate new experiences and technology into an existing framework of Christian education. Spirits appear as if at a slideshow of the moral past life. The beatified repentant, soberly attired spirit indicates high points of the soul's earthly tenure. "What a consolation to believe that...repentance for any vicious deeds may secure the removal...of such deeds from this gallery...." In this scheme spirit visitation is as innocuous as the family portrait gallery. Photographic ephemerality -- already uncanny -- is reinstated into a heavenly context where the spooky is reassuringly domesticated. All the grandmothers (in all their nightcaps) peacefully people eternity -- offering picture-book guidance to their earthly progeny.

Rev. Crosland, although he does not *ask* it as such, offers us a beguiling question: What (kind of) an idea of infinity and divine government does it give us, to suppose that after death we shall move through a grand picture-gallery of our own deeds self-delineated? It gives us a divine government that, in fact, does not substantially differ from earthly government: hegemonically inscribed grannies eternally wearing their aprons. The celestial imitates and celebrates the terrestrial. No revolutionary changes or acts are required; heaven is a well-edited strolling gallery run by the divine government with angel-docents. Christian *telos* is nothing but the divine reinscription of a pre-existing respectable England.

Even as odd as the technology Newton alludes to -- spirit photography -- may seem, it turns out in practice to be something rather ordinary and traditional. England's first spirit-photographer, Mr. Fred A. Hudson, of 177 Holloway Road, London, experienced a booming business in the Spring of 1872. Fritz, in his book *Where are the Dead?* notes,

> Mr. Hudson has taken a great number of spirit photographs, and his rooms for many months in the summer of 1872 were crowded with Spiritualists from all parts of the country, anxious to be photographed....the form of a spirit came out distinctly upon the plate immediately on the likeness being "developed" (Fritz 81-82).

The verb "developed" is duly noted to emphasize, no doubt, the Victorian trope of development. One striking feature of the description of Mr. Hudson's business is the likelihood that the sitter will recognize the spirit that is developed beside him or her on their photographic plate. Often one's dead children, as for the Swedenborgian medium, Mr. Howitt, or ancestors whose likeness is only known to the sitter and not to Mr. Hudson, will appear in the spirit photograph. The lesson of the photograph seems to be that it will document that ancestral ties and familial identity persist beyond the vale. The photograph serves as evidence, as a material record to preserve lineage.

There were other spiritualist theologies and practices that counter such conservative assumptions as ur-perfectibility (the object-lesson of virtuous ancestors) and the survival of family ties. Take, for instance, the conviction that time does not matter or come to bear upon the existence of a thing. Professor G.G. Zerffi writes,

> Kant's theory is confirmed by many facts that are adduced. For if time is not essential to the reality of a *thing*, past and future have no signification with reference to it. According to this any event may be seen whether it has already happened or not (Zerffi 67).

In this fashion, temporality and the reality that comes with it have no bearing on what does or does not exist or on what has or has not occurred. Taking this as a possible assumption creates a wildly different view of the spiritual from those upheld by Rev. Crosland or the photographer, Mr. Hudson.

Without temporality, history becomes a non-issue. The removal of history makes the contemplation of what society is or might be a vital question for some spiritualist theologians. For Mrs. Camilla Crosland, who in the mid-1850s became quite taken up with Spiritualism, a reconsideration of temporality accompanied a reconsideration of all physical laws. Mrs. Crosland gives the following surprising depiction of natural law:

> The laws of the spiritual world do -- under certain conditions, and finding, there is reason to suppose, their *tertium quid* in magnetism or electricity -- very often control and supersede the common laws of matter. And thus it comes to pass that I, with hundreds of others, am able to testify that heavy articles are frequently suspended in the air by invisible means; that a musical instrument has been played by invisible fingers; that by those peculiar concussions which spiritualists agree to call raps, messages proceeding from disembodied intelligences are frequently delivered; and, in short, to certify to more interesting phenomena than it would be easy to catalogue or classify (C.Crosland 81-82).

Why, we may ask, should this commotion be necessary? In another place Camilla responds that if the spirits came with more solemnity they would overawe (19). There also seems to be a gendered program fulfilled by this spectacular supersession of natural law. Science and nature in this theology seem to cooperate in an effort to thwart the presumptions of catalogues and classifications. Camilla speaks of woman as being closer to the spiritual than man. It seems that with this claim Camilla expresses a desire to overturn the power of a professionalized science that insists on a knowable, ordered, classifiable, hierarchical world.[3] Instead, the "laws of the spiritual world" "supersede the common laws of matter." Her rhetoric subjects the centralized dominion of a recordable natural history. Nature and the history of civilization with it become a radically changeable record that is subject to arbitrary and entertaining uncanny performances that Camilla calls "spiritual laws." These laws, by which instruments are invisibly played and heavy furniture is lifted, reorganize and vitalize domestic space. Camilla Crosland's view of the inexplicable but superior spiritual powers of women challenge the concept of a knowable and recordable historical world.

Of different domains and functions of men's and women's powers, Camilla writes,

> On a particular occasion Vastness gave us the following message: "To man was given wisdom, the first spiritual gift, and that is represented in the spiritual world by the colour blue. Wisdom gives government and therefore blue is always a governing type. The woman, the last created terrestrial being, approaches more nearly to the celestial than any form of the terrestrial creation. Therefore, the first spiritual gift given to the woman is love, for she is the representative of it. Love rules. So the union of love and wisdom gives dominion -- the type of which is purple, -- and unto humanity was given dominion over all created things and beings. But woman also represents the church. The church is militant, and woman is militant; when the church is triumphant, woman will be triumphant" (C.Crosland 94).

This vision makes loving women spiritually closer to the divine and destined for dominion through their affiliation with the church. Thus, private women actually adhere to a revolutionary "woman is militant" public, institutional future. These women, unlike the Rev. Newton Crosland's, do not people heaven in caps and aprons.

A further sign of an inverted terrestrial order is apparent in the structure of the seance itself. Mrs. Crosland notes,

> I must observe that the dictation was taken down from the lips of the seeress in my presence, the gentleman -- a clergyman of the Church of England -- who was the amanuensis, being the only person besides ourselves present....The spirit who showed this vision is known to us by the name Vastness -- (C.Crosland 83).

We may wonder whether, in fact, the amanuensis from the Church of England is the Reverend Newton Crosland. He is busy, in any event, transcribing the lived vision into a written record. His job is one of transcription, not of interpretation, and his source is not the familiar Biblical text of his profession, but is, instead, the sensual seeress' lips. He is a scribe involved in a distinctly non-professional act. Even the exegesis of the vision is reserved for Camilla. The representative of the Church of England has been subsumed by Camilla's higher spiritual laws.

What seems to me to be most striking about the spiritual realm with which Camilla presents us is not so much the content of the visions she describes but rather the implied structure of the higher spiritual realm that she depicts. In the practice of the vision, the clergyman of the Church of England is only an amanuensis; spiritual laws control natural ones; women are natively closest to the celestial and will rule; and even the vision itself is viewed through the vehicle of a crystal likened to a hen's egg -- rather an undignified object[4] not only for its barnyard provenance but also for its proximity to the hen and its low status in the food chain. Mrs. Crosland explains the seance's material detail as follows:

> A novice in spiritualism will very naturally inquire the manner in which the foregoing vision was presented to the seeress. I answer, through an oval crystal about the size and shape of a hen's egg.... I may describe that when a vision is about to be presented the crystal appears to expand, and then that it disappears; nay, that surrounding objects seem likewise to give way, and only the spiritual world to be visible....The phenomena, however, of clairvoyance, and even of ordinary dreaming, suggest how completely the spirit eye can see, totally unaided by outer light, which is necessary to the use of the physical organ...(C.Crosland 91-92).

The rather homely hen's egg crystal becomes transcendent -- serving as the gateway to inner-vision and higher law. In fact, no shortage of dignitaries appear to the seeress in this fashion. Surprisingly, included on this distinguished list is Christ. The simultaneous orthodoxy and heterodoxy of this Christ serve as the basis of a compelling, original, revolutionary theology. Let us meet this Christ:

> THE BEARDED CHRIST: "I am that I am....I was rejected, I was betrayed, I was misrepresented, I was slandered, -- even more, I was crucified. I was buried, I was resuscitated, I was made evident unto woman, being the nearest approach to the spiritual; through her I was made evident unto man in the outer; through the two, or the perfect humanity, I was enabled to show My final ascent into

heaven....To another in the body, in the last or the closing of the outer upon the inner world, I gave in charge the keeping of My mother. She lived seven epochs, or years, according to your calculation of time; after that she was translated, but her spirit descended in various ways to help in the Christianizing or polarizing of the earth and its inhabitants to God....I, by the telegraphic communication between the Father, His Spirit, and Myself, preserved My own oneness....I was linked with God,....with everything that exists in creation, because they are from and part of God, the Outer and the Inner....I will marry the outer to the inner, and the innermost; I will etherealize, I will spiritualize, I will mentalize My chosen, My predestined, My pre-called. They are many, they are numerous; they are more than many, -- they are great" (Crosland 136-138).

The first somewhat surprising statement this Christ makes is that he was "made evident unto woman, being the nearest approach to the spiritual." The Bearded Christ who speaks through Vastness attributes woman with the capacity for correct interpretation. In fact, this narrative states that Christ's crucifixion occurred because he was "misrepresented." As if to foreground the issue of representation, Christ goes on to note, when speaking of the Virgin Mary's Assumption into heaven, that "she was translated, but her spirit descended in various ways to help in the Christianizing or polarizing of the earth and its inhabitants to God...." Again, as before, representation is at the fore; the Virgin Mary is reinscribed into a new language system: translated, as if staying just the same in meaning while changing form into a sign only fleetingly or occasionally recognizable to her old sphere, the world.

In Crosland's document the Passion becomes a series of perpetually reiterated statements that are available to interpretation; not a set of previously narrated historical events. In this new language system, seeresses and the female attendants of seances become the ideal exegetes. Also noteworthy about the "translated" Mary is that her intercessions and appearances on earth involve her in an act of "polarizing" (or "Christianizing") "of the earth and its inhabitants to God." Mary is no free-will missionary; her mission, if it can be termed as such, is one of magnetic "polarization." Her function is naturalized and raised to the technical realm of professionalized science. Like a magnet or a cathode ray, she polarizes and upholds the contemporary Victorian view of progressive science. Also of note is that her polarizing could scarcely be considered an act of volition, but is rather a mechanistic inevitability. Again, according to Camilla's account, events are as they may be and only become "Christianized" through women's interpretation. This take on religious history has a certain undeniable Calvinist tone. Crosland has found an antinomian Christ who remarks that he "will etherialize, ...spiritualize...mentalize [His] chosen, [His] predestined, [His] pre-called." Just as spiritual laws can control natural ones, Christ can supersede free-will. In fact, for Camilla, human history becomes solely a part of the mind of God in a massive project of unification.[5] Christ was linked to "everything that exists in creation, because they are from and part of God" (C.Crosland 134).

The new language system that Camilla Crosland upholds is not only one in which women's interpretation subsumes Biblical history, it is also one that makes claims for whole new types of divinely-inspired writing. In *Light in the Valley*, Camilla Crosland documents and explains her belief in Spirit Writing and Symbolic Spirit Drawing as types of additional revelations to the Bible. In her explanations of automatic writing and drawing, Camilla Crosland presents her surprising view of woman as crucified Christ and prophesies the intellectual union of man and woman and their joint polarization to the eye and heart of God. Additionally, in this work, Crosland theorizes new modes of spirit communication. First of all, she naturalizes these interactions, claiming that "the spirits have declared that magnetism and electricity, though not spirit, are the media by which spirit acts on matter....It would appear that there is a soul...which permeates through the body in life, and it is on or by this atmosphere that disembodied spirits are permitted to communicate with mortals" (C. Crosland 31, 33). She goes on to elevate the topic of spiritualism and to protect it from its critics by saying,

> The truth is, that talking of spiritualism to those whose spiritual faculty is thickly encrusted with materialism, is something like talking of flashing jewels to one who has never seen; but the blinded eyes have often been couched, and the light let in, and none should despair of a human mind, sooner or later, shaking off its encarnalizing scales (C. Crosland 39).

Her theological beliefs are thus protected from the onslaught of detractors by her claim that such critics are physically unable to comprehend spiritualism -- because of materialist encrustations. She presents an alternative, naturalized representational system as she suggests an alternative theology.

The real Victorian world is assumed under the ideal umbrella of the mind of the Godhead in Camilla's scheme. While the Rev. Newton's spirit world is a photographic record of the past, of the celestial turned terrestrial, Camilla's, as well as many other Victorian women theologians', is firmly in the present tense, with pre-destination more specifically having become destination.

If Camilla's invisible is the most truly real and volitional category, we may well wonder what happens when human history becomes spectral or what changes take place in the day to day lives of women with similar mystical theological beliefs. If the "ideal" becomes more tenable to a Victorian woman in her theology than the "real," then how does this affect her subjectivity, her definition as a political self? Let us look at two other case studies of Victorian women whose identities are radically and distinctly re-routed through their mystical, antinomian world views.

First, we will consider Harriet Martineau's remarkable cure from grave illness. Secondly, we will observe how the spiritual superseded the natural for novelist Florence Marryat in her intriguing relationship to a trance medium named Miss Showers. All three of these women, Crosland, Martineau and Marryat, shared a belief in the superior reality of the unseen world; it led them to dramatic cure, to surpassingly strange friendships, and to new theologies. In all three cases, mystical fringe theologies profoundly shaped and changed these women's lives and community membership.

HARRIET MARTINEAU AND MESMERIC CURE

Socialist and political economist Harriet Martineau was quite ill in the early 1840s and felt she was cured by mesmerism -- a practice which relies upon one person having sway over the mind and body of another. Harriet Martineau, who was originally under the care of the mesmeric physician, Mr. Spencer T. Hall, gives us the following account of her cure:

> First, the outlines of all objects were blurred; then a bust, standing on a pedestal in a strong light, melted quite away...I feared to move my eyes, lest the singular appearance should vanish, and I cried out, 'O! deepen it! deepen it!' supposing this the precursor of the sleep. I could not be deepened, however; and when I glanced aside from the luminous point, I found that I need not fear the return of objects to their ordinary appearance. While the passes were continued, the busts reappeared ghost-like, in the dim atmosphere, like faint shadows, except that their outlines and the parts in the highest relief, burned with the same phosphoric light. The features of one, an Isis with bent head, seemed to be illumined by a fire on the floor, though this bust has its back to the windows. This appearance continued during the remaining twenty minutes before the gentlemen [Mr. Hall and a male assistant] were obliged to leave me. The other effects produced were, first, heat, oppression, and sickness, and, for a few hours after, disordered stomach, followed, in the course of the evening, by a feeling of lightness and relief, in which I thought I could hardly be mistaken (Hall 71).

The mesmeric passes do not make the room disappear for Martineau; they only change the appearance and function of the room's elements. Isis, for instance, the famous Egyptian corn goddess begins to glow and illumine a fire on the floor. Frazer in his *The Golden Bough* notes that "Isis, goddess of corn, was revered for increasing fruitfulness of the earth in many ways" (Frazer 314, facing page.) It is interesting that a goddess of fruitfulness and harvest food should become illumined for Martineau who, by the descriptions, sounds as if she is suffering from a severe stomach disorder. The mesmeric state creates a receptive place for the literal, rather than symbolic, interaction of myth and medicine.

What may be stranger to ponder, though, is that Martineau's maid then takes over her medical care. This switch in primary provider I found somewhat surprising. No reasons are given; the new "doctor" is only parenthetically noted. Martineau reports:

> Within one minute (after the maid began) the twilight and phosphoric lights appeared; and in two or three more, a delicious sensation of ease spread through me -- a cool comfort, before which all pain and distress gave way, oozing out, as it were, at the soles of my feet. During that hour, and almost the whole evening, I could no more help exclaiming with pleasure, than a person in torture crying out with pain. I became hungry, and ate with relish, for the first time these five years. There was no heat, oppression, or sickness during the seance, nor any disorder afterwards. During the whole evening instead of the lazy hot ease of opiates under which pain is felt to lie in wait, I experienced something of the indescribable sensation of health, which I had quite lost and forgotten. I walked about my rooms, and was gay and talkative. Something of this relief remained till the next morning; and then there was no reaction. I was no worse than usual; and perhaps rather better. Nothing is to me more unquestionable and more striking about this influence than the absence of all reaction (Hall 73-74).

Then, she reports, "...her maid had carried on the cure pretty far, when a benevolent lady came to her aid, out of pure zeal and kindness, and proceeded with it." She said she could not "feel sufficiently thankful for such a resurrection." And finally, in a letter to Mr. Hall, that she had "the day before walked nearly five miles" and that she "continued quite well, feeling *nothing* whatever of her late complaints" (Hall 74).

Harriet Martineau not only recounts a remarkable recovery, she also lists a remarkable host of makers and witnesses to her cure, from doctor to maid to "benevolent lady." Her switch in primary health care provider from

Doctor to maid and then to lady marks an affront to the growing professionalization of medicine in the nineteenth-century. Professional expertise becomes less important for Martineau and she, instead, favors the amelioration of pain through mesmerism from her maid at home. Direct spirit communication does more for her than professionalized medicine. Her case is also a record of ecstasy: "I could no more help exclaiming with pleasure, than a person in torture crying out with pain."[6] It would seem to be a success story for the efficacy of trance and the unquestionable power of one person's head and hands, whether those of Doctor or servant, to overpower and control the patient. It is also an instance which asks interesting questions of other seances.

If we read "medium" for Harriet Martineau and "spirit" for the Doctor, maid, or lady, we quickly realize how promiscuous the claims of the seance table are. The respectable housewife turned medium or control for the table is inviting anyone from the beyond, whether "good" or "bad", "high" or "low" to have the total use of her body. In the example of Harriet Martineau, the entranced subject, just like every other medium, is the completely open recipient of outside influence. It is also interesting to me because Harriet Martineau, as Miss Showers' case will also indicate, paints a very different picture of female subjectivity. It is only by the community of women mesmerists and statues overseeing fires in her home that her cure comes to pass. It is also only through a state of ecstasy where pleasure is not distinguishable from pain that she ritualistically passes into wellness -- is this a non-narratable "state" of orgasm? It is as if her "doctors" remain nameless to emphasize their significance as maid and lady; as women enacting on her body a certain type of pleasurable "torture." Furthermore, a symbolic sexual act here becomes associated with healing Martineau's body. Unlike pregnancy and childbirth, which increased the probability of a Victorian woman's mortality, this sexually pleasurable, non-procreative act makes Martineau well again, "gay and talkative" in all of her rooms. In "fancy," the long infancy of her illness is ended. Through her membership in a radically mystical, mythical female community, Martineau regains health and connection to the larger human family. Like the seance situation that Camilla Crosland presents, Martineau also experiences a radically enlarged present tense in which the efficacy of mystical intervention seems boundlessly influential. In Martineau's account, we get a strong sense of spiritual laws superseding natural ones.

FLORENCE MARRYAT, THE PROFESSIONAL MEDIUM, AND PROMISCUOUS COMMUNITY

An equally unexpected situation is depicted by Victorian novelist Florence Marryat and her depiction of seance life. Here, too, we see the spiritual superseding the natural with a compelling antinomian flair. The medium plays no small role in this particular spiritual supercession. Miss Showers, the medium, is the passive receptacle for the spiritual "other" while, at the same time, she is also the producer of the spectral. The medium wavers, being, at once, both subject and object. Present at the table, while vacantly waiting for an unseen spirit to employ her body, the medium embodies a complex system of exchange. The invoking, flaming lips of the medium produce spectra creating an imaginary host of spirits, who evoke amazingly complex and diverse relations with and within the medium's body.

Florence Marryat, daughter of the famous Victorian adventure novelist, Captain Marryat, herself was a romance writer, spiritualist, and close friend of certain mediums, including the well-known public (professional) medium Miss Showers. In her work of 1891, *There Is No Death*, Florence Marryat recounts her personal experiences with several trance mediums. In one account, Marryat is instructed by materialized spirit emissaries to explore the body of the entranced medium:

> Then someone else grasped my other hand, and Peter's voice said, "We've got you safe. We want you to feel the medium." The two figures led me between them to the sofa on which Miss Showers was lying. They passed my hands all over her head and body....When my hands were placed upon it [her heart], it was leaping up and down violently, and felt like some rabbit or some other live animal bounding in her bosom.... There was no doubt at all of the abnormal condition into which the medium had been thrown, in order to produce these strong manifestations, which were borrowed, for the time being, from her life, and could never (so they informed me) put the *whole* of what they borrowed back again (Marryat 152).

I think this description is not only noteworthy for its depiction of Marryat's non-interactive bodily contact with materialized ectoplasms and the medium, but also because it promotes a scenario in which Miss Showers, while still Miss Showers, is also inhabited by another creature (like a rabbit) and that this life-force is stealing away or "borrowing" her own and not leaving her body as the spirit found it. Her identity is not at this moment single or fixed. The use of the verb "borrowing" is common in describing what the medium gives in many accounts. This verb also places the seance in the realm of economic exchange. Certainly, it seems with Miss Showers that what is "borrowed" from the body is lost in speculation. I mean "speculation" both in the sense of insight and in the sense of some sort of strange futures market.

It is also interesting how the audience becomes implicated in this show. Florence Marryat is not, after all, stopping this life-stealing practice -- she is aiding and abetting it. Is she a type of broker? Like the active force within

Miss Showers' body, something active and "abnormal" or, perhaps, atypical also is going on outside her body that is busy being publicly (or beyond-privately) observed and touched in a scene of active frottage. Miss Showers is a stock exchange, of sorts. It is unclear, though, what is being bought/sold/exchanged at this market. Florence Marryat also remains outside Miss Showers' body, to prove that there is no more room *inside* the medium's body: Miss Showers is not alone. Her body is an active bus(y)ness.

If the medium's body has become the site of spiritual exchange and a place that Marryat believes spirits to inhabit, we must inquire as to the theological implications of such a state. If, as Marryat believes, Miss Showers' body becomes a locus of spiritual interdigitation, and if, as she also assumes, this takes away part of Miss Showers' life, we must ask what Miss Showers gets in return: what is her new identity? Considering this question theologically yields an interesting possible reply. In effect, through Miss Showers' mystical practices as a medium, she is removed from a context of private, domestic space, on a sofa in a *boudoir*, and replaced into an active, public community, placed amongst rather busy and energetic spirits. The seance room, while semi-private, transforms through seance practices of calling up and embodying spirits, into a public, imaginary, democratic space, where any number of spirits, with any number of opinions, descend upon the entranced body for a congress of sorts. The answer, then, to our theological question is that the mystical medium, in turn for her body and her role in domestic space, gets an imaginary spiritual life elsewhere in turn for her other-worldly commitment and practices. The theological implication is that a woman, by renouncing or complicating her ties to this world, gets an active role in a concurrent, extra, spiritual world.

Important to note here, though, is that I am not suggesting that Victorian women who engaged in mystical practices were (1) crazy, or (2) submissively, subalternly, renouncing possible political, and personal engagement with Victorian society. I am suggesting that their mystical identification fundamentally changed their identities and made them, according to their beliefs, directly interactive with the ostensible emissaries of the godhead from beyond the vale. They placed themselves then, not in the separate sphere of the domestic, but in the extra sphere of a theologically-inflected, mystical imaginary community.

Also important to mention is the way in which Marryat, herself, theorized the theology of mediumship. Three years after publishing *There Is No Death*, Marryat published a sort of *apologia* for this work titled, *The Spirit World* (1894). She directly (unlike Camilla Crosland some forty years earlier) pitted spiritualism against the promise of Christianity and of history. She writes,

There must be a big screw loose somewhere in the various religions presented to us, which profess to give us everything but this -- vague hopes, threatening fears, promises of reward, and dread of punishment, but not *an atom of proof* that, having passed out of this body, we shall exist either to enjoy the one, or endure the other....And though history may be sufficient for us, when we are asked to believe that William the Conqueror landed in England in the year 1066 (because, if the truth were told, we do not care one jot nor tittle if he ever landed here at all), it is *not* enough to rest all our hopes of a future life upon, for ourselves and those we love (*Spirit World* 7,9).

In this work she goes on to argue that the Catholic Church knows of and denies the power of spiritualism because it would reduce its power (*Spirit World* 12-13) and that spirits supersede the Church's spiritual authority. She writes, "They [spirits] come to teach us, not to be treated like servants to run messages, or gratify idle curiosity. They are the higher powers, we the lower. They the preachers, we the congregation" (*Spirit World* 14). Marryat, then, defines her own mystical practices and writings as a direct theological challenge to the authority of the Church.

On another occasion, Miss Showers, busy at work as a medium, asks Florence Marryat "to put [her] hands up her skirts and convince [her]self that she was half-dematerialized" (Marryat 152). Marryat did as she told her "and felt that she had no legs, although she had been walking around the room a few minutes before. [She] could feel nothing but the trunk of a body, which was lifted completely off the ground" (Marryat 152). These are but two of numerous examples of Miss Showers' and Florence Marryat's physical union during the act of mediumship. It is as if Marryat were appointed body-guard to keep the spirits from carrying off her friend entirely. The *rapport* between Marryat and Showers extended beyond the seance room. She writes,

And I may mention here that Miss Showers and I were so much *en rapport* that her manifestations were always much stronger in my presence. We could not sit next each other at an ordinary tea, or supper table,...A hand that did not belong to either of us, would make itself apparent under the table-cloth between us -- a hand with power to grasp ours...(Marryat 148).

The spirits in this narrative seem to play the role of constant third-party "Lucky Pierre" or chaperone (not that Lucky Pierre and chaperone would be synonymous roles) between or over these two women. The spirits, in these accounts, are constantly demanding, facilitating, or creating physical contact between the two. Perhaps they seek, in this narrative, to keep Miss Showers in the material world or to convince Florence Marryat that the immaterial can embody and replace the material or to illustrate that the immaterial may be materially known.

It also cannot be overlooked that the acts of these two friends may be slipping into a category of Victorian sexual practices between friends -- and same-sex desire or romantic friendship. It is as if, though, their eroticism works literally in two ways at once. In one sense, as I have mentioned, theirs is the passionate yet strangely chaperoned/monitored/encouraged (by the ostensibly disembodied, yet materialized, spirits) romance. On the other hand, this same scenario could be interpreted with many players. As I noted above, one of Florence's functions is to prove that there are others in Miss Showers' body. Perhaps Marryat is just a witness and/or one of the many who are erotically inhabiting Miss Showers' body. In this interpretation, for instance, we could consider that Showers' and Marryat's union serves as a metaphor for the union of spirits and the medium during the seance. In this metaphor, their physical contact is no longer solely about a same-sex erotic act, but is also about an "auto"-erotic mystical community all (self-)contained by Miss Showers' flesh. How can we describe the multiple subjectivities that form an identity within a single body?

Here, perhaps, we return to the words of Camilla Crosland's Christ who claims that all of creation is joined in the mind and body of God. This could lead us, no doubt, to an interesting new viewing of some Victorian women's lives in comparison to the Passion. Being rejected, betrayed, misrepresented, slandered, crucified, buried, resuscitated, made evident, made ethereal, made spiritual, made mental, found chosen, militant and triumphant, becomes a map not only of Christ's passion, but also of a Victorian woman's domestic life. The passions at home, the crucifixion of the marriage bed, or the resuscitation of the drawing room seance become Christ-like and involve Victorian women in complicated, mystical subjectivities. In fact, these subjectivities are not only defined by interaction, but also sometimes become the preserve of the imaginary: a transcendent place of hiding.

In the previous examples we have explored the private side of mediums. We have seen what spirits (or mesmerists) do to and through their medium/control/object. What is most interesting to me about these examples is the way in which these experiences changed the category of subjectivity. Not only did they make a single identity impossible and replace it with a plural one, they also turned a person from an "is" to a "does." No longer could these Victorian women of the mystical fringe be appended to a fixed definition of identity. A person became a *process* of exploring different identities within the one body, as well as becoming a place, a space where the promiscuous (mixing of the unlike) live in community. The woman's body became uncanny; unfamiliar at the place where it once seemed at home.

The seances in these examples affected the medium, who became plural - - such as Crosland's seeress who was also Christ. Through this we see that the Victorian woman who was a mystical practitioner is allowed a lot of latitude in terms of identity and identification. Perhaps such a woman in not unlike a hero from a Sacher-Masoch novel. Gilles Deleuze, in his discussion of the same, notes that the masochistic hero always and only has a contract with himself. The masochistic hero is always in control because he only keeps an imaginary contract with himself. He always has the option of choosing a different fantastic role (Deleuze 22).[7] The same can be said for the Victorian woman theologian of the mystical fringe. She invented the system; she was not circumscribed by a pre-existing Christan *telos*, and she was always able to choose a new spirit-control with whom she could continue her theological discussion.

Through these examples we see three women actively writing their own nonconformist theologies. These were notable Victorians who wrote for a living: three professional writers. In the domain of biographers, political economists, and novelists, perhaps it is not surprising to find that we also have three theologians of the mystical fringe, women who devoted their lives to religious and gender reformation and to political intervention through their mystical practices and writings. Whether their lives were lived in the shadow of the Church of England (Camilla Crosland), in the realm of radical politics at mid-century (Harriet Martineau), or in the world of the later Victorian popular press (Florence Marryat), the explicit experiences of theology of the mystical fringe had a huge effect on these Victorian women's lives. The consideration of Victorian women's theology is important because theirs was an intervention into a primarily masculinist discourse that was based too often on a logic of fixed dominance and submission. Victorian women's mystical fringe theology, however, was invested in creating an alternate sphere of discourse. The extra spheres of mystical women's theology contained challenging ideas concerning the nature of God and of history. These women's primary identification with this "extra space" necessitates thinking about new and more accurate models of a mystical woman's subjectivity. I have only been able to touch upon a few diverse examples of these practices and issues in this essay. I offer these remarks to the growing conversation concerning Victorian women's theologies and lives.

NOTES

1. For example, see Ruskin, John, "Of Queens' Gardens," in *Sesame and Lilies* (1865) and Armstrong, Nancy, *Desire and Domestic Fiction* (1987).

2. Eighteen forty-eight marks the publication of the *Communist Manifesto*, the March revolutions in central Europe, the first Paris Commune, the last Chartist protests in London, the first railway book stalls, and the formation of the PRB.

3. For a discussion of the masculinization of thought, professionalism, and science, see, for instance, Bordo, Susan, "The Cartesian Masculinization of Thought," *Signs* 11.3 (1986) 439-456.

4. For an interesting discussion of Spiritualism and the undignified, especially as it pertains to the challenge popular religion posed to professionalism, see Cottom, Daniel, "On the Dignity of Tables," *Critical Inquiry* 14 (Summer 1988) 765-783.

5. For a very detailed depiction of this philosophical trajectory, see Bray, Charles, *Illusion and Delusion; or, Modern Pantheism versus Spiritualism* (London: Thomas Scott, 1873). Bray was friend and correspondent of George Henry Lewes and George Eliot.

6. It is also modelled like the myth of the corn goddess on succeeding phases of death and rebirth -- or loss and gain, winter and festival.

7. See also Sacher-Masoch, *Venus in Furs*, in *Masochism* (New York: Zone Books, 1991).

WORKS CITED

Armstrong, Nancy. *Desire and Domestic Fiction*. Oxford: Oxford University Press, 1987

Bordo, Susan. "The Cartesian Masculinization of Thought." *Signs* 11.3 (1986): 439-456.

Bray, Charles. *Illusion and Delusion; or, Modern Pantheism versus Spiritualism*. London: Thomas Scott, 1873.

Browning, Elizabeth Barrett. *A Note on William Wordsworth with a Statement of Her Views on Spiritualism*. London: Printed for Private Circulation Only by Richard Clay and Sons, 1919.

Cottom, Daniel. "On the Dignity of Tables." *Critical Inquiry* 14 (Summer 1988): 765-783.

Crosland, Camilla (Mrs. Newton). *Light in the Valley. My Experiences of Spiritualism*. London: G. Routledge, 1857.

Crosland, Newton. *Apparitions; a New Theory*. London: Effingham Wilson, 1856.

Deleuze, Gilles. "Coldness and Cruelty." In *Masochism*. New York: Zone Books, 1991.

Frazer, J.G. *The Golden Bough: A Study in Comparative Religion*. London: Macmillan, 1890.

Fritz. *Where are the Dead? Or, Spiritualism Explained*. London: Simpkin, Marshall, 1873.

Hall, Spencer T. *Mesmeric Experiences*. London: H. Bailliere, 1845.

Marryat, Florence. *The Spirit World*. Leipzig: Berhard Tauchnitz, 1894.

---. *There is No Death*. London: Kegan Paul, Trench, Trubner, 1891.

Ruskin, John. "Of Queens' Gardens." *Sesame and Lilies*. 1865.

Sacher-Masoch, Leopold von. *Venus in Furs*. In *Masochism*. New York: Zone Books, 1991.

Zerffi, G.G. *Spiritualism and Animal Magnetism*. London: Robert Hardwicke, 1871.

Decadence, Evolution, and Will:
Caroline Rhys Davids's "Original" Buddhism

Susan Thach Dean
University of Colorado

Since the publication of Edward Said's groundbreaking *Orientalism* (1978) it has become a widely accepted idea that commentators on cultures other than their own often reveal as much, if not more, about their own assumptions and attitudes as they do about the objects of their scrutiny. The study of Buddhism by the British from the late eighteenth to the mid-twentieth centuries is a particularly informative case in point. The voluminous public discourse on an alien religion that was conducted in scholarly and religious works and, increasingly after the middle of the nineteenth century, in the popular press and lecture halls, expresses fundamental concerns about the nature of religion, Christianity's status as divinely revealed truth, and humanity's own capacity for growth and progress. In the many treatments of nineteenth-century religious controversies, relatively little attention has yet been paid to the development of knowledge about Buddhism in Britain and to the effect that this knowledge had on the Victorians' view of religion and of the world.[1]

Thomas William Rhys Davids (1843-1922) and his wife, the former Caroline Augusta Foley (1857-1942), were arguably the two best known and most productive British investigators of Buddhism in the late nineteenth and early twentieth centuries. Not only were both scholars of international reputation, they claimed a popular audience as well. Their nearly herculean efforts in acquiring, translating, and publishing the books of the Buddhist canon written in Pali made the original literature of the Theravada (sometimes called Hinayana or Southern) School of Buddhism widely available in the West for the first time. In large part through their influence, the tenets of Theravada Buddhism came to be accepted, particularly by the British, as the purest, most genuine form of the Buddha's teaching.

Although T.W. and Caroline Rhys Davids both sought to determine the earliest, least adulterated form of Buddhism, their ultimate conclusions differed. T.W., an agnostic from a Nonconformist background, consistently maintained that, while Buddhism was admittedly a religion, its primary concerns were ethical and philosophical. Caroline, in contrast, gradually developed theories about the original teachings of the Buddha that diverged significantly not only from the views of her husband but also from those of most contemporary scholars. While the majority of her controversial explications of Buddhist doctrine did not appear in print until the last decades of her long life, they were the result of many years of study and contemplation and were firmly rooted in Victorian assumptions about religious truth and the essential nature of human beings -- assumptions that, for her as for many others, were severely shaken by the carnage of the first World War.[2] The work of Caroline Rhys Davids links the religious questioning of the Victorian period with the era of disillusionment and religious eclecticism that followed.

Two apparently contradictory yet inseparably connected themes pervade Rhys Davids's writing on Buddhism. Her search for the original teachings of the Buddha was based on the assumption that those teachings were corrupted as they progressed, first from an oral tradition to a written one, then into various countries and languages. To compensate for this inevitable decay, she eventually postulated a form of Buddhism (which she called Sakya, to distinguish it from later teachings) that existed before the texts were written and whose tenets differed in many respects from those contained in the texts. At the same time, she believed that although the transmission of the Buddha's teaching had decayed, humanity was simultaneously and continually evolving on a spiritual level, both as a species and individually, in this world and in a sphere beyond our perceptions. The human will was a crucial element in this long process of "becoming." Unlike many Victorians who felt that Buddhism taught passivity and the elimination of all desire, Caroline Rhys Davids was convinced that the Buddha had advocated aspiration and exertion as the means by which humanity would develop. The concepts of decadence, evolution, and will gave Rhys Davids a framework for explicating Buddhist doctrine that enabled her to incorporate Victorian ideas into her view of Buddhism and to express unfamiliar tenets in a language easily comprehended by her readers.

The work of T.W. and Caroline Rhys Davids grew out of the increasing knowledge by the British of Asian classical languages, beginning in the late eighteenth century, and the simultaneous study of Asian religious beliefs that eventually grew into the discipline of comparative religion. Sanskrit, the ancient literary language of India, was first investigated by colonial administrators who desired a clearer understanding of traditional Indian law. The founding of the Asiatic Society of Bengal in 1784 and the Royal Asiatic Society of Great Britain and Ireland in 1823 encouraged research and aided its dissemination. The Royal Asiatic Society's London Headquarters also housed an important collection of Asian manuscripts, among them the Sanskrit manuscripts of Buddhist texts collected in Nepal by Brian Houghton Hodgson during the 1820s and 1830s. Hodgson's discovery of this previously unknown Buddhist literature was, as the renowned philologist and scholar of religion Friedrich Max Müller pointed out in 1862, "the real beginning of an historical and critical study of the doctrines of Buddha..." (Rev. of *Le Bouddha* 384). Meanwhile, Pali, the ancient literary language of Ceylon, was also being investigated by scholars, but extensive work by the British was frustrated for several decades by the lack of a Pali dictionary or grammar.

The first scholar to learn both Sanskrit and Pali and to apply that knowledge to Buddhist literature was the Frenchman Eugene Burnouff. A modern critic has called his *Introduction a l'Histoire du Buddhisme Indien* (1844) the first "'scientific' study of Buddhism" (Clausen 1), and Horace Hayman Wilson, the first holder of an endowed chair of Sanskrit at Oxford, described Burnouff in 1856 as "the only scholar...equally familiar with the Buddhist authorities of the north and south of India" (229). Burnouff approached the perplexing question of whether the Sanskrit texts from Nepal or the Pali texts from Ceylon contained the most accurate representation of Buddhism by suggesting that the oldest tenets must be those that appeared in both (de Jong 1: 73).

The issue of whether the Sanskrit or Pali texts were earlier preoccupied scholars until the mid-1870s. Implicit in the controversy was the belief that the earliest texts provided the truest, most accurate version of the doctrines. Philip Almond, in *The British Discovery of Buddhism*, has related this search to "the obsession throughout the middle and latter part of the nineteenth century with the quest for origins -- biologically, geologically, and historically" (95). In addition, he has also pointed out, by mid-century Buddhism as it was then practiced in Asia was viewed as "being in a general state of decay" (37), a religion that had radically diverged from the original vision of its founder. In 1869 Max Müller presented the "principle problem" of Buddhist scholarship as the question, "'Is it possible to distinguish between Buddhism and the personal teaching of Buddha?'" ("Buddhist Nihilism" 137). In general, he argued, it was impractical to attempt to do so except in cases where different parts of the canon contradicted each other. There, he revealingly suggested, the scholar had "the right to choose, and the liberty to accept *that* view as the original one, the one peculiar to Buddha, which *least* harmonizes with the later system of orthodox Buddhism" (139).

Max Müller's formula for determining the "personal teaching of Buddha" vividly illustrates what Almond has identified as the developing tendency, after 1850, to view Buddhism as "less a living religion of the present...and more a religion of the past bound by its own textuality" (25). As Buddhism was increasingly "defined, classified, and understood as a textual object" (25), physical possession of the texts led to the presumption that their contents could be "ideologically controlled" (24) by those who studied them. Scholars appropriated the power to determine which portions of the texts represented the Buddha's actual teachings and which were distortions or later accretions. Even in cases where these efforts were genuinely disinterested, the commentator's own views inevitably affected the result. In this manner, the "Buddhism" that the Victorians studied became their own creation, a reflection of their attitudes, ideals, and assumptions about what a religion ought to be. T.W. and Caroline Rhys Davids, both of whom were children of clergymen growing to maturity in the post-Darwinian intellectual ferment, brought their own preconceptions and experiences to bear on their interpretation of Buddhism.

Thomas William Rhys Davids, born in 1843, was the son of a Congregationalist minister. He studied Sanskrit at the University of Breslau and entered the Ceylon Civil Service in 1864. It was there that he began the study of Pali with Yatramulle Unnanse, an elderly monk with whom another civil servant, Robert Caesar Childers, whose Pali dictionary would be published in 1872-75, had also studied. In his Hibbert Lectures of 1881, Rhys Davids spoke movingly of the "thin and diseased-looking monk" suffering from "a painful and incurable malady," who nevertheless traveled some distance to share his knowledge. "There was an indescribable attraction about him, a simplicity, a highmindedness, that filled me with reverence" (*Lectures on the Origin and Growth of Religion* 186-87). Rhys Davids's Civil Service career came to an abrupt end in 1872, when a dispute with his superiors led to his resignation and return to England as, according to Caroline Rhys Davids, "a man still young in years, but thrown back, saddened and ill" ("India and the Pali Text Society" 889).[3] He began the study of law and was called to the bar in 1877 but never practiced, having begun to establish himself as an authority on Buddhism.

One of T.W. Rhys Davids's obituarists, Lord Chalmers, described the state of knowledge about Buddhism at that time as "a mere jungle of doctrines and legends derived from sources as multifarious as they were disconnected" (540). Rhys Davids began, with prodigious skill and energy, to organize and clarify the extant information on Therevada, or Southern, Buddhism, always emphasizing the need to rely on original texts. His article for the ninth edition of the *Encyclopedia Britannica* (1877), was a lucid summary of what was then known. *Buddhism*, the volume that he wrote for the series on non-Christian religious systems published by the Society for Promoting Christian Knowledge (1878) was so popular that it continued to be reprinted for years and had sold 21,000 copies by 1907. In these early writings Rhys Davids asserted the belief, which he held to the end of his life, that while the Pali texts had been written over a period of time beginning some centuries after the death of the Buddha, they contained no evidence of "growth and change in fundamental ideas" (*Buddhism* 87) but embodied the teachings of the Buddha as he had transmitted them to his disciples.

While writing these expositions of doctrine, Rhys Davids never lost sight of what he considered to be the essential requirement for the advancement of Buddhist studies, accurate editions and translations of the original Pali texts. In his series of Hibbert Lectures, delivered in May 1881 and published as *Lectures on the Origin and Growth of Religion* in 1882, he announced the formation of the Pali Text Society "in order to render accessible to students the rich stores of the earliest Buddhist literature now lying unedited and practically unused in the various MSS. scattered throughout the Public and University Libraries of Europe" (232). As it transpired, Buddhist texts already in Europe were not the only ones utilized. In the Society's first annual report, printed in the *Journal of the Pali Text Society* for 1882, Rhys Davids announced a financial contribution from the Buddhist Order of Ceylon that was being applied to the purchase of additional manuscripts in that country. "It is no slight thing," he wrote, "that an established clergy should have come forward so readily to support the publication of the sacred books of their religion in an alien alphabet and by scholars of an alien faith" (2). This spirit of cooperation persisted, eventually resulting in such endeavors as the joint translation of several texts, beginning in 1910, by Caroline Rhys Davids and the Burmese scholars, Shwe Zan Aung and Pe Maung Tin[4], the earliest of which she described as "the first attempt to treat of Buddhist philosophy by East and West working hand in hand" (*Compendium of Philosophy* xii-xiii). During the forty years of T.W. Rhys Davids's presidency, the Pali Text Society published 64 texts in 94 volumes, a remarkable accomplishment for an international organization funded entirely by voluntary contributions.[5]

In 1894 T.W. Rhys Davids married Caroline Augusta Foley, daughter of an Anglican clergyman. She had achieved distinction at University College, London, in psychology and philosophy, winning the John Stuart Mill and Joseph Hume scholarships in philosophy in 1889. In addition, she had worked with societies promoting the welfare of working women and children and advocating women's suffrage. From 1893 to 1897 she wrote and translated articles and reviewed books for *The Economic Journal*. According to Mabel Bode, a friend and fellow Pali scholar, Caroline Foley first began the study of Pali at Rhys Davids's suggestion in 1884, "but put it aside in favour of more instantly pressing collegiate claims" (82). She resumed its study in 1891, having learned Sanskrit in the interval. When the Ninth International Congress of Orientalists was held in London in 1892, T.W. Rhys Davids read a summary of her paper, "Women Leaders of the Buddhist Reformation," which was published in full in the proceedings of the congress (344-61).[6] The stories of the earliest women Buddhist practitioners seem to have greatly influenced her interest in Buddhism. She later published her translation of their devotional poems, accompanied by a perceptive and sympathetic introduction, in *Psalms of the Early Buddhists, I. Psalms of the Sisters* (1909).

After their marriage, T.W. and Caroline Rhys Davids worked both independently and in collaboration to make the Pali texts available in the West and to explicate the doctrines they contained. Mabel Bode, in 1911, paid tribute to "the splendid energy, the fidelity to an idea and the tenacity in work that have gone with them through every undertaking of their lives" (84). From 1887 to 1905 T.W. Rhys Davids was the Secretary and Librarian of the Royal Asiatic Society, while holding the honorary post of Professor of Pali and Buddhist Literature at University College, London. In 1905 he resigned his position with the Royal Asiatic Society to accept the newly created Chair of Comparative Religion in Victoria University, Manchester, the first such professorship in England, which he held until his retirement in 1912. Caroline Rhys Davids was Lecturer on Indian Philosophy, Victoria University, Manchester, from 1910 to 1913 and Lecturer on the History of Buddhism in the School of Oriental Studies, London, from 1918 to 1933. Sir E. Denison Ross, the first director of the School described her in his autobiography as "one of the most versatile and gifted women I have known....As Reader in Pali she was one of the ornaments of the School, attracting students from many countries" (171). It was, however, as an editor, translator, and controversial explicator of Buddhist texts that she was most distinguished.[7]

The Buddhist canon consists of three large groups of texts known as Pitakas. The Vinaya Pitaka is a compilation of the rules to be followed by monks and nuns. The Sutta Pitaka, divided into five Nikayas or collections, brings together treatises on Buddhist ethics and philosophy, some of which are represented as the actual words of the Buddha. The Abhidamma Pitaka consists of works that analyze mental processes.[8] From 1900 to 1942 Caroline Rhys Davids, alone or in collaboration, translated or edited all six books of the Abhidamma and one commentary on it, as well as twenty books from the Sutta Pitaka. Such work was agonizingly painstaking, requiring her "to wear eyes and patience in deciphering undivided lines of alien scripts on palm-leaves of mellow ochre, unsuited to readers in this light-starved climate" (*Psalms of the Early Buddhists, II: Psalms of the Brethren* xix). In addition, the palm-leaves written in Pali often needed to be collated with variants of the same texts written in Sinhalese, Burmese, or other South Asian languages.[9] Rhys Davids's expertise as a Pali scholar formed the basis of her discussions of Buddhist doctrine and enabled her to cogently refute common misinterpretations. And, although the inaccuracy of the texts became a major theme of her later writings, she seems never to have rejected the texts entirely, since she continued to use philological arguments to prove her points.

It was to the Abhidamma Pitaka that the most important of Caroline Rhys Davids's efforts as an editor and translator were devoted, and she became arguably the greatest Western authority of her time on this difficult work. In the introduction to her translation of the first book of the Abhidamma, published as *A Buddhist Manual of Psychological Ethics* in 1900, she recorded that when T.W. Rhys Davids suggested in 1893 that she translate it, she was "at once attracted by the amount of psychological material embedded in its pages" (xxii). Her background in psychology was an undoubted asset in working with texts that were abstruse yet essential for an understanding of Buddhism.

Unlike many of her fellow scholars, Rhys Davids realized that the system of detailed mental analysis contained in the Abhidamma was the basis of Buddhism, that the Buddhist "system of personal self-culture" was the result of "studying the processes of attention, and the nature of sensation, the range and depth of feeling, and the plasticity of the will in desire and in control..." (xxiii). Caroline Rhys Davids's interpretations of Buddhist doctrine often explicitly referred to portions of the Abhidamma and, even when they did not do so, were almost always influenced by it.

Although the issue of the relative priority of the Sanskrit and Pali texts was extensively debated through mid-century, by the late 1870s it was generally agreed that the Pali canon antedated the Sanskrit canon. In 1877 T.W. Rhys Davids described the relationship of the Sanskrit texts to those in Pali as "resembling in many respects that of the apocryphal gospels to the New Testament" ("Buddhism," *Encyclopedia Britannica* 4: 381). Mahayana, or Northern, Buddhism, whose teachings comprised the Sanskrit texts, was considered a degenerate form of Buddhism, a radical departure from the early purity and simplicity of the Buddha's teachings.[10] According to T.W. Rhys Davids, the relative isolation of Ceylon protected the form of Buddhism practiced there and incorporated in the Pali texts so that it "retained almost its pristine purity to modern times" (*Encyclopedia Britannica* 4: 391). Caroline Rhys Davids originally accepted this point of view. In her earlier works she argued that, although the Pali canon was not compiled in writing until approximately 80 B.C., having been introduced into Ceylon in 241 B.C., it had nevertheless been accurately transmitted through the "splendidly trained memories" of those who recited it (*Buddhism: A Study of the Buddhist Norm* 19). She did, however, disagree almost from the beginning with certain common interpretations of Buddhist doctrine.

In an essay titled "On the Will in Buddhism," published in the *Journal of the Royal Asiatic Society* in 1898, she asserted that "many hasty generalizations and one-sided conclusions concerning the nature of Buddhist ideals and discipline" needed to be revised in the light of information being discovered in the Pali texts (47). In particular, she argued vehemently against the commonly held view that the ultimate goal of Buddhism was the elimination of suffering to be achieved by "self-restraint and the extinction of desires" (Monier-Williams 35). In part, she suggested, this idea had arisen from inaccurate translations where "the one English word 'desire' is made to do duty for no less than seventeen Pali words, not one of which of which means desire taken in its ordinary general sense, but rather in that of perverted, morbid, excessive desire" (54). But more than a lack of appreciation for the subtleties of Pali was involved. The entire concept that Buddhism required the elimination of desire was false:

> ...if there be one feature in Buddhist ethics eminent for the emphasis attached to it, it is not only that will as such, desire as such, are not to be repressed, but that the culture and development of them are absolutely indispensable to any advance towards the attainment of its ideals...(50).

Buddhism actually strove "to *divert the current of desire* to aims intellectual and ethical...and then *to foster and strengthen* aspiration and resolve in the effort to persevere towards...the noblest kind of life" (57). The "outward calm of mien of the Buddhist sage" did not represent "stony, stultified, self-centered apathy," but instead concealed "a passion of emotion and will not paralyzed or expurgated, but rendered subservient to and diffused around deep faith and high hope" (55).

The question of what "high hope" Buddhism extended to its followers was a source of continued controversy throughout the nineteenth century. Nirvana, the "great end and object of life," was generally held to be "utter extinction...literally a blowing-out, as of a candle, -- annihilation..." (Wilson 256). Other interpretations occasionally surfaced, as when Francis Barham, responding in 1857 to Max Müller's article "Buddhist Pilgrims," argued in a letter to the *Times* that Nirvana meant "absorption of the soul into God, but not its annihilation..." (8). Max Müller put an end to the discussion with the tart rejoinder that since Buddhism recognized the existence of neither the soul nor God, the "most charitable view" that could be taken of Nirvana was that it was "self-ness, in the metaphysical sense of the word -- a relapse into that being which is nothing but itself" ("The Meaning of Nirvana" 289). In his 1869 lecture "Buddhist Nihilism" Max Müller modified his position to the extent of suggesting that Nirvana might "mean the extinction of many things -- of selfishness, desire, and sin, without going so far as the extinction of subjective consciousness" (141).

It was not until 1877 that a strikingly different interpretation of Nirvana appeared in an article written by T.W. Rhys Davids for the *Contemporary*

Review. He argued that previous commentators had erred when they attempted "to understand Nirvana without understanding the *system of thought* of which Nirvana is the last conclusion..." ("On Nirvana" 249). After a lengthy discussion of such foundations of Buddhist philosophy as the concepts of karma, rebirth, the Four Noble Truths, and the eight parts and four stages of the Path, Rhys Davids concluded that what was actually extinguished in Nirvana was "*that sinful, yearning, grasping, condition of mind and heart which would otherwise, according to the great mystery of Karma, be the cause of renewed individual existence.*" Nirvana was "a moral condition, a pure, calm, clear state of mind," best translated as "holiness...in the Buddhist sense -- *perfect peace, goodness, and wisdom*" (263). It was attainable in this life by the Arahat, the follower of the Path of the Holy Ones, who at death would have eliminated the forces that could create a new being and who would then enter the state of Parinirvana, or extinction without rebirth (264). European writers on Buddhism had, Rhys Davids argued, failed to distinguish between Nirvana and Parinirvana since they "naturally" assumed "that the highest happiness, the aim of a religious man, *must* be some state to be attained *after* death" (264). "The Buddhist heaven," in contrast, was "not death, but a perfect life here and now," extolled in the Pali texts as "the highest happiness, the noblest aim, the most elevating hope, for mankind" (265). Throughout the remainder of his life, in numerous books and articles, T.W. Rhys Davids maintained his conviction that Buddhism was a complete ethical and philosophical system whose goal was the attainment of "the state of intellectual and moral perfection called Nirvana" that could be reached "by inward self-culture and self-control" ("The Ancient Buddhist Belief Concerning God" 223). This argument carried no implicit threat to Victorian religious beliefs, since the moral qualities thus cultivated were clearly admirable. Christopher Clausen has pointed out that Rhys Davids's "emphasis on moral striving -- 'self-control,' 'self-discipline,' 'modification of character' -- ...placed Buddhism in an altogether more favorable light for the Victorian reader" (12).

Caroline Rhys Davids's view of the ultimate goal of Buddhism, one that would become increasingly difficult for her contemporaries to accept, was considerably different. She gradually came to believe that the repeated cycles of existence postulated by Buddhism were, rather than being the negative result of clinging and grasping, in fact the means by which a long process of evolution, whose final end was beyond comprehension, took place. Her knowledge of the Abhidamma enabled her to understand the Buddhist belief that the individual "self" was in fact a series of transient mental processes. In a 1903 article, "The Soul-Theory in Buddhism," she related this idea to Heracleitus's "flux of becoming" and Aristotle's "theory of soul as informing energy" (589). Extending the argument to the Buddhist concept of rebirth, she pointed out that for the relatively static and material notion of an indivisible soul-monad dwelling in one concrete perishable cage after another, Gotama substituted the idea of a of a series of wholly transient compounds....Living revealed itself as a congeries of manifestations...of becomings and extinctions (589).

The early Buddhists were, she declared, "feeling out after a dynamic conception of things -- after a world-order of becoming, movement, process, sequence, force" (588). She realized that such a view did not come naturally to European readers, despite its similarities to some trends in Greek thought. "Our perspective is based on space rather than on time; on substance statically filling space, rather than on movements and moments; on permanence and identity, rather than on change and transmitted force" (Preface, *Compendium of Philosophy* xv). But, she also argued, if Buddhist concepts of the nature of reality "could be adequately expounded so as to be intelligible to Western philosophy," ideas might emerge that would be "not a little sympathetic" to current trends in science (xvi). The Buddha did not merely transmit his own hard-won insights into the best way to live the ideal life, he described "something that was cosmic law, eternal, necessary, omnipresent, whether discerned or not" (*Buddhism* 33). The Buddhist law of causation, known as *paticcasamuppada*, that described the series of actions and results creating the cycle of existence, was not just "a mechanical succession of moments," but "one moment or state being wrought up into, and informing the next with a ceaseless pulsation" (246), and "ultimate reality" consisted of "throbbing energies whirling in ordered rhythm, whether of solar systems or our own hearts and intelligences..." (246-47).

Since Buddhism saw "the individual life as an immensely prolonged self-transmitting and evolving force" it also "saw in every individual at any given moment a phase of that evolution" (Introduction, *Psalms of the Early Buddhists, II. Psalms of the Brethren* (xlv). Rhys Davids argued that because karma, the motive power of this evolutionary process, was self-created, "self-fecundating flux" ("The Buddhist Principle of Change" 230), human beings were not passive victims of a force outside themselves but were capable of shaping and directing their own development. This could be accomplished, she believed, through the agency of thought. Rhys Davids was unusual among her contemporaries in apparently having some understanding of the importance of meditation, an aspect of Buddhism that, as Douglas Brear has indicated, the Victorians "infrequently described, rarely discussed, and hardly ever understood..." (137).[11] In a reference to the practice of *metta*, the "psychic suffusion of...man or beast or spirit with benign, fraternal emotion...," she wrote of the Buddhist belief "that 'thoughts are things,' that psychical action, emotional or intellectual, is capable of working like a force among forces" (Introduction, *Dialogues of the Buddha, Part III* 186).

Aspiration and exertion, operating through an effort of will, were essential elements of this force. In her 1898 essay "On the Will in Buddhism," she wrote that Nirvana was not to be attained "by bare quiescent meditation,...but by rational discontent, strong anguish, longing, followed by a forward leap of the mind into peace and calm -- *then* again by joyous strenuousness..." (51). In writing of the early Buddhist nuns she spoke of their poetic "testimony to high quest, to devoted heart, to indomitable resolve," particularly pointing out the importance of "Resolve and its persistent efficacy throughout rebirths" (Introduction, *Psalms of the Early Buddhists, I. Psalms of the Sisters* xix). She then went on to discuss the further development of this concept, in Mahayana Buddhism, as the "aspirations of persistent effect, formed when, in any human being, the *bodhicitta* (or heart of intelligence) awakes and transforms him into a nascent Bodhisattva," one who not only seeks his or her own enlightenment but also aspires to bring all living beings to that state. Rhys Davids's emphasis on the power of will in this lengthy process of spiritual development inevitably led her to the examine the question of what entity was doing the willing and, indeed, what entity was developing. The conclusions she reached became the most controversial of her doctrinal interpretations.

The Buddhist doctrine of *anatta*, or the non-existence of a soul, was extremely difficult for the Victorians to grasp. Douglas Brear has commented on

> ...the extent to which the complete novelty and apparent oddness of the doctrine was simply too much for many to assimilate, the result being either an inability to understand [it] at all, or even a deliberate and reasoned refusal to accept the doctrine at face value (147).

T.W. Rhys Davids was perhaps the most convincing articulator of *anatta*, discussing the theory in many of his published works. In "On Nirvana" (1877), one of his earliest and most important articles, he stated categorically that according to Buddhism "there is in man no soul, no abiding principle whatever" (253), but he also acknowledged the difficulty "a mind impregnated with Christian ideas" (254) experienced in comprehending and accepting such a doctrine. To make it more understandable to his readers, he generally included *anatta* as part of a discussion of the Four Noble Truths on the prevalence, origin, and path to cessation of suffering. It was precisely "the struggle necessary to maintain individuality," that was "the essence of sorrow" and the cause of all future suffering ("Buddha's First Sermon" 904). He also argued that the doctrine of *anatta* was fundamental in promoting ethical development since "so long as men were harassed by doubts and fears about their 'souls,'" they could not achieve "the emancipated state of mind essential to a calm pursuit of the higher life;...a perfect life here and now, in this world..." (*Buddhism: Its History and Literature* 41-42). T.W. Rhys Davids's predilection toward viewing Buddhism as a rational system of ethics colored his interpretation of *anatta*, making the doctrine one more building block in the Buddhist "Palace of Good Sense" (41) and thus somewhat more intelligible to his contemporaries. His view that *anatta* was developed essentially as a means of encouraging Buddhists to focus on attaining perfection in this life rather than in some future state enabled him to incorporate the concept into his own theories about Buddhism but failed to acknowledge the complexity of the issue.

Caroline Rhys Davids struggled for many years to understand the doctrine of *anatta* and to reconcile it with her vision of Buddhism as a lengthy path of spiritual evolution. In "The Soul-Theory in Buddhism" (1903) she discussed the apparent conflict between the doctrines of *anatta* and karma, pointing out that "to Western minds the nihilism of the one tenet and the persistent individuality implied in the other" seemed indicative of "muddle-headedness, or sophistry, or esotericism, or all three in early Buddhism" (587). She resolved this contradiction by arguing that in the Pali texts the "soul-entity" was considered to be a series of "psychological processes" and that "a future personal complex or self like unto, and the effect of, yet not identical with the present self" would bear the fruition of the karma created by that present self (590). Sounding much like her husband, she concluded that the Buddha proposed the doctrine of *anatta* for reasons that were "profoundly ethical and social," in order to oppose "priests and gods and sacrificial ritual" (591).

By 1917 Rhys Davids had taken a major step in her efforts to reconcile *anatta* and spiritual evolution. In "The Buddhist Principle of Change" she declared that *anatta* applied only to "the belief in an *unchanging divine* soul that transmigrated, as the soul in other cults is held to do," not to "the belief in a changing, growing soul, that could yet, unlike all other mental and physical phenomena, defy death ..." (221). She first justified this conclusion by analyzing the Buddha's statements about the soul, arguing in 1924 that the "merely speculative" language in which he discussed the matter in his second sermon made it "utterly incredible" that he placed any importance on being "known as a teacher of No-soul" ("Development of the Anti-Soul Attitude" 285). In fact, "the meaning of the idea 'self, soul, being,' was fluctuating, confused, and not very consistently expressed" in the texts (294). Little help could be obtained from either European scholars or from practicing Buddhists, since they knew too little of the original language of the Suttas to make an accurate judgment on this important point, being "much like Christians into whose hands their scriptures in the vernacular have not yet been placed" (293). Rhys Davids had emphasized the significance of textual evidence during her entire scholarly career, but the development of her own beliefs about the evolution of the soul and her increasing difficulty in finding textual substantiation for them began to lead her to deny the authenticity of the very texts to which she had devoted years of painstaking work. In the conclusion to "Development of the Anti-Soul Attitude" she stated that "even with more light of internal evidence we shall not know clearly what Gotama taught, so is he smothered" (294). The differences between "original" Buddhism and the Buddhism presented in the Pali texts became a major theme in the remainder of her writing.

Shortly after her husband's death in 1922 Caroline Rhys Davids began to publicly assert the belief that the Buddha's teachings had been significantly changed when they were committed to writing and that the texts represented a decadent and corrupted form of Buddhism that had been codified in the monasteries but had not been advocated by the founder.[12] In the chapter on Buddhism in *Old Creeds for New Needs* (1923), she explicitly stated that scholars needed to "seek out" the Buddha's "real message amid monastic doctrines put forward as central, not by him, but by his church" (98). The monks, having removed themselves from the daily concerns of ordinary people, inhabited "an inner, artificial world, a world...of 'half-men'" ("Buddhism Not Originally a Negative Gospel" 626).[13] In *Gotama the Man* (1928) a biography of the Buddha written as if it were spoken by him, she included both the concept of the monastic corruption of the teachings and that of rebirth as the means of spiritual evolution by having the Buddha say:

> ...the teaching came to be shaped by the monk's ideal, and that was not mine. The monk saw life as ill. I saw it as growing in the better....The monk looked on rebirth as bringing ever more woe. I looked to rebirth as holding the promise of ever more happiness (235).

The "rectifying editors" who gathered and collated the spoken versions of the texts "adapted these to fit and express the view they themselves had come to hold of a given doctrine" ("Buddhism Not Originally a Negative Gospel" 625). Rhys Davids argued that the original teaching, which she called "Sakya" to distinguish it from the corrupted "Buddhism," could be discerned "under the Pali palimpsests, but only if we refuse to take these at the face-value given in them, by compilers and editors, to their own standpoint and their own standing" (625).[14] Rhys Davids's position on this issue can be seen as the logical culmination of the sense of ideological control that physical ownership of the Buddhist texts conferred, as Philip Almond has pointed out, on Western scholars (24-25). While other scholars attempted to distinguish degrees of accuracy among various texts, she rejected the texts altogether, creating a Buddhist doctrine for which she could find relatively little written justification but which seemed to her to more truly embody the spirit of the Buddha's teachings.

Rhys Davids's primary quarrel with the texts was their "denial of the spiritual 'man' as existing in a real, ultimate sense" ("Buddhism Not Originally a Negative Gospel" 626). As she continued to examine the nature of the spiritual component in human beings, the "changing, growing soul" that evolved and progressed, she formulated a theory about the Buddha's original teaching on the subject that reached back to the period before Buddhism, to the earlier doctrine of Brahmanism. The Buddha was generally considered to have been either "certainly an Atheist," (Max Müller, "The Meaning of Nirvana" 288) or "an Agnostic" (T.W. Rhys Davids, "The Ancient Buddhist Belief Concerning God" 222), and Buddhism had "no God higher than the perfect man" (Monier-Williams 14).[15] Caroline Rhys Davids argued that the Pali texts contained no explicit denial of the existence of either God or the soul, that in fact "the then current terms for Deity -- *Brahman* (neuter) and *attan* (masculine) -- occur very often..." ("Silence and Emphasis in Buddhism," 129). In order to clearly understand the position of Buddhism on the subject of God it was necessary for the West to

> ...come apart from lands and times where it was, or is, taught that God is separate being from human being, or where man was, or is, taught as 'having a soul.' In India the 'man' (*purusha*) *was* soul, *was* self, and was (and is) in and of God (130).

At the time of the Buddha, God was "worshipped, not as external, but as the ideal self or spirit within, somehow within, each man" ("The More in Man: A Hallmark of Man and of Religion" 1025). The Buddha did not discuss God because "a very great mandate had been taught, before he came, and accepted: that of the Divine Being Brahman, as immanent in man's self, and as thus his ideal...". The Buddha's contribution was to formulate the "finer deeper view" of this immanent divinity as "not static, but as an inner dynamic urge..." ("Buddha and Not Buddhists" 1082).

Rhys Davids thus identified the divine principle in human beings with the very soul, or spiritual entity, that evolved through innumerable lifetimes toward a transcendence that was as yet beyond comprehension. She called that transcendent state *attha* and described it, not as a static and definable goal, but as "that which man, in seeking, ever figures as the Best, the Most he can as yet conceive" ("An Historical Aspect of Nirvana" 654). The Buddha intended, not to show the way to a state of perfection in this life and to extinction of the self after death, but to teach the continuing evolution of the divine principle, to show "man how, as a wayfarer in the worlds he might, seeking his *attha*, finally *become* That" (658). While Rhys Davids's discussions of the spiritual principle in human beings were couched in overtly theistic language, she nevertheless came closer than her fellow scholars to a description of the Buddhist concept of *tathagatagarbha*, the inherent "Buddha-nature" that makes enlightenment possible. And her willingness to acknowledge that the ultimate state she discussed could not be described contrasts sharply with the limited, frequently simplistic views of Nirvana presented in most nineteenth and early twentieth-century works on Buddhism by Europeans.[16]

Caroline Rhys Davids's conception of the true goal of Buddhism also influenced her view of the nature of religion in general. In "Popular Errors About Buddhism" (1932) she discussed T.W. Rhys Davids's critique of Max Müller's list of the essential components of a religion presented in *Lectures on the Science of Religion* (1873). Max Müller had enumerated those elements as "the belief in a divine power, the acknowledgement of sin, the habit of prayer, the desire to offer sacrifice, and the hope of a future life" (qtd. in T.W. Rhys Davids, "Cosmic Law in Ancient Thought" 288). T.W. Rhys Davids pointed out that several Asian systems of belief, including Buddhism, contained none of the elements listed by Max Müller, and he proposed that those religions be classified as "Normalistic," since their underlying principle was "the belief in a certain rule, order, law" (282). Offering another view of the essential elements of a religion, Caroline Rhys Davids argued that all religion involved the "tremendous quest...to see in attainment of Godhead the birthright of every man," which could only be achieved as the result of "a very long period of becoming" (470). Organized Buddhism, in reducing "the idea 'man,' or 'soul'" to "his 'vehicle,' the 'beminded body'" had forfeited "the right to be any longer called a religion..." (471). The Buddha, she asserted, had originally "taught the 'man,' i.e. the 'soul,' as not a fixed static 'is,' but an ever-moving 'becoming.'" She, therefore, defined the "irreducible fundamentals of religion" as "a belief in a Highest and a belief in man as a Less, identical in nature with the Highest, but ever in process of becoming a More travelling towards that highest, that Most" (475). Caroline Rhys Davids's declaration that the defining characteristic of a religion was its belief in the ability of humans -- not to attain union with the ultimate -- but to develop the ultimate that already existed within them, that was "identical" with them, unequivocally removed religion from the sphere of ethics and propelled it into the realm of mysticism.

Rhys Davids's later books and articles provoked objections during her lifetime and have since been commonly dismissed as misguided at best and deliberate falsifications at worst. Rhys Davids herself noted that she was "stigmatized by Buddhists as 'she who calls the great non-self teacher the teacher of the self'" ("An Apologist in Buddhism" 873). In 1932 *The British Buddhist* reprinted an article by one Ariya-Dhamma titled "Mrs. Rhys Davids and the Higher Criticism," originally published in *The Mahabodhi* (Calcutta), preceded by an anonymous editorial headed "Scholarship Run

Mad." Both the article and editorial brutally criticized the "perverse view of the Buddha's teaching" (115) propounded by Rhys Davids in *Gotama the Man* and *Sakya, or Buddhist Origins*, arguing that she had "assumed the role of a true-blue and even vociferous atmanist, having recanted her previous reasoned conclusions and jettisoned her former cherished beliefs" (117). The death of her husband, both writers strongly implied, had removed the restraint that had held her unruly intellect in check while "she remained a learner (*sekha*) under the tuition and guidance of her mentor..." (117). A true understanding of the Buddha's teaching, the editorial writer admonished, could only be achieved by "humble, patient willingness to learn, simple, quiet readiness to be taught" (115-16). Both the exaggerated condemnation and the patronizing advice identify this jeremiad as one of the reprimands typically delivered to women whose ideas differ from those of their male colleagues. While the language of more recent writers has been somewhat less inflammatory, the ideas conveyed have not changed. T.R.V. Murti, in 1960, described Rhys Davids as "elaborat[ing] her pet theme with tiresome repetition" (20), and Guy Richard Welbon, writing in 1968, criticized her for going "to absurd lengths after the death of her husband to show that earliest Buddhism was not at all what he had taken it to be" (226), as if her works were merely a marital squabble carried beyond the grave. Such pronouncements have undoubtedly contributed in large part to the obscurity into which she has now fallen.

Welbon commented that Caroline Rhys Davids's "belief in what a religion ought to be...determin[ed] what she 'discovered' earliest Buddhism to be" (246). While he was no doubt correct, the issue is more complex than he acknowledged. Rhys Davids struggled to discover what it was that made spiritual development in human beings possible. Her intensive study of the Abhidamma may have precipitated this quest. If, as the Abhidamma predicated, the only "self" was a series of fleeting mental processes, how could such development take place? The answer she found was a "self" that transcended any conventional idea of "self": a self that was never static but was constantly evolving, a self whose possibilities for development were limitless, beyond conception, but whose eventual end would be complete identification with the ultimate that already existed within it. Since the existence of this "self" seemed to her the only means by which spiritual development could occur, she sought evidence for it in the Pali texts, sometimes resorting to convoluted philological arguments and, in other instances, rejecting the texts altogether. But her search was a genuine one, impelled by the desire to understand both the nature of religion and the nature of human spirituality.

Reginald Ray has pointed out that, in contrast to the nineteenth and early twentieth century quest for the "original" teachings of the Buddha, it has now "come to be widely agreed that nothing definitive can be known about the Buddha himself or the Buddhism he founded" (9). Perhaps it is time to focus, not on the relative "correctness" of the doctrinal interpretations proposed by early Western students of Buddhism, but on what those interpretations reveal about the intellectual history of the West as it encountered and attempted to understand a radically different system of thought. The Victorians and their successors developed versions of Buddhism that, in general, enabled them either to assimilate it or to reject it. The examples of rejection are legion, and T.W. Rhys Davids's creation of a Buddhism that was, in some respects, Protestantism without God is perhaps the clearest instance of assimilation. Caroline Rhys Davids propelled her contemporaries into entirely new territory. She postulated a theory of evolution that was more radical than Darwin's, one that not only required an immensely long period of spiritual development to attain an incomprehensible end, but that also, in a very real sense, eliminated the boundary between the human and the divine.

NOTES

1. Almond provides the most comprehensive treatment to date. Earlier articles by Brear and Clausen also give useful background. Thomas's overview is brief but cogent, focusing on Victorian approaches to the study of non-Christian religions. Peiris's chapters on Britain are historical rather than critical and concentrate on the period after 1880. Humphreys's two works focus on the growth of Buddhism as a religion in England, primarily after 1900. Fields, Jackson, and Tweed discuss the influence of Buddhism in America while providing some information on Britain. DeJong and Welbon include European scholars of Buddhism. Batchelor covers Western interactions with Buddhism beginning with the ancient Greeks. Schwab's wide-ranging history describes the European encounter with many aspects of Asian culture.

2. Rhys Davids's ideas took their most radical form after World War I, when she began to believe that established religions could no longer satisfy the needs of the modern world. In *Old Creeds and New Needs* (1923) she declared of the Buddha that "many, who have in these days come to know something of the teachings ascribed to him, will have found it an all but barren quest to find in them guidance to meet the problems of the great war" (91).

3. For details, see Wickremeratne 109-139.

4. *Compendium of Philosophy, Points of Controversy, The Expositor.* Caroline Rhys Davids also jointly translated *The Book of the Kindred Sayings, Part I* with Suriyagoda Sumangala, a Ceylonese monk.

5. See "The Passing of the Founder" 10.

6. See "The Ninth International Congress of Orientalists" 861.

7. In addition to the sources cited in the text, the preceding biographical information has been derived from *Who's Who, 1937*; Chalmers, *D.N.B., 1922-30*; Stede, "Caroline Augusta Foley Rhys Davids" and "T.W. Rhys Davids"; "Thomas

William Rhys Davids," *JRAS*; Ridding; Pe Maung Tin; "The Passing of the Founder"; Davids, C.A.F. Rhys, "Report of the Pali Text Society for 1922"; "Interpreter of Buddhism"; Waterhouse; Horner. The available biographical information on Caroline Rhys Davids is very limited.

8. For consistency, the Pali form of words is used, although the Sanskrit form is often similar and may be more familiar; i.e., *Sutta* (Pali) instead of *Sutra* (Sanskrit). An exception is *Nirvana* (Sanskrit) instead of *Nibbana* (Pali).

9. According to Caroline Rhys Davids's introductions to several of these texts, a number of British women who were Pali scholars assisted her in editing them. Among the names she mentions are Mabel Bode, Cecilia Dibdin, Mabel Hunt, May Smith, Mary C. Foley, Mary E. Lilley, and Miss Chalmers. Little information is available about these women, but a greater knowledge of this group is highly desirable.

10. The similarity of Mahayana Buddhist rituals to those of Catholicism was often noted and may have been the source of the British prejudice against the Mahayana. See Almond 123-26 and Clausen 7.

11. For a description of several British writers' views of meditation see Almond 122-23.

12. Almost two decades after her husband's death Caroline Rhys Davids expressed regret that they did not more often "hammer out" their interpretations of texts together, acknowledging that until almost the time of his death she "was too much just pupil. . . " ("Enemy Action: Dialogues of the Buddha and a Bomb" 966).

13. Caroline Rhys Davids's negative view of Buddhist monasticism was not unusual. The institution was severely criticized by most British writers on Buddhism. For a summary see Almond 119-23.

14. Rhys Davids argued that the Buddha was, in India, "ever known as Sakya-muni," and his disciples were called "the Sakya-sons." Sakya only began to be called Buddhism when it "was lingering on in India as a moribund cult, as a decadent quasi-philosophy" (*Sakya, or Buddhist Origins* 1).

15. The American writer on Buddhism, Albert J. Edmunds, noted that "[T.W.] Rhys Davids wrote when Victorian agnosticism was at the crest of its wave, and could not resist the temptation of making poor old Buddha the great agnostic of antiquity" ("The Psychic Elements in Buddhism," *Two Worlds* 42 (10 May 1929): 1; qtd. in Tweed 124).

16. It is likely that some of Caroline Rhys Davids's later theories about Buddhism were influenced by Theosophy. The movement expanded significantly after World War I, and the Theosophical Society reached its peak membership of 45,000 in 1928 (Johnson 9). Theosophy also taught that the body was "the temporary vehicle for an eternal spirit, which in its evolutionary progress passes through all material forms from the mineral to the angelic, and reincarnates innumerable times in male and female guises" (Burfield 35). Diana Burfield has noted that Theosophy was particularly attractive to women because it offered them opportunities for leadership not available in established churches (35-36). Several of Rhys Davids's later essays (collected in *Wayfarer's Words*, 3 vols., 1940-42) were originally published in such

Theosophical periodicals as *The Quest* and *The Theosophist* or were delivered as lectures to branches of the Theosophical Society.

WORKS CITED

Almond, Philip C. *The British Discovery of Buddhism*. Cambridge: Cambridge UP, 1988.

Ariya-Dhamma. "Mrs. Rhys Davids and the Higher Criticism." *The Mahabodhi* (1932); Rpt. in *The British Buddhist* 6 (1932): 117-19.

Barham, Francis. Letter. *Times* (London) 24 Apr. 1857: 8.

Batchelor, Stephen. *The Awakening of the West: The Encounter of Buddhism and Western Culture*. Berkeley: Parallax, 1994.

Bode, Mabel. "Thomas William Rhys Davids; Caroline Augusta Foley Rhys Davids; The Work of Professor and Mrs. Rhys Davids in Pali Literature." *The Buddhist Review* 3.2 (April-June 1911): 81-86. Nendeln, Liechtenstein: Kraus Reprint, 1968.

Brear, Douglas. "Early Assumptions in Western Buddhist Studies." *Religion: Journal of Religion and Religions* 5.2 (1975): 136-59.

Burfield, Diana. "Theosophy and Feminism: Some Explorations in Nineteenth-Century Biography." *Women's Religious Experience*. Ed. Pat Holden. London: Croom Helm; Totowa, NJ: Barnes & Noble, 1983. 27-56.

Chalmers, Robert, Baron Chalmers. "Thomas William Rhys Davids, 1843-1922." *Proceedings of the British Academy* 10 (1921-23): 540-44.

---. "Davids, Thomas William Rhys." *Dictionary of National Biography*. 1922-30 supplement.

Clausen, Christopher. "Victorian Buddhism and the Origin of Comparative Religion." *Religion: Journal of Religion and Religions* 5.1 (1975): 1-15.

Davids, Caroline Augusta Foley Rhys. "An Apologist in Buddhism." *The Theosophist* [Adyar] (1940). Rpt. in *Wayfarer's Words*. Vol. 3. London: Luzac, 1942. 870-79. 3 vols. 1940-42.

---. "Buddha and Not Buddhists." *Indian Culture* 3.3 (1937). Rpt. in *Wayfarer's Words*. Vol. 3. London: Luzac, 1942. 1079-83. 3 vols. 1940-42.

---. *Buddhism: A Study of the Buddhist Norm*. NY: Holt; London: Williams and Norgate, 1912.

---. "Buddhism Not Originally a Negative Gospel." *Hibbert Journal* 26 (1928): 624-32.

---. "The Buddhist Principle of Change." *The Quest* (Oct. 1917). Rpt. in *Buddhist Psychology: An Inquiry into the Analysis and Theory of Mind in Pali Literature*. 2nd ed. London: Luzac, 1924. 213-43.

---. "Development of the Anti-Soul Attitude." *Buddhist Psychology: An Inquiry into the Analysis and Theory of Mind in Pali Literature*. 2nd ed. London: Luzac, 1924. 278-95.

---. "Enemy Action: Dialogues of the Buddha and a Bomb." *Wayfarer's Words*. Vol.3. London: Luzac, 1942. 962-72. 3 vols. 1940-42.

---. *Gotama the Man*. London: Luzac, 1928.

---. "An Historical Aspect of Nirvana." *Indian Culture* 2.3 (1936). Rpt. in *Wayfarer's Words*. Vol. 2 London: Luzac, 1941. 642-58. 3 vols. 1940-42.

---. "India and the Pali Text Society." *Jubilee Number of the J. Bhandarkar Oriental Research Institute* (1942). Rpt. in *Wayfarer's Words*. Vol. 3. London: Luzac, 1942. 889-94. 3 vols. 1940-42.

---. Introduction. *A Buddhist Manual of Psychological Ethics*. 1900. Trans. C.A.F. Rhys Davids. Pali Text Society Translation Series 41. 3rd ed. London: Pali Text Society, 1974. xxi-ciii.

---. Introduction. *Psalms of the Early Buddhists, I. Psalms of the Sisters*. Trans. C.A.F. Rhys Davids. Pali Text Society Translation Series 1. London: Pali Text Society, 1909. xiii-xlii.

---. Introduction. *Psalms of the Early Buddhists, II. Psalms of the Brethren*. Trans. C.A.F. Rhys Davids. Pali Text Society Translation Series 4. London: Pali Text Society, 1913. xix-lii.

---. Introduction to the Atanatiya Suttanta. *Dialogues of the Buddha, Pt. III.* Trans. T.W. and C.A.F. Rhys Davids. Sacred Books of the Buddhists 4. London: Humphrey Milford, 1921. 185-87. 3 vols. 1899-1921.

---. "The More in Man: A Hallmark of Man and of Religion." *The New Indian Antiquary* 1.1 (1938). Rpt. in *Wayfarer's Words.* Vol. 3. London: Luzac, 1942. 1022-27. 3 vols. 1941-42.

---. *Old Creeds for New Needs.* London: T. Fisher Unwin, 1923.

---. "On the Will in Buddhism." *Journal of the Royal Asiatic Society* 3rd ser. (1898): 47-59.

---. "Popular Errors About Buddhism." *London Quarterly and Holborn Review* 157 (1932): 464-75.

---. Preface. *Compendium of Philosophy.* Trans. Shwe Zan Aung. Ed. Rhys Davids. London: Pali Text Society, 1910. vii-xxiv.

---. "Report of the Pali Text Society for 1922." *Journal of the Pali Text Society* (1920-23): 22-34.

---. *Sakya, or Buddhist Origins.* London: Kegan Paul, 1931.

---. "Silence and Emphasis in Buddhism." *Hibbert Journal* 32 (1933): 129-32.

---. "The Soul-Theory in Buddhism." *Journal of the Royal Asiatic Society* 3rd ser. (1903): 587-91.

Davids, Caroline Augusta Foley Rhys, ed. *Compendium of Philosophy.* Trans. Shwe Zan Aung. London: Pali Text Society, 1910.

---. *The Expositor,* Vols. I, II. Trans. Pe Maung Tin. Pali Text Society Translation Series 8,9. London: Pali Text Society, 1920-21.

Davids, Caroline Augusta Foley Rhys, trans. *The Book of the Kindred Sayings,* Pt. I. With Suriyagoda Sumangala Thera. Pali Text Society Translation Series 7. London: Pali Text Society, 1917.

Davids, Caroline Augusta Foley Rhys and Shwe Zan Aung, trans. *Points of Controversy, or Subjects of Discourse.* Pali Text Society Translation Series 5. London: Pali Text Society, 1915.

"Davids, Caroline A.F. Rhys." *Who's Who.* 1937 ed.

Davids, T.W. Rhys. "The Ancient Buddhist Belief Concerning God." *Modern Review* 1 (1880): 219-23.

---. "Buddha's First Sermon." *Fortnightly Review* 32 (1879): 899-911.

---. "Buddhism." *Encyclopedia Britannica.* 9th ed. Vol. 4. Philadelphia: Stoddart, 1877. 381-92. 25 vols. 1875-90.

---. *Buddhism: Being a Sketch of the Life and Teachings of Gautama, the Buddha.* London: Society for Promoting Christian Knowledge, 1878. Rev. ed., 1907.

---. *Buddhism: Its History and Literature.* NY & London: Putnam's, 1896.

---. "Cosmic Law in Ancient Thought." *Proceedings of the British Academy.* 8 (1917-18): 279-89.

---. *Lectures on the Origin and Growth of Religion.* N.Y.: Putnam's, 1882.

---. "On Nirvana, and on the Buddhist Doctrines of the 'Groups,' the Sanskaras, Karma, and the 'Paths'." *Contemporary Review* 29 (1877): 249-70.

---. "Report of the Pali Text Society for 1882." *Journal of the Pali Text Society* 1 (1882-84): 1-14. Rpt. London: Pali Text Society, 1978.

Fields, Rick. *How the Swans Came to the Lake: A Narrative History of Buddhism in America.* Boulder, CO: Shambhala, 1981.

Foley, Caroline A. "Women Leaders of the Buddhist Reformation." *Transactions of the Ninth International Congress of Orientalists Held in London, 5th to 12th September 1892.* Ed. E. Delmar Morgan. Vol. 1 London: Committee of the Congress, 1893. 344-61. 2 vols.

Horner, Isaline B. "Caroline Rhys Davids." *Hibbert Journal* 41 (1942-43): 172-73.

Humphreys, Christmas. *The Development of Buddhism in England: Being a History of the Buddhist Movement in London and the Provinces.* London: The Buddhist Lodge, 1937.

---. *Sixty Years of Buddhism in England (1907-1967): A History and a Survey.* London: The Buddhist Society, 1968.

"Interpreter of Buddhism." *Times* (London). 1 July 1942: 7e.

Jackson, Carl T. *The Oriental Religions and American Thought: Nineteenth-Century Explorations.* Contributions in American Studies 55. Westport, CT: Greenwood, 1981.

Johnson, K. Paul. *Initiates of Theosophical Masters.* SUNY Series in Western Esoteric Traditions. Albany: SUNY Press, 1995.

de Jong, J.W. "A Brief History of Buddhist Studies in Europe and America." *The Eastern Buddhist* 7.1 (1974): 55-106; 7.2 (1974): 49-82.

Monier-Williams, Sir Monier. *Buddhism, in Its Connexion with Brahamanism and Hinduism and in Its Contrast with Christianity.* NY: Macmillan, 1889.

Müller, Friedrich Max. "Buddhist Nihilism." *Lectures on the Science of Religion.* N.Y.: Scribner's, 1893. 131-47.

---. "Buddhist Pilgrims." *Times* (London) 17 Apr. 1857: 5; 20 Apr. 1857: 6. Rpt. in *Chips From a German Workshop.* Vol. 1 NY: Scribners, 1881. 232-75. 5 vols.

---. "The Meaning of Nirvana." *Times* (London). 28 Apr. 1857: 10. Rpt. in *Selected Essays on Language, Mythology, and Religion.* London: Longman's, 1881. 280-291.

---. Rev. of *Le Bouddha et sa Religion*, by J. Barthelemy Saint Hillaire. *Edinburgh Review* 115 (1862): 379-408.

Murti, T.R.V. *The Central Philosophy of Buddhism: A Study of the Madhyamika System.* 2nd ed. London: Allen, 1960.

"The Ninth International Congress of Orientalists." *Journal of the Royal Asiatic Society.* 3rd ser. (1892): 855-76.

"The Passing of the Founder." *Journal of the Pali Text Society* (1920-23): 1-21.

Pe Maung Tin. "T.W. Rhys Davids: The Scholar." *Bulletin of the School of Oriental Studies* 111 (1923-25): 207-210.

Peiris, William. *The Western Contribution to Buddhism.* Delhi: Motilal Banarsidass, 1973.

Ray, Reginald A. *Buddhist Saints in India: A Study in Buddhist Values and Orientations.* NY: Oxford UP, 1994.

Ridding, C. Mary. "Professor T.W. Rhys Davids." *Bulletin of the School of Oriental Studies* 111 (1923-25): 201-207.

Ross, Sir E. Denison. *Both Ends of the Candle.* London: Faber and Faber, 1943.

Said, Edward W. *Orientalism.* N.Y.: Pantheon, 1978.

"Scholarship Run Mad." Editorial. *The British Buddhist* 6 (1932): 115-16.

Schwab, Raymond. *The Oriental Renaissance: Europe's Rediscovery of India and the East, 1680-1880.* Trans. Gene Patterson-Black and Victor Reinking. NY: Columbia UP, 1984.

Stede, William. "Caroline Augusta Foley Rhys Davids." *Journal of the Royal Asiatic Society* 3rd ser. (1942): 267-68. Nendeln, Liechtenstein: Kraus Reprint, 1969.

---. "T.W. Rhys Davids." *The Asiatic Review* 19 (1923): 359-62.

Thomas, Terence. "The Impact of Other Religions." *Religion in Victorian Britain.* Ed. Gerald Parsons. Vol. 2. Manchester: Manchester UP, 1988. 280-98. 3 vols.

"Thomas William Rhys Davids." *Journal of the Royal Asiatic Society* 3rd ser. (1923): 323-28.

Tweed, Thomas A. *The American Encounter with Buddhism, 1844-1912: Victorian Culture and the Limits of Dissent.* Religion in North America. Bloomington: Indiana UP, 1992.

Waterhouse, E.S. "Caroline Rhys Davids--The Woman and Her Work." *London Quarterly and Holborn Review* 168 (1943): 130-35.

Welbon, Guy Richard. *The Buddhist Nirvana and Its Western Interpreters.* Chicago: Chicago UP, 1968.

Wickremeratne, Ananda. *Genesis of an Orientalist: Thomas William Rhys Davids and Buddhism in Sri Lanka.* Delhi: Motilal Banarsidass, 1984.

Wilson, Horace Hayman. "On Buddha and Buddhism." *Journal of the Royal Asiatic Society* 16 (1856): 229-65.

Contributors

Kimberly VanEsveld Adams is Assistant Professor of English at Rutgers University. She is completing a book on the Madonna and three nineteenth-century feminist writers -- Anna Jameson, Margaret Fuller, and George Eliot -- and has recently published articles on this subject in the *Journal of Feminist Studies in Religion* and *Women's Studies*.

Virginia Bemis is Assistant Professor of English at Ashland University in Ohio. Her dissertation at Michigan State University was entitled "A Critical Introduction to Charlotte M. Yonge." She has recently written numerous entries for the *Dictionary of Literary Biography, British Bibliographers and Book Collectors*.

Susan Thach Dean is Head of the Special Collections Department of the University of Colorado at Boulder Libraries. She has published articles and curated exhibitions on Victorian book and periodical illustration and the history of printing. Her work on Caroline Rhys Davids is part of a more extensive project on the study of Buddhism in England from 1889 to 1942.

Lucretia A. Flammang is Associate Professor of English at the United States Coast Guard Academy in New London, Connecticut. A Commander in the Coast Guard, she is the first and presently only woman member of the Permanent Commissioned Teaching Staff at the Academy. She recently received her Ph.D. in English from the University of Iowa. Her doctoral research and current scholarship in the Victorian period and rhetorical theory have focussed on the life and work of Josephine Butler.

Mark M. Freed earned his doctoral degree from Michigan State University in Victorian literature and cultural theory. He is currently Assistant Professor of Literary Theory at Central Michigan University.

David Goslee is Professor of English at the University of Tennessee, Knoxville. His previous publications include *Tennyson's Characters: "Strange Faces, Other Minds"* and *Romanticism and the Anglican Newman*, as well as numerous articles on Tennyson, Browning, Newman, and Arnold.

Robert M. Kachur is Assistant Professor of English at the University of Massachusetts, Lowell. He is currently writing a book entitled *Getting the Last Word: British Women and the Authoritative Apocalyptic Voice, 1845-1900*, which examines literary uses of the biblical Apocalypse. His publications include "Repositioning the Female Christian Speaker: Christina Rossetti as Biblical Reader in *The Face of the Deep*" (*Victorian Poetry*, Summer 1997) and "A Closer Look at Authentic Interaction: Profiles of Student-Teacher Talk in Two Classrooms" in *Opening Dialogue* (Teachers College Press, 1997).

Julie Melnyk received her M.Phil. from Oxford University and her Ph.D. from the University of Virginia. She is now Assistant Professor of English at Central Methodist College in Fayette, Missouri. Her publications include reviews for *Victorian Prose* and an article on Evangelical magazines for *Victorian Periodicals Review*. She is currently co-editing, with Nanora Sweet, a volume of essays on Felicia Hemans.

Susan Mumm teaches for the Department of Religious Studies of The Open University, Milton Keynes, England. Her publications include "'Not Worse than Other Girls': the Convent-based Rehabilitation of Fallen Women in Victorian England" (*Journal of Social History*, 1996).

Frederick S. Roden is a doctoral candidate at New York University, where he is working with John Maynard on a dissertation entitled "Behind Cloister Walls: Gender, Spirituality, and Victorian Medievalism." His publications include "'Sisterhood is Powerful': Christina Rossetti's *Maude*" in *Women of Faith in Victorian Culture* (Macmillan, 1998) and "Two 'Sisters in Wisdom': Hildegard of Bingen, Christina Rossetti, and Feminist Theology" in *Hildegard of Bingen: A Casebook* (Garland, 1998).

L. Robert Stevens took his Ph.D. at the University of Oklahoma in 1963. He is author of a book *Charles Darwin*, published in G.K. Hall's Twayne Series. He has written numerous articles on Victorian subjects and is currently Regents Professor and Chair of the English Department at the University of North Texas.

Sarah Willburn is a doctoral candidate in English at Duke University. Her dissertation "Mystical Writing by Victorian Women, 1860-1890," directed by Eve Kosofsky Sedgwick, will be completed in 1997.

Index

A., C.J. ("The Divine and Human in the Book of Revelation") 18-19
abolition 74, 79 n.15, 80 n.19
Abraham 65, 120 n.1
Academy of Fine Arts, Philadelphia 76
Aelred of Rievaulx 50
afterlife xvii, 6, 217
Albion Hill Home 167
Almond, Philip 211, 221, 225 n.1, 226 n.10,11,13
Amalie, Princess of Saxony 78 n.5
anatta 219-220
Anderson, Bernhard W. 9
angels 12, 19, 32, 70, 77, 101, 151, 161, 191-192
Anglican Church/Anglicanism. See Church of England.
Anglo-Catholicism. See High Church.
animal rights 86-7
Anna, mother of Virgin Mary 62
Anselm 41, 54 n.6
Anson, Peter 54 n.7
Anthony, Susan B. 75, 78 n.7
Apocalypse xv, xvi, xvii, 3-34 (*passim*), 38, 55 n.15, 160-161, 189, 234
Apostolic Succession 110, 118
Aquinas, Thomas 85
Aristotle 85, 217
Ariya-Dhamma 223
Armstrong, Nancy 206 n.1
Arnold, Julia Ward 135
Arnold, Matthew 133, 135, 137, 145, 145 n.6, 234
Arnold, Thomas (Jr.) 135
Arnold, Thomas (Sr.) 109, 135
Ashton, Rosemary 145 n.5
Asiatic Society of Bengal 210
Atonement 130, 166-167, 169, 182

Augustine 85
Austen, Jane 101

B., L. (*Short Notes on the Revelation*) 12, 15, 19-20, 24-25, 26-27
Bacon, Margaret Hope 79 n.15, 80 n.19
Bakhtin, Mikhail 7
Banks, Olive 161
baptism 23, 108, 124, 125, 127, 128, 129, 130, 181
Barham, Francis 216
Baring-Gould, Sabine 54 n.6
Barrett, Rosa M. 166, 171, 182
Batchelor, Stephen 225
Baur, F.C. 143, 145-146 n.8
Baxter, Mrs.M. (Elizabeth) 15, 18, 25, 31-32
Bede 114
Bell, E. Moberly 157, 163 n.2
Bernard of Clairvaux 206
Besant, Annie 162
Bible 5, 6, 13, 14, 19, 21, 24, 31, 66, 74, 83-86, 88, 117, 133, 135, 137-139, 152, 166, 167, 185, 197
Blackwell, Elizabeth 166
Blanchard, Paula 76
Boddington, Gracilla 33 n.11
Bode, Mabel 213, 226 n.9
Bodichon, Barbara 59, 67, 78 n.6 & n.7, 80 n.20
the body in theology 37-55 (*passim*), 86
Book of Common Prayer 126, 128, 130
Bordo, Susan 206 n.3
Boston Museum of Fine Arts 80 n.18
Boswell, John 55 n.14
Boyd, Nancy 152